ANAÏS NIN

a reference guide

A
Reference
Publication
in
Literature

Ronald Gottesman
Editor

ANAÏS NIN

a reference guide

ROSE MARIE CUTTING

G.K. HALL &CO.

70 LINCOLN STREET, BOSTON, MASS.

Library of Congress Cataloging in Publication Data
Cutting, Rose Marie.
    Anais Nin: a reference guide.

    (A Reference publication in literature)
    Includes index.
    1. Nin, Anaïs, 1903-1977 — Bibliography.   I. Series.
Z8628.945.C87   [PS3527.I865]   016.818'5'209   78-13505
ISBN 0-8161-8001-6

This publication is printed on permanent/durable acid-free paper
MANUFACTURED IN THE UNITED STATES OF AMERICA

Contents

Introduction

BIOGRAPHY

Anaïs Nin was born in Paris on February 21, 1903--under the astrological sign of Pisces. Her parents were Rosa Culmel Nin, a singer of French and Danish ancestry, and the Spanish composer and concert pianist Joaquin Nin.

When her parents separated in 1914, Nin went with her mother and two brothers to live in New York. During the voyage to America, the little girl began her diary, originally as an extended letter to her father which she hoped might lure him to rejoin his abandoned family.

Nin attended the New York public schools, but dropped out at fifteen, apparently in rebellion against her first unfavorable critic-- a teacher who assailed her style as too stilted and literary. The girl pursued her own education by selecting a course of reading which embraced both the Catholic philosophers and a list of books officially proscribed by the Church. At sixteen, she became a model for artists and fashion designers. She studied Spanish dancing but eventually decided against a professional dance career.

Nin married Ian Hugo when she was twenty. Aside from a few professional collaborations--her acting in his films, and his designs which illustrate her novels--little is known about their relationship. All mention of her husband has been omitted from the published portions of Nin's diary, and Nin refused to discuss her marriage or even name her husband in interviews.

During her early twenties, Nin lived in Louveciennes, near Paris. Here she wrote D. H. Lawrence: An Unprofessional Study (1932), her first book. Edward W. Titus, the lawyer who negotiated the publisher's contract for that book, introduced Nin to another writer friend, Henry Miller. Volume one of Nin's diary, covering the years 1931-1934, traces the beginnings of the literary and personal friendship between Nin and Miller, and Nin's involvement with the other members of

Miller's circle. Nin developed an intense fascination with June Miller, Henry's beautiful wife. In 1934, Nin paid for the publication of Miller's Tropic of Cancer.

The diary also recounts Nin's psychoanalysis, first under Rene Allendy and then with Otto Rank. The latter's theories of creativity were influential in developing Nin's sense of artistic identity; her disagreement with him on the proper creative channels for women prompted her to formulate her own theories about women's art. In 1935, Nin went to New York to work as a lay analyst with Rank but after a few months decided to return to Paris and her literary career.

In 1936, Nin's poetic novel House of Incest was published in Paris by Siana. Another novel, Winter of Artifice, followed in 1939, published by the Obelisk Press in Henry Miller's Villa Seurat Series.

During World War II, Nin returned to the United States. When her books were turned down by commercial publishing houses, she established her own press, the Gemor Press. With the help of a friend, she hand-set and printed limited editions of Winter of Artifice (1942), Under a Glass Bell (1944), and House of Incest (1947). In The New Yorker, Edmund Wilson praised Under a Glass Bell, a collection of short stories, and Nin was soon offered a contract with E. P. Dutton.

Dutton published Ladders to Fire in 1946, the first book of Nin's roman fleuve or continuous novel, Cities of the Interior. The other volumes of this series were Children of the Albatross (1947), The Four-Chambered Heart (1950), A Spy in the House of Love (1954), and Solar Barque (1958). In 1959, the publisher Alan Swallow put out a one-volume edition of Cities of the Interior. Seduction of the Minotaur, published by Swallow Press in 1961, was actually an enlarged version of Solar Barque and replaces the earlier title in reissues of the series. Swallow also issued Collages, another collection of fiction, in 1964. Waste of Timelessness and Other Stories, a collection of Nin's early fiction, was published posthumously in 1977 by the Magic Circle Press. Delta of Venus, a collection of erotica, was published in the same year by Harcourt Brace Jovanovich and became a posthumous best seller.

Most of Nin's work in later years was devoted to editing her diary for publication. Volume one was published in 1966 (The Swallow Press and Harcourt, Brace and World). Five other volumes were issued up through 1976. The Novel of the Future, Nin's theoretical work on criticism and fiction writing, was published in 1968 by Macmillan.

During her last years, Nin lived in California. She died in Los Angeles on January 14, 1977. Her ashes were scattered over the Pacific.

THE REPUTATION OF ANAÏS NIN'S WRITINGS

Nin's literary reputation has been one of the most sharply divided in literary history. From the earliest reviews of her works, readers and critics have tended to fall into two camps: strong admirers, whose praise for her life and work sometimes has gone so far as to make a saint of her; and bored or angry detractors, whose rejection of Nin's work and values sometimes reaches extremes of unreasonable loathing.

The admirers and the detractors often agree that Nin's works are assertively feminine. The disagreement tends to be over whether the individual critic or group finds either or both of these qualities attractive or abhorrent. Nin's diction as a novelist has been described as "lyrical" and "poetic" but also as "pretentious" and "stilted." She has been praised for making the dream world real and damned for ignoring facts and falsifying reality. Her sexual politics as expressed in her writings have taken abuse from one group for being man-rejecting, even man-hating—and from another for being too accepting of the nurturing, feminine, and passive traditional roles vis-à-vis men. She has been praised for her personal courage in enunciating her vision, and condemned for showing an overwhelming ego in so doing.

Nin's support of Henry Miller—even giving him her only typewriter to work on—is frequently cited as evidence of her excesses in nurturing. But Miller repaid the debt at least in part by publishing in 1939 the essay "Un Être Étoilique," which praised Nin for the first time to an American audience. This essay may have gone a long way toward setting the tone for later high praise. Certainly, Miller gave the critical world what is probably the most frequently-quoted encomium to Nin's diary:

> ...a monumental confession which when given to the world will take its place beside the revelations of St. Augustine, Petronius, Abelard, Rousseau, Proust, and others.

Although rumors about the diary began circulating early, Nin made no attempt to publish it until rather late in her life. She used it as a sourcebook, a tool, perhaps as some friends and associates charged, as a crutch; but for publication she was writing criticism (D. H. Lawrence: An Unprofessional Study) and fiction. While she lived in Paris, she was able to find publishers among the smaller presses for her work. French culture was no stranger to the lyrical, psychological, and "feminine" in literature, and she belonged to a distinguished circle of literary friends who took notice of each other's writings (the Villa Seurat Circle, which included Henry Miller, Michael Fraenkel, Walter Lowenfels, Lawrence Durrell, and Alfred Perlés).

For years, however, Nin could not find an American publisher who would issue her works, and she eventually set up her own small press and self-published two novels and a collection of short stories. Finally, in 1944, a good review in The New Yorker provided a break. Edmund Wilson, one of the most eminent American critics, praised the collection Under a Glass Bell and declared that Nin deserved a commercial publisher. Dutton offered Nin a contract to publish her books, and reviewers gave them attention in a wide number of publications.

Many of these reviews were intensely unfavorable. In 1948, Elizabeth Hardwick chastised Nin for being "pretentious" and escapist, mystical, abstract, obscure, and boring. But a school of admirers also began to emerge from the American literary public. In 1970, a newsletter, Under the Sign of Pisces: Anaïs Nin and Her Circle, was founded at Ohio State University to provide a forum for readers of Nin's works.

Because Nin was known to have been keeping a record of her interactions with a host of distinguished associates, and because of advance praise from Miller and others who had been shown portions of the diary, the critics were predisposed to tackle the published diary. Debates raged about the sincerity and accuracy of the various volumes, and whether they were more literary or factual. Many charged Nin with egotism, and there were complaints about both omissions and inclusions.

In general, however, the diary fared better with reviewers than the novels had. Between Diary II and Diary III, Nin published The Novel of the Future, her second book of criticism, in which she explains her fictional method and places her own fiction in historical and critical context. It has been clear to critics who compared the novels with the diaries that the plots of the novels are drawn directly from journal materials. Nin's fictional characters are pronounced to be variations on herself, her father, and a selection of her friends and associates. By publishing materials taken directly from the manuscript diaries, Nin dropped the mask of fiction--or at least one of the veils.

A recent trend in Nin criticism deals with the diary as literature, sometimes in the context of the journal as a feminine literary genre. The question arises whether the portrait Nin paints of herself in her diary, and in the frequent lectures she made in later years, did not itself become a literary persona. Certainly, Nin's persona becomes more and more frequently the subject of reviews, often in terms of the role model it provides for young, struggling artists and for women on the road to self-actualization. A self-admitted cult or magic circle has grown up around the Nin legend, focused on the values Nin developed in her lifetime and espoused in her works: grace, integrity, the reality of the inner universe, and the power of psychological verities to transform the world.

THE FICTION

In 1936, Nin published <u>House of Incest</u>, followed in 1939 by <u>Winter of Artifice</u>. Two reviews of Nin's fiction in the 1930s provide a key to later reactions. Stuart Gilbert wrote a "Foreword" to the <u>House of Incest</u>,[1] praising the book for characteristics that later were considered significant in Nin's writing: her focus on the subconscious, on moments of intensity, the themes of love as projection or incest. Gilbert likewise complimented Nin for her use of language and rhythm and her special quality of "clairvoyance." For Gilbert, Nin was so exceptional that in earlier times she "would have been burned at the stake." Gilbert, as one of Nin's literary associates, had an insider's certainty about what Nin was doing and took the position of an advocate.

Emily Hahn (1939.B1), on the other hand, was writing about an author she did not know and who was not known to the general public; she could only speculate about whether the individual stories in <u>Winter of Artifice</u> were written at different times. Hahn labeled <u>Winter of Artifice</u> "real literature," but she believed <u>House of Incest</u> was "difficult" and "opaque."

<u>Winter of Artifice</u> received more attention in the early 1940s. Alfred Perlès, another Nin associate, recommended the novel in words that echo Gilbert's: Nin's style is "clairvoyant"; she is an artist and also a "seer"; she "knows too much" and her writing is a form of black magic (1940.B1). In 1942, William Carlos Williams (1942.B3) ranked Nin's work very high on the literary scale because it showed an "authentic female approach to the arts" through its microscopic concentration on the fluctuations of the individual.

In contrast to these tributes, reviewers representing two prestigious journals showed less enthusiasm for <u>Winter of Artifice</u>. Writing for the <u>New York Herald Tribune</u> (1942.B1), Elaine Gottlieb found some of the characters vivid and some of the language good but judged the book too "mystic" and the plot hard to follow. Paul Rosenfeld in <u>The Nation</u> (1942.B2) acknowledged Nin's strength of individuality but otherwise did not praise the book.

Nin credited Edmund Wilson with making her work better known in America and helping her secure a commercial publisher. Wilson's first review (1944.B4) commended <u>Under a Glass Bell</u>, comparing it to the work of Virginia Woolf. Like William Carlos Williams, Wilson emphasized the "feminine perception and fancy" in Nin's writing. Although he objected to the surrealistic imagery, he granted Nin the status of a "very good artist" and called some of the stories "really

---

1. <u>See</u> 1974.B36. Robert Zaller included this article in <u>A Casebook on Anaïs Nin</u> as one of the earliest pieces of criticism on Nin's fiction. According to Zaller, Nin claimed that the Gilbert article was published in the 1930s, but no source of publication has been located.

beautiful." Like many later Nin admirers. Wilson described her as a being apart from ordinary mortals, "a superterrestial being who feels things we cannot feel."

In 1945, Wilson reviewed This Hunger,[2] once again stressing Nin's "feminine point of view," and her picture of a woman's struggle to live in a male-dominated world while creating her own reality. Wilson compared the "excessive abstraction" and repetition of Nin's style (targets for later attacks) to the style of D. H. Lawrence. He concluded that Nin deserved a commercial publisher and many readers.

One month after Wilson's review, Isaac Rosenfeld (1945.B1) objected to the psychoanalytical style of This Hunger as an inadequate basis for creating fictional characters, noted that Nin shows women's relationships with men as generally painful, and declared that Nin offers no solutions other than protest for the problems she portrays.

The claim that Wilson's review of Under a Glass Bell helped to establish Nin's reputation appears to be justified, since in 1946 Nin's work was discussed in eight journals, including many of the standard sources for book reviews. Diana Trilling, in The Nation, chided Nin for the "sexual chauvinism" of This Hunger, interpreting the book as saying we should pity women and resent men.

The other seven reviews in 1946 were all of Ladders to Fire (the first Nin novel to be published by a commercial press).. Only Wilson's in The New Yorker was positive. Again he applauded Nin's "perceptive" studies of women. The other reviewers criticized Nin's style as obscure and abstract, as too emotional and Freudian. Most noted that she focuses on women; these women characters were attacked for their desire to enter a man's world (1946.B4), and their passionate emotionalism (1946.B1). One reviewer believed them little short of witches (1946.B2). Some objected to the fact that male characters play only minor roles or are weak (1946.B3, B5). Reviewers did not hesitate to cavil at Nin on the basis of sexual stereotypes: in the Saturday Review, for example, Harrison Smith (1946.B5) compared Nin to "any woman in a permanent tantrum...any woman...who had lived too long in the art colonies of the world, and had too little to do with children, cooking and the garden in the backyard."

Children of the Albatross was published in 1947. The five reviews showed mixed reactions. The New Yorker lauded Nin's images and metaphors; Hart acclaimed her "psychologically probing prose" and treatment of relationships; McLaughlin pointed out the lushness and symbolic quality of the work. But, as in previous reviews, Nin was criticized for her psychoanalytical style, unreal characters, lack of plot, and remoteness from everyday life. One of the most laudatory pieces on Children of the Albatross is Lawrence Durrell's 1959 preface

---

2. This Hunger, published in 1945 by Nin's Gemor Press, contains a "Prologue," "Hejda," "Stella," "Lillian and Djuna."

to the British edition (1959.B1). Durrell described Nin as a writer
of "real force" who belongs to "the great subjective-feminine tradition."

Under a Glass Bell was originally published in 1944 by Nin's
Gemor Press; the first British edition came out in 1947; the first ;
commercial American edition in 1948. Wilson's review of 1944 was
followed by one review in 1947 and six in 1948. The Kirkus review
(1947.B1) branded the book as plotless erotica, with vague and in-
comprehensible language.[3] Others found some merit in the book.
Young (1948.B6) said that at her best Nin is equaled only by Lawrence. Garoffolo (1948.B3) noted Nin's "sincerity." But most reviews were disparaging. Nin was upbraided for being too absorbed in
the world of women and for not creating good male characters; for
being monotonous; abstract and obscure; and for avoiding reality.

In 1950, the first American edition of The Four-Chambered Heart
was published. Two advance reviews in 1949 and eleven reviews in
1950 endorsed and denounced the novel with about equal frequency and
vehemence. Attacks focused on the eroticism of Nin's writing
(1949.B1, 1950.B3), her lack of action and plot (1950.B1), her style
--as pretentious and "feverish female" writing (1950.B1-B3, B9).
Six of the reviewers recommended the book for aspects such as the
language, character of Djuna or Rango, interest for women, insight
into the inner life, understanding of male/female relationships
(1949.B2; 1950.B4, B5, B7, B8).

In 1954, the first edition of A Spy in the House of Love was
printed. Over a two-year period, there were only four reviews, but
these were in significant review publications (Atlantic Monthly,
Hudson Review, Saturday Review, The Nation). Again the critics showed
a pronounced split, either lauding Nin's work or damning it totally.

The negative reviews were uncompromising: Nin lacks imagination
and profundity, has a "dreamy" literary style (1954.B3); the book is
"breathingly trite," a survival of the 1920s; Sabina is only "a girl
in search of an ideal mate" and the male characters are stereotypes
(1955.B3). On the other hand, one commentator liked Nin's humor, a
quality she is usually condemned for lacking, compared her honesty to
that of D. H. Lawrence, and defended her for giving as serious attention to women as is usually given to men (1954.B1). Another positive
reviewer noted the dance-like structure (1954.B2). Later praise of
A Spy in the House of Love appeared in a French article by Jean Fanchette (1959.B3), where it was praised as Nin's best work.

In 1959, five Nin novels were published together as Cities of the
Interior (Ladders to Fire, Children of the Albatross, The Four-

---

3. With only an occasional exception, Kirkus conscientiously reviewed
each Nin publication as it came out from 1946 to 1977 and thoroughly and con-
sistently damned it.

Chambered Heart, A Spy in the House of Love, Solar Barque). Only
Baldanza in the Minnesota Review (1962.B2) condemned the series: it
is pointless and rambling, abstract sentimentalizing, cloying eroticism, soap opera, and undisciplined writing. Chase (1960.B1) and
Stern (1968.B19) esteemed Nin's feminine vision and revelation of
women's feelings. Evans (1962.B4) called Nin a pioneer in the search
for identity, relentless in searching out the motivation of characters. Spencer (1971.B47, 1974.B67, 1976.B36) investigated the structure of the novels and their functioning together as an "architectonic" or "continuous novel" with an "open form" resembling a mobile.
Balakian's introduction to the Anaïs Nin Reader (1973.B3) studied
Nin's relationship to symbolism and surrealism, Nin's images and symbols, her use of the dream, and the relationship between the fiction
and diary. The French-Canadian Ouellette (1962.B6) and Frenchman
Brodin (1964.B5) praised Cities of the Interior. The latter compared
the complex style, symbols, and characters to the work of Virginia
Woolf.

Seduction of the Minotaur was first published in 1961 (in America
by Swallow, in England by Peter Owen). The British reviews were generally favorable. Only Colin Murray called it a "bit of a bore"
(1961.B4). The others approved of Nin's use of setting and sense of
truth (1961.B1), her sensitivity "like that of Woolf and Stein"
(1961.B2), and "finely controlled prose" (1961.B3). In The Village
Voice, Margoshes (1962.B5) extolled the depiction of landscape, characterization, style, and the feminine sensibility. Similarly, Wayne
McEvilly (1969.B22) said the book delivers the world of women's wis-
dom and shows the anima expressing itself.

The introduction to the French translation of Ladders to Fire
(1962.B3) paid tribute to Nin, calling her as "rich" as Durrell and
Miller and more truly a pioneer and declaring that her work requires
multiple readings. The French-Canadian reviewer Ouellette (1963.B4)
agreed that Nin is a great writer and has written a great novel. On
the other hand, Cabau, in the Paris L'Express (1963.B3), reproached
Nin for writing that is too vague and uncertain and too narcissistic.

The British reviews in response to the Peter Owen edition of
Ladders to Fire (1963) were overwhelmingly negative: "tangled chronicle of erotic attachments (mainly lesbian)" (1963.B2); the characters are "Mrs. Dalloways under mescalin" (1963.B5) and inhabit a
"dreamy, girlish world" (1963.B6).

The Swallow and Peter Owen editions of Collages came out in 1964.
The British reviews were negative: "fictionalized hash" (1964.B6);
"avante-garde writing at its worst" (1964.B9). A few of the American
reviews were unfavorable. In Critique (1965.B4), Korges damned the
style for verbal inaccuracy, puppet-like characters, (all the same
woman seeking love), the abstractness of the theme, and "solipsism
without irony." But most American reviews were favorable; they
ranged from William Goyen's defense of Nin's "unique feminine vision"

Introduction

and "vital artistry" (1964.B8) to the Lerman review in Mademoiselle
(1965.B5), where readers were introduced to the "intense, hot sensitive and sensitized lives" of Nin's characters. Spencer's articles
on Collages (1973.B46 and 1975.B28) and her book (1977.A1) analyzed
the techniques of Nin's book in relation to the techniques of the
visual arts.

When the first Owen edition of Under a Glass Bell appeared in
1968, the British reviews were once again more negative than positive,
dismissing Nin as a "minor" writer with a "limited vision" (1968.B8)
and calling her obvious and trivial (1968.B12).

Two British reviews of the Owen edition of A Spy in the House of
Love (1971) took opposing stands. The London Observer said the style
would make the reader's head ache; the Times Literary Supplement extolled the style and recommended the work as "championing the emanci-
pation of women's psyche."

The first British edition of House of Incest was published by
Peter Owen along with Winter of Artifice in 1974. Typically, the reviews were mixed in reaction. The book was criticized for not making
sense (1974.B55) and for "tastelessness" (1974.B78); recommended for
images resembling Klee's or Chagall's (1974.B8) and for its strange
beauty (1974.B55). Like House of Incest, Winter of Artifice received
a few reviews in 1974 and 1975. Vaughan, in the London Observer,
applied the same "tastelessness" to it as to House of Incest. The
other reviews are neutral or mixed. Stubbs (1975.B30) called the
novel "illuminating but claustrophobic."

A posthumous collection of fiction, Waste of Timelessness and
Other Stories was published in 1977. These previously unpublished
stories were written by Nin in her twenties. One commentator declared they are for Nin fans only (1977.B8). But other reviewers
believed the book worth reading in itself and important for the light
it sheds on Nin's later work (1977.B16).

Delta of Venus was Nin's first best seller, a collection of erotica written for money for a client in the 1940s but likewise not published until after Nin's death in 1977. None of the reviewers was
harsh, although several note weaknesses or see the book primarily as
a "literary curiosity."

Reviewers often commended Nin for showing her love of beauty and
poetry and refusing to separate sex from feeling even in pornography
written for hire (1977.B2, B28, B31). Nin was lauded for writing
from a feminine perspective in a field of literature usually dominated by the male point of view (1977.B7, B28, B34). Zinnes called
the book the first American work written by a woman to openly extol
sexuality. Alice Walker (1977.B33) similarly recommended Delta of
Venus as "the boldest, most useful" of Nin's books because it is "so
distinct an advance in the depiction of female sensuality."

THE DIARY

"Un Être Étoilique," Henry Miller's 1937 panegyric acclaiming Nin's diary as equal to the confessions of St. Augustine, Rousseau, and Proust was the first published description of the diary; it has been quoted and requoted throughout the four decades the diary has been discussed. The applause of Miller and other Nin associates made the diary a legend, and most articles written about Nin before publication of the first volume in 1966 speculated about the autobiographical, historical, or literary value of the diary.

Diary I drew widespread attention. In 1966 alone there were over thirty reviews, with favorable reviews outnumbering negative ones by two to one. Reviewers frequently asserted that the character of Nin is the most absorbing aspect of the diary; they complimented her for writing from a woman's point of view and constructing a detailed picture of a woman's psyche (1966.B7, B10, B23-B24, B35). Several valued Nin's portrait of the artist as young woman (1966.B13, B18, B19, B31).

For many commentators, Nin's incisive portraits of her friends and associates--Henry and June Miller, Artaud, Allendy, Rank--constituted one of the chief strengths of the diary (1966.B16, B21, B25, B33). Some esteemed the diary for vividly recreating the life of the 1930s (1966.B8-B9, B14, B33).

Some commentators admired Nin's style for its poetic qualities and fluid movement (1966.B8-B9, B23-B25, B31); for its personal and subjective qualities (1966.B29); for its sincerity and frank revelation of Nin's life (1966.B17, B21, B33). The diary was also studied as a source for clarifying Nin's fiction (1966.B8-B9, B19, B23-B24).

Tributes to the diary ran from grudging admission of Nin's "talent" (1966.B3) to descriptions of it as a "great book" (1966.B8-9, B21, B29), "one of the finest works of its types in modern literature" (1966.B33), and "a definitive statement on the life of the twentieth-century artist" (1966.B19).

Unfavorable reviews generally spotlighted Nin's egotism as her chief sin. "Nothing exists but the self" (1966.B5) in Nin's world of "narcissistic self-indulgence" (1966.B1). (See also 1966.B4, B20, B27, B28 for further censure of Nin's supposed egotism.) Buckmaster and Jones denounced Nin for inhabiting a fantasy world in which she could not separate illusion from reality. Heppenstall amd MacAdam judged the omission of characters such as her husband as an irritating flaw. Nin's style was condemned for being too subjective and too analytical (1966.B6, B15, B27); for its emotional, poetic quality, ("monumental gush," 1966.B1; B20); and for being verbose and pretentious (1966.B27, B28).

Introduction

There was considerable foreign interest in Nin's diary. The
French edition of Diary I elicited a friendly response. Of ten French
reviews from 1969 to 1970, only one was hostile, reproaching Nin for
setting up a mutual admiration society with Miller (1969.B4). The
other reviewers lauded the diary for the same reasons as the American
and British reviewers: understanding of the female world, view of the
artist, and portraits of others. Nin was rated an attractive, exceptional, and intriguing woman. The diary was proclaimed an "exemplary document" of female art (1969.B21).

Other foreign notice of the diary was likewise largely favorable.
A Dutch writer (1967.B27) praised the diary's great literary value
and its revelation of a fascinating woman. A Japanese writer
(1971.B43) analyzed Nin's diary as an important example of the transformation of a diary into a work of art. In the "Afterword" to his
translation of Diary I into Japanese (1974.B39) and in two articles
on the diary (1977.B20-B21), Hara discussed the theme of womanhood
in the diary.

The interest manifested in Diary II, although less than for Diary
I, was still high. In 1967-1968 there were slightly over twenty reviews. The proportion of positive to negative responses was roughly
three to one. Most commentators emphasized the same aspects of style
and content that were examined in volume one. However, special note
was taken of Nin's themes of creativity and the dream, her opposition
to the destructiveness of war, and her preferring personal to political solutions (1967.B7, B13, B14, B18, B20, B23).

The number of reviews of Diary III during 1969-1970 showed only a
slight decline in comparison with the number for volume two; favorable opinions outweighed unfavorable opinions by two to one. The
number of reviews for volume four during 1971-1972 and volume five
during 1974-1975 remained constant but showed a slight decline from
the number for volume three. Positive and negative responses to
Diary IV and V were nearly equal in number. The former focused on
aspects singled out in earlier volumes: appreciation for Nin's picture of an era or a place and for the image of herself as a "liberated" and self-liberating woman (1971.B35; 1972.B6, B50). Attacks
continued on Nin's style ("sub-Lawrentian gush," 1972.B5) and especially on the egotism of her work (1971.B8; 1974.B43; 1975.B24).

In 1976, the standard reviews gave attention to volume six.
There was little harsh criticism, although some writers noted flaws
such as the inclusion of items of little interest or implied the volume is for light reading rather than a serious literary work. A number of reviewers judged the last volume as the best: it is more
entertaining; less narcissistic and more accepting; the most successful and artistic volume to date, according to Joyce Carol Oates
(1976.B32).

THE CRITICISM

Most of the attention given to Nin's criticism emphasizes two books, D. H. Lawrence: An Unprofessional Study and The Novel of the Future. The work on Lawrence was Nin's first published book (1932), but most comments on it were written only after the book was reissued (in England in 1962, in America in 1964). One reviewer (1964.B2) chided Nin for apparent inaccuracy. Generally, however, writers spoke highly of Nin's work. Several honored Nin for producing one of the most significant critical works on Lawrence during the years after his death (1964.B11, 1971.B38). Nin was commended for recognizing Lawrence's "almost feminine sensibility" (1962.B1); for studying the texture of Lawrence's work; for producing a "sensitive" study (1964.B11). Her book was appraised as "one of the most valuable" on Lawrence (1964.B7). Many reviewers wrote that Nin's ideas on Lawrence cast as much light on her own books as on Lawrence.

One of the more detailed critiques of D. H. Lawrence: An Unprofessional Study was done by Paul West for The Southern Review (1965.B8). West declared that Nin analyzes on the basis of intuition or feeling but also sometimes does less "impressionistic" criticism. West credited Nin with perceptive views on Lawrence's picture of male friendship, Lawrence's female characters, Lawrence's resemblance to Whitman, his view on love, and his techniques of imprecision.

Evelyn J. Hinz' book, The Mirror and the Garden: Realism and Reality in the Writings of Anaïs Nin (1971.A1), studied Nin's criticism in detail. Hinz devoted a chapter to D. H. Lawrence: An Unprofessional Study, defending the book as a "creative" rather than critical work. Nin's purpose is not to explicate Lawrence so much as to prove the superiority of intuition as an "objective" and "realistic" form of knowledge.

The Mirror and the Garden included chapters on two more of Nin's critical works: Realism and Reality (1946), a work that Hinz likewise examined in an article (1973.B35) as showing Nin's opposition between objective truth and subjective reality; The Novel of the Future (1968), which Hinz compared to D. H. Lawrence: An Unprofessional Study and to Realism and Reality, in order to prove that Nin did not change her basic attack on realists and her defense of the subjective, poetic way of knowing and of creating art.

Several reviewers of The Novel of the Future strongly condemned Nin for approaching criticism intuitively rather than logically (1968.B5; 1969.B1, B9). Critics also assailed Nin for waging unnecessary battle over currently accepted techniques such as symbolism and for a tone that was described as patronizing or self-righteous (1968.B5-B6; 1969.B1).

Nevertheless, the proportion of favorable to unfavorable reviews ran almost three to one. The Novel of the Future was applauded for daring to substitute criticism that works through illustration and

image for criticism by argument (1969.B34); for working to create a
new sensibility in the reader (1972.B11); for analyzing particular
writers' works with skill (1968.B17; 1969.B15); for probing deeply
into every aspect of the creative process (1970.B2); for casting important light on Nin's own work (1968.B17; 1969.B27); for clarifying
the tradition of literature written by women writers (1971.B6); and
for ruthlessly exposing the weaknesses of male culture (1973.B28).
The Novel of the Future was called a "valuable guide" (1969.B18), an
important book (1969.B10), and one of the most important studies of
modern fiction (1972.B11).

Hinz continued her scrutiny of Nin's criticism in two 1972 articles that examined Nin's diary as another work in which Nin argued
her theory of reality, castigated realists, and defended subjective
experience. In Diary IV Nin confronted "objective" critics such as
Edmund Wilson and Diana Trilling and advocated a "humanistic" philosophy of criticism.

THE GROWTH OF NIN'S REPUTATION

Nin's growing popularity and the development of a body of criticism on her work were manifested through a number of sources from the
late 1960s through the 1970s. In 1970, Under the Sign of Pisces:
Anaïs Nin and Her Circle was founded, a quarterly newsletter edited
at first by Richard Centing and Benjamin Franklin V and then from
1973 by Centing alone. Under the Sign of Pisces provided reviews of
works by Nin and the "circle" of writers associated with her (such as
Henry Miller, Lawrence Durrell, Anna Kavan, Barbara Kraft, Marguerite
Young), and biographical and critical articles on Nin and related
writers. It became the principle vehicle for following Nin's progress as a writer and the work of Nin scholars and critics.

During the 1960s and early 1970s, Nin drew large audiences for
the lectures she frequently gave at college campuses and literary
events. Under the Sign of Pisces covered Nin's public addresses and
other events in her personal and professional life (such as her
birthday, honors, and contacts with friends). In addition, college
newspapers and the daily press also reported Nin's many doings.

Nin was undoubtedly one of the most frequently interviewed of
twentieth-century authors. The interviews clump thickly at the end
of the 1960s and run through the first half of the 1970s--interviews
in American and French newspapers, underground presses, popular
women's magazines such as Mademoiselle and Vogue, interviews on cas-
sette tape, and interviews in journals with more serious literary or
social purposes (The New Woman, Ramparts, Shantih, Under the Sign of
Pisces). The topics discussed vary widely and cover much territory;
some of the most popular are the diary, Nin's famous friends and associates, her critical theories, her views on the special problems

and strengths of women and women writers, the relationships between the sexes, her personal development and liberation, and her views on the women's movement.

In 1968, the first book-length study of Nin was published--Oliver Evans' Anaïs Nin (1968.A1). Evans devoted separate chapters to an analysis of each of Nin's works of fiction, from House of Incest through Collages, and noted the relationship between the fiction and the diary. In 1971, Evelyn J. Hinz produced the second critical book on Nin; The Mirror and the Garden: Realism and Reality in the Writings of Anaïs Nin (1971.A1) emphasized the "theme" of realism versus reality in Nin's criticism, her fiction, and Diary I-III. Sharon Spencer completed the third critical book on Nin in 1977. Collage of Dreams: The Writings of Anaïs Nin (1977.A1) studied Nin's use of the techniques of nonverbal art forms, her use of the dream, her exploration of woman (especially woman as mother and artist), Diary I-VI, and Nin's exoneration of the symbol of Narcissus.

In 1973, Benjamin Franklin V published a book-length bibliography of Nin's publications (1973.A1). Nin's publishing history is complex and confusing because of the number of presses--including private presses--that published her works. In addition, Franklin discussed Nin's bibliography and the publishing history of her books in several articles (1973.B23, B25; 1974.B34). Franklin and Richard Centing regularly compiled a series of articles on primary and secondary sources relating to Nin for Under the Sign of Pisces. This newsletter also printed other articles and bibliographies showing Nin's foreign and American reputation.

In 1973, Valerie Harms edited and published A Celebration with Anaïs Nin (1973.B30-B33), an anthology of personal responses to Nin and critical discussion of her work contributed by those who attended a weekend retreat with Nin. In the same year, Robert Snyder produced his film study of Nin, "Anaïs Observed: A Film Portrait of a Woman Artist." Snyder later edited a book largely composed of scenes from the film (1976.A1).

Beginning in 1970, a series of dissertations studied Nin and her work. The first was Catherine Broderick's "A Comparative Thematic Study of François Mauriac's Génitrix and Anaïs Nin's The Four-Chambered Heart" (1970.B10), which studied the themes of the story and of the plot, examined dominant linking images, and compared Nin's themes with Mauriac's. In 1973, Margaret Lee Potts completed "The Genesis and Evolution of the Creative Personality: A Rankian Analysis of The Diary of Anaïs Nin, Volumes I-IV" (1973.A2), which argued that the diary exhibits the creative stages outlined by Rank--self definition as an artist; identification with masters or schools; and creation of an individual style. Also in 1973, Nancy Scholar Zee produced "Anaïs Nin: Beyond the Mask" (1973.A5), examining major metaphors of Nin's works, her "seductive" style, and the "persona" of the diary.

Ellen McKee Peck, in "Exploring the Feminine: A Study of Janet Lewis, Ellen Glasgow, Anaïs Nin, and Virginia Woolf" (1974.B59), viewed Nin as "the chronicler of the ultra-feminine woman's progress." In "Sense and Sensibility in Woman's Fiction: Studies in the Novels of George Eliot, Virginia Woolf, Anaïs Nin, and Doris Lessing" (1974.B76), Lynn Sukenick concluded that Nin accepts society's view of female roles and association of femininity with emotional responsiveness more readily than the other woman writers studied. Deanna Madden "Laboratory of the Soul: The Influence of Psychoanalysis on the Work of Anaïs Nin" (1975.A1), studied psychoanalytic elements such as the dream, the unconscious, the writer as analyst and the novel as therapeutic experience.

The growth of Nin's reputation was announced by an increase of significant critical articles written for journals or as introductions to Nin's books. A Casebook on Anaïs Nin (1974) gives clear evidence of this development. Edited by Robert Zaller, this collection printed twenty essays on Nin's diary and fiction. Some are reprints of comments from the 1930s and 1940s (Gilbert, Miller, Wilson). Others are from the 1950s and 1960s (Durrell, Zinnes, McEvilly). But the majority of the articles are appropriately from the 1970s, the decade when Nin's work received the most careful critical scrutiny. Many of the writers represented in A Casebook on Anaïs Nin are among the most prolific students of Nin: Richard Centing, Benjamin Franklin V, Wayne McEvilly, Deena Metzger, Duane Schneider, Sharon Spencer, Daniel Stern, Harriet Zinnes.

NIN AS A WOMAN WRITER

Much of the criticism on Nin focuses on the fact that she wrote about women's lives and problems, particularly the problems of woman as artist, and about areas of experience that are usually important to women, such as the emotional life and search for good relationships.

Many critics complain that Nin's diary persona and the women characters in her fiction are too traditional and too ready to accept the conventional stereotypes of woman's nature and roles. Stone, (1976.B37) writing for The Village Voice, argued that many women critics denounced Nin (a pattern seen dating from the early reviews of Diana Trilling and Elizabeth Hardwick) because Nin's defense of traditional "female" qualities such as the personal, emotional, and intuitive threatened women who chose to be "intellectual, concrete, political as a way of being new and free."

Other scholars defended Nin for studying the pressures put on women to be good and unselfish (1972.B44; 1974.B67); or believed that Nin dramatized the conflict and ambivalence women feel over being socialized to play a nurturing role for others rather than seek independent goals for themselves (1971.B46; 1972.B43; 1973.A5, B53).

Frequently, readers applauded Nin's diary for showing growth from a traditional and restrictive background to liberation. These commentators saw Nin as a role model for modern women (1972.B6, B50; 1974.B40, B42; 1976.B18; 1977.B24). Spencer declared that Nin's diary provides "the most complete record of the psychic life of the woman as creator...the most daring and powerful portraits of woman as artist" (1973.B45). Harms said the diary makes Nin "the most important representative of the questing female writer" (1975.B18).

Moreover, Nin's fiction was praised for showing early examples of emancipated women. Both Spencer and Brians (1974.B67; 1977.B9) acknowledged Nin's pioneering work in creating the sexually aggressive Sabina who breaks out of traditional sex roles. Brians lauded Nin's exploration of sex roles and of such "advanced" themes as bisexuality. Spencer announced that Nin studied "radical" topics such as incest, lesbianism, friendships between heterosexuals and homosexuals, and the neurotic aspects of woman's goodness long before such subjects became fashionable.

Members of the women's movement took a strong interest in Nin. Many feminist publications (for instance, Amazon Quarterly, Chrysalis: A Magazine of Women's Culture, The New Woman Magazine, Notes from the Third Year, MS., Spokeswoman, Women's Studies) published articles on Nin, interviews with her, or reports on talks she made to women's groups. Nin herself claimed that her diary spoke for the mute women of the world. Some women disagreed strongly. Nin's "lack of feminist consciousness is staggering," said Snitow (1971.B45). Others paid tribute to the diary as "political in the most classic sense...working out solutions to the oldest political question: the woman question...[Nin] was the first to discover consciousness raising" (1971.B25).

In addition, a substantial number of diverse periodicals printed articles on Nin which emphasized her views on the nature and social roles of women, and her opinions on the changes being brought about by the women's movement: American journals, College English, Glamour, Hudson Review, Journal of the Otto Rank Association; French periodicals, Elle, Les Nouvelles Littéraires, Votre Beauté; Japanese periodicals, Bokushin, Eureka, Gakuto, Weekly Playboy.

Many commentators saw Nin's writing as especially feminine in both style and content (1942.B3; 1960.B3; 1968.B15). Spencer said Nin's work is "decidedly and unashamedly feminine writing" (1974.B67). The diary form was seen as particularly appropriate for a woman writer (1974.B76; 1976.B10), and Nin was praised for showing reality through a woman's senses (1963.B7). Nin was singled out for promoting a "revolutionary" philosophy of love that would unite female with male strengths (1974.B30); and for insisting on the strength of female qualities and demanding that they be regarded equal to male qualities (1974.B59).

ANNOTATION AND INDEXING

Effort was made to include all books and articles in English and foreign languages on Nin. I have included interviews of Nin because the questions asked often show significant trends in criticism of Nin's work. It was impossible to separate interest in Nin as a woman from interest in Nin as a writer; hence biographical articles have been annotated. I have included articles on Nin in daily presses and attempted to cover articles on her in college newspapers, although the latter were difficult and sometimes impossible to locate. Few histories of American literature give space to Nin; hence such secondary sources are generally not represented in this book.

The annotations are descriptive rather than evaluative. The book is indexed by titles of Nin's works, titles of secondary sources on Nin, authors of these sources, and subjects frequently discussed in secondary works on Nin.

ACKNOWLEDGMENTS

I express gratitude to the University of Texas Research Institute for two grants to cover expenses in preparing the manuscript; to Judith Jackson for patient and persistent help in locating most items included in the book and annotating one-third of the items; to Caroline Byrd for generous and resourceful help at all stages of the book; to Frieda Werden for aid in editing the annotations and the introduction; to Rose Bruckbauer Cutting for patient and untiring work in typing and proofing the manuscript and preparing the index; to Bobbye Delafield for typing the manuscript; to Diana Oliva for careful work on the index; to the interlibrary loan staffs of the University of Texas at Austin and St. Mary's University of San Antonio; to Catherine Broderick for supplying Japanese materials; to Richard R. Centing for thoughtful and prompt aid throughout the preparation of the manuscript.

Major Writings by Anaïs Nin

D. H. Lawrence: An Unprofessional Study, 1932*

House of Incest, 1936

Winter of Artifice, 1939

Under a Glass Bell and Other Stories, 1944

Realism and Reality, 1946

Ladders to Fire, 1946

On Writing, 1947

Children of the Albatross, 1947

The Four-Chambered Heart, 1950

A Spy in the House of Love, 1954

Solar Barque, 1958

Cities of the Interior (Includes Ladders to Fire,
    Children of the Albatross, The Four-Chambered
    Heart, A Spy in the House of Love, Solar
    Barque), 1959

Seduction of the Minotaur, 1961

Collages, 1964

The Diary of Anaïs Nin, Volume One: 1931-1934, 1966

The Diary of Anaïs Nin, Volume Two: 1934-1939, 1967

*Dates refer to first editions.

Major Writings by Anaïs Nin

The Novel of the Future, 1968

The Diary of Anaïs Nin, Volume Three: 1939-1944, 1969

The Diary of Anaïs Nin, Volume Four: 1944-1947, 1971

The Anaïs Nin Reader, 1973

The Diary of Anaïs Nin, Volume Five: 1947-1955, 1974

A Woman Speaks: The Lectures, Seminars, and Inter-
    views of Anaïs Nin, 1975

The Diary of Anaïs Nin, Volume Six: 1955-1966, 1976

In Favor of the Sensitive Man & Other Essays, 1976

Delta of Venus, 1977

Waste of Timelessness and Other Early Stories, 1977

Writings about Anaïs Nin, 1937-1977

1937 A BOOKS - NONE

1937 B SHORTER WRITINGS

1   MILLER, HENRY. "Un Être Étoilique." The Criterion, 17 (Octo-
     ber), 35-52.
         Nin's diary is "a monumental confession which when given
     to the world will take its place beside the revelations of
     St. Augustine, Petronius, Abelard, Rousseau, Proust, and
     others." "The diarist is not concerned with truth but,
     like the novelist, with self-realization." In Nin's work,
     "life assumes the aspect of a labyrinth into which the
     seeker is plunged." Nin enters "to stay her old self."
     The earliest pages of the diary show the conflict between
     the old, inadequate self which was attached to the father
     and the budding, unknown self which she was creating. To
     make herself worthy for her father, she unknowingly made
     herself an artist. "Throughout the diary the amazing thing
     is this intuitive awareness of the symbolic nature of her
     role." "It is a great pageant of the times patiently and
     humbly delineated by one who considered herself as nothing."
     Nin's "relentless spirit of elaboration" shows her struggle
     to create a world. The whole diary "assumes the nature of
     the record of a second birth...the story of death and trans-
     figuration." In the earlier volumes, the dominant mood is
     sadness and disillusion; "joy and fulfillment" dominate the
     later volumes. "The old obsessional desire to devour every-
     thing in sight, in order that it be preserved in her own
     private tomb is gone." Three successive volumes of the
     diary take place "entirely within the confines of the female
     world." "It is the first female writing I have ever seen;
     it rearranges the world in terms of female honesty. The
     result is a language...which bears no resemblance to any of
     the masculine experimental processes with which we are
     familiar. It is precise, abstract, cloudy and unseizable...
     the opium of woman's physiological being, a sort of cine-
     matic show put on inside the genitourinary tract." Re-
     printed 1938.B1; 1939.B2; 1974.B58; translated 1977.B27.

1938

1938 A BOOKS - NONE

1938 B SHORTER WRITINGS

    1   MILLER, HENRY. "Une Être Étoilique." The Phoenix, 1 (June-
        August), 67-94.
            Reprint of 1937.B1.

1939 A BOOKS - NONE

1939 B SHORTER WRITINGS

    1   HAHN, EMILY. "Winter of Artifice." T'ien Hsia Monthly, 9
        (November), 435-438.
            Unlike the difficult, opaque House of Incest, Winter of
        Artifice has a "straightforward and forceful style."
        Nin's prose is never "meaningless" or "commonplace." It
        includes an "interesting and fair picture of what is fool-
        ishly called 'homosexuality,'" and the ending is "beauti-
        fully done" with the "perfect amount of restraint." The
        stories seem to show "growth" and suggest they were written
        far apart in time. The first story sounds "immature and
        romantic" while the last is "perhaps the only one which
        does not jar in this period of trouble and panic and an-
        guish." During this time of war, literature has been crit-
        icized for focusing exclusively on the personal. Nin's
        book is "real literature" that has not been overwhelmed by
        war.

    2   MILLER, HENRY. "Un Être Étoilique," in his The Cosmological
        Eye. Norfolk, Conn: New Directions, pp. 357-364.
            Reprint of 1937.B1

1940 A BOOKS - NONE

1940 B SHORTER WRITINGS

    1   PERLÈS, ALFRED. "Fathers, Daughters and Lovers." Purpose,
        12 (January-March), 45-48.
            Review of Winter of Artifice. Nin handles the father-
        theme in the "Lilith" portion of the story with "consum-
        mate skill." Her style is "clairvoyant" and "transmogri-
        fying." Her language is "climatic." It is the "style of
        the artist reinforced (and in a way weakened) by the
        'seer.'" The part entitled "The Voice" describes the se-
        crets of the analyst's consulting room by creating the

"sensation of impending miracle." The reader feels that Nin "knows too much"--that "no woman should ever be endowed with such knowledge." She deals with subjects that "should not be dealt with," approaching the "portals of magic--black magic." The book is written as if by "some nereid or dryad," not by a human being. Winter of Artifice is "one of the strangest books I have ever read." It is valuable not for its subject matter but for its "atmospheric, seasonal qualities."

1942 A BOOKS - NONE

1942 B SHORTER WRITINGS

1   GOTTLIEB, ELAINE S. "New Fiction of America." New York Herald Tribune Books (8 November), p. 14.
      Review of Winter of Artifice. Both parts of the book are continuations of the diary, in which Nin talks to herself or God. "Winter of Artifice" is basically a good story that "loses itself in the telling." "The Voice" offers personality contrasts. Lillian and Mischa are vivid but dropped too soon. "All the people in the book are united by their failure to live normally." "The Voice" is "a little overfull" of mystic statements, stories about stories, conclusions before facts. Over all, there is "a rather piquant icing of good language," but "The Woman in the Myth" and "Birth" are better examples of Nin's gifts.

2   ROSENFELD, PAUL. "Refinements on a Journal: Winter of Artifice by Anaïs Nin." The Nation, 155 (26 September), 276-277.
      Begun as an attempt to make the loneliness of her father's desertion bearable, the diary of Anaïs Nin grew into a revelation of her true feelings and spirit. Winter of Artifice distances the diary's material and examines Nin's realization that the image of her father was an incomplete fulfillment of the diary's "imago." The novel portrays the temporary rejoining of father and daughter for a stay in France, showing that the break between the two was inevitable because of the disharmony of their styles of living. The child-daughter realizes her need for the father has outgrown the actual person. In the novel, another revelation comes through psychoanalysis, the discovery of the two personal poles of warmth and coldness. But Nin will not accept normality in the orthodox sense; she still favors her original situation. Nin's representative in the

1942

> novel keeps allegiance to the diary despite pain or pleas-
> ure, fashioning it so that it is indelibly marked with her
> own individuality.

3   WILLIAMS, WILLIAM CARLOS. "Men...Have No Tenderness: Anaïs
     Nin's 'Winter of Artifice,'" in New Directions No. 7.
     Edited by James Laughlin. Norfolk, Conn.: New Directions,
     pp. 429-436.
         Winter of Artifice shows Nin's ability to "give" from
     her female experience. Female artists have tended to be on
     the defensive; many have wanted to write only with a "male"
     style. Nin struggles to overcome the bitterness of the
     female writer. Her female characters look for a love which
     will envelop them; as they search, they create capabilities
     for love. There is an "authentic female approach to the
     arts," and without it the "male" approach lacks balance.
     The female writer studies the infinite variety of one par-
     ticle. The association of weakness with everything female
     has prevented a study of the female's approach to writing.
     Nin's style has assurance; it shows the freedom of enjoy-
     ment. It is not without violence and struggle, but its
     violence is not a straining after effects. Female writing
     occasionally suffers from wordiness; Nin is praiseworthy
     for her ability to say what she feels in her unique way and
     then stop.

1944 A BOOKS - NONE

1944 B SHORTER WRITINGS

1   ANON. "Nin, Anaïs," in Current Biography 1944. Edited by
     Ann Rothe. New York: H. W. Wilson, pp. 493-495.
         Nin chose to "write sincerely" and print her own books.
     Although commercial publishers rejected it, Nin's work has
     been praised by other writers such as Henry Miller and
     William Carlos Williams. Rebecca West is quoted on Winter
     of Artifice: "I think the whole thing quite marvelous,
     particularly in its use of absolutely new material. You
     seem to me to have real and unmistakable genius." Biogra-
     phy of Nin. Nin has been keeping a journal since the age
     of eleven. In 1920 she married Ian Hugo. In 1944, Nin
     "announced her plan to convert and transpose the diary of
     sixty-five volumes into a full, long novel of the thirty
     years between 1914 and 1944--between two wars." Describes
     Nin's private printing of Winter of Artifice and Under a
     Glass Bell. Nin says her work has been successful with many

readers, including those without much education. Describes Nin physically: "slender...red-brown hair, green eyes, pale mat skin."

2   MILLER, HENRY. "Letter to Anaïs Nin Regarding One of Her Books," in his Sunday After the War. Norfolk, Conn.: New Directions, pp. 284-297.

   Miller will not suggest changes in Nin's work, for her English is intimately her own and "plays on raw nerves with effects of delirium and ecstasy." "Beyond the masks stands a woman stripped of all femininity...the all-sufficient self." The character of Mona in the diary is "obscene," distorting relationships and sex. Nin's work puzzles Miller because it makes an artificial unity of many layers and there are "holes between her utterances." Images of fear and despair intermingle in her work, and its central "calamity" is the discovery that peace and security cannot be found. Losing everything, Nin's strength to go on living comes from the artist within her. Nin must rid herself of the demon, the woman one step away from madness, looking for suffering; but there is no way to separate us from our suffering, for suffering is "the disease which has produced all our art."

3   MILLER, HENRY. "Letter to William Bradley, Literary Agent, August 2, 1933," in his Sunday After the War. Norfolk, Conn.: New Directions, pp. 276-284.

   Miller condemns the taste, judgment, and vision of literary agent William Bradley, who requested Nin to make changes in her diary for the sake of making it totally palatable to the public. The diary is a "painfully naked exposal of a woman's soul," a cross-section of modern life that has universal human appeal. Parts which do not appeal to Bradley could appeal to other readers. Such quest of truth in literature never leads to "nullity." The basic theme of the diary is pain of isolation; it reflects struggle in Nin's past and offers a framework for future drama. "The book and the woman are one"; this record of her life will save posterity the labor of researching it. Possibly no publisher wants to risk a fortune to publish Nin's diary but it will eventually come into print regardless of considerations about public reception.

4   WILSON, EDMUND. "Books--Doubts and Dreams: Dangling Man and Under A Glass Bell." The New Yorker, 20 (1 April), 78-82.

   Praises Under a Glass Bell. Nin's earlier books, "rather fragmentary examples of a kind of autobiographical fantasy [are] a little disappointing." The pieces in Under

1944

a Glass Bell belong to a genre Virginia Woolf also used:
"half short stories, half dreams...they mix a sometimes ex-
quisite poetry with a homely realistic observation." They
transpire in "a world of feminine perception and fancy."
Passages suffer from the tendency of the surrealists to a
"mere reeling-out of images," but in Nin's work the imagery
has meaning. "Half woman, half childlike spirit," the
writer is "likely at any moment to be volatilized into a
superterrestrial being who feels things that we cannot
feel." Nin "is a very good artist," unlike the other literary surrealists. Some of the pieces in the collection
are "really beautiful." Reprinted 1974.B82.

1945 A BOOKS - NONE

1945 B SHORTER WRITINGS

1   ROSENFELD, ISAAC. "Psychoanalysis as Literature." The New
      Republic, 113 (17 December), 844-845.
          Review of This Hunger. Nin's preoccupation with the
      problems of the feminine soul shows concern for human val-
      ues in general; however, her psychoanalytical style of
      writing is "inadequate." Her unconscious "systematization"
      of her characters distorts their reality. She takes the
      results of psychoanalysis, the splitting up of the person-
      ality into its drives, and uses these drives for the total
      motivation of her characters. Hence the characters of This
      Hunger remain as "personifications of neurotic anxiety."
      Nin illustrates the sexual dangers which impede women's
      development. This theme is found in each of the stories of
      This Hunger. Women fear expressing sexuality to men, who
      will not allow women to express their nature or who fail
      in their own masculine role. Fear leads to aggression and
      women try to take dominance away from men. Nin creates
      "great emotional pictures," but her only weapon against
      aggression and detachment is protest. Women are pictured
      in pain and retreat or recoil from relationships; as if it
      were "a natural law," women are expected to fail in their
      efforts to deal with men. The events of the novel "do not
      illustrate Nin's aim of describing woman's efforts to un-
      derstand her own nature."

2   WILSON, EDMUND. "Books--Isherwood--Marquand--Anaïs Nin." The
      New Yorker, 21 (10 November), 97-102.
          Nin's This Hunger is not polished but explores important
      new areas. She attempts to express the feminine point of
      view while handling the conflict of living half in a male-

controlled world and half in a world she is making for herself. Each of the three sections of the novel represents
a different woman in relationships with others. None of
the groups interconnect; probably they all are part of a
longer novel of unknown design, dealing with woman's self-
destructive aspect. The excessive abstraction of character
relations and a repetitiousness that obscures Nin's own
personal voice are reminiscent of Lawrence. The world of
this novel is one where "semi-independent" men and women
engage in "the capriciousness of passion and friendship."
Nin creates a dynamic picture of our confusion from identi-
fying imagined love with actual sexual contacts. Nin has
not yet begun to use all her intelligence and talent in her
work; hopefully a commercial publisher will accept her next
work so that she will have the general reading audience she
deserves.

1946 A BOOKS - NONE

1946 B SHORTER WRITINGS

1   ANON. "Ladders to Fire." The Virginia Kirkus Service, 14
      (15 August), 396.
          Ladders to Fire is the "mystic erotica" of woman warring
      with herself. It is frenzied, passionate, and Freudian.
      Public libraries should "pass it firmly by."

2   KAY, KEITH. "Ladders to Fire." San Francisco Chronicle
      (8 December), "This World" Section, p. 11.
          Henry Miller has called Nin a genius, "but then he says
      that to all the girls--all the girls, that is, who write a
      little bit like Henry Miller." Most critics agree Nin is
      "a good writer who combines the impressionism of Virginia
      Woolf with an intellectual searching never native to Blooms-
      bury." In life Nin has been an actress in surrealistic
      movies and a practicing psychiatrist, work which plays the
      greatest part in her new novels. The trio of women in Lad-
      ders to Fire--Stella, Lillian, and Djuna--"almost comes
      complete with cauldron and spoon." It is good that Dutton
      has taken over the job of printing Nin's books and is mak-
      ing them available.

3   LYONS, HERBERT. "Surrealist Soap Opera." The New York Times
      Book Review (20 October), p. 16.
          Review of Ladders to Fire. Nin's work has long been the
      preserve of an enthusiastic circle of friends who read her
      privately printed books. It appears that her avant-garde

1946

friends were more enthusiastic than critical. The story
concerns the struggles of a woman to understand her nature;
man appears only dimly, since the woman is at war with herself and relates only to the child in the man. The stories
of Stella, Lillian, and Djuna are reminiscent of radio soap
operas in which pale, weak, young men revolve around women
who endlessly seek their "independence and self-creation."
Nin writes that she wants her readers to receive her works
through their senses like painting and music, but her work
is so obscure and abstract, her canvas looks like a used
palette. Nin's work merely echoes Djuna Barnes, Henry
Miller, and Edmund Wilson. This novel has interest only
as "a pastiche of contemporary preciousness."

4   MARTIN, JEX, JR. "Modern Version of Old Fable: Woman Loses
        Femininity When She Enters Man's World." The Chicago Sun
        (17 November), "Book Week," p. 14.
          Patronizing and negative review of Ladders to Fire, the
        first of Nin's books to be published by a commercial press
        (Dutton). Nin is "a Franco-Spanish American exotic...
        doyenne of the Village's experimental writers." The theme
        of the book is the "modern 'incomplete woman' who in seek-
        ing to enter the masculine creative world has lost her
        femininity and destroyed her own nature." Nin's "somnam-
        bulistic prose" is influenced by Djuna Barnes and Gertrude
        Stein and Henry Miller. "It's pretty but is it art?" The
        average reader will not call it "either life or art," but
        Nin's coterie (Edmund Wilson, Kay Boyle, William Carlos
        Williams) will probably approve.

5   SMITH, HARRISON. "Ladies in Turmoil." Saturday Review, 29
        (30 November), 13.
          Review of Ladders to Fire. Counsels Nin that she should
        worry about "bursting into flame" if the prose of Ladders
        to Fire is typical of her work. All the women in the book
        are in "the throes of passion, convulsed by pity," strong
        personalities paired with such timid male companions that
        they seek female friends. The personalities of the women
        characters and their dreams are material for a "psychoana-
        lyst's holiday." Nin is no more a surrealist, imagist, or
        "modern," than "any woman in a permanent tantrum...any
        woman...who had lived too long in the art colonies of the
        world, and had too little to do with children, cooking and
        the garden in the backyard." Ladders to Fire is the "il-
        legitimate child" of Wilson's "Memories of Hecate County."

*6   STEPANCHEV, STEPHEN. Review of Ladders to Fire. New York
      Herald Tribune Weekly Book Review (20 April), p. 396.
          Unlocatable. Cited in Zee, Nancy Scholar. "Anaïs Nin:
      Beyond the Mask." Ph.D. dissertation, Brown University,
      1973, p. 266.

7   TRILLING, DIANA. "Fiction in Review." The Nation, 162 (26
      January), 105-107.
          Review of This Hunger. Nin's works have not been com-
      mercially published to any great extent, but privately
      printed copies have been praised by her friends. The three
      short stories in This Hunger are each about "a gravely mal-
      adjusted woman hungering for affection." The writing style
      is based on psychoanalysis; stories are like case his-
      tories. The "surrealist" quality of Nin's work is merely
      a by-product of a style which abstracts the characters and
      provides specific detail only when it is necessary for anal-
      sis of emotions. Nin's method is that of "clinical history"
      with two specific differences: she has literary ability
      and her intention is to make a "comment about life," not
      just an addition to the knowledge of the clinical method.
      Objects to Nin's philosophy that women are hurt by men and
      the reader should feel resentment against men and pity for
      their victims. Nin uses psychoanalysis for the singular
      purpose of supporting her sexual "chauvinism" and self
      pity; however, when she employs the straight prose of ob-
      servation, Nin shows potential ability to produce good
      fiction.

8   WILSON, EDMUND. "Books--A Note on Anaïs Nin." The New
      Yorker, 22 (16 November), 114.
          Ladders to Fire is the first book by Nin to be published
      by an American commercial publisher. The first two sec-
      tions of the book were originally published in This Hunger;
      the new chapter, "Bread and Wafer" is better than the
      others, blending "poetic imagery with psychological por-
      traiture." The story is rather amorphous in its aim, but
      the reviewer's judgment is limited since this tale is only
      part of a longer, several-volume novel. Nin's studies of
      women remain "perceptive and disarming."

1947 A BOOKS - NONE

1947 B SHORTER WRITINGS

1   ANON. "Children of the Albatross." The Virgina Kirkus Serv-
      ice, 15 (15 August), 440.

1947

Children of the Albatross continues the "vagaries" of
the same four characters found in Ladders to Fire. "This
time the facts are a little more visible...although the
same dream-like and erotic handling of words and phrases is
prevalent." Lacking plot and resolution of the problems
depicted, the book is not a novel but a collection of
scenes from the lives of people in pre-war Paris.

2 ANON. "Briefly Noted--Fiction." The New Yorker, 23 (8 November), 131-132.
Review of Children of the Albatross. Nin only partially
succeeds in illuminating the hidden areas of her characters' personalities. With total disregard for the conventions of the novel, she writes of a group of "delicately
strung young people thrashing their way through adoles-
cence." She frequently uses "incandescent metaphors and
images," but the book rambles.

3 ANON. "Under a Glass Bell and Other Stories." The Virginia
Kirkus Service, 15 (15 December), 678.
Under a Glass Bell contains nebulous, poetic, and in-
comprehensible phrases creating a montage of impressions of
the dream world; like the other Nin works, it is erotica
with only a tenuous plot.

4 BURFORD, WILLIAM. "The Art of Anaïs Nin," in On Writing, by
Anaïs Nin. The "Outcast Chapbooks," Number 11. Yonkers,
New York: Oscar Baradinsky, pp. 5-14.
Nin's art needs "definition," but current standards are
inadequate to judge such new writing. Critics and writers
of the present still cling to traditional forms of order.
Young writers turn to Nin because of her ability to create
order valid for the modern world. Nin represents the opposite of the negative qualities of the realists of the day.
"Creation is more important to her than destruction, order
more desirable than confusion, reality more valid than
realism." In Nin's work the "distinction between literature and life" disappears; "the order which Anaïs Nin has
perfected is the equality of literature and life." Nin
"has shown her readers the modern woman and the modern
man." Nin's fictional characters are hungry for "destruction and creation." Destruction means loss of individuality, inability to act according to feeling, intuition or
desire. Creation means liberation so that nothing separates achievement from desire. For Nin's characters "the
requisite of happiness is a perfect human relationship."
All her fiction shows the theme of this search for perfection. Nin makes a distinction between life (moments of

high tension in which lives are at stake), and living (periods of boredom and uneventfulness). Nin's "successful
people are always those who do not cling to their safety."
Nin is traditional and modern because she makes us aware
of "the myths of human nature."

5   DAVIS, ROBERT GORHAM. "Anaïs Nin's Children of Light and
    Movement." The New York Times Book Review (23 November),
    p. 36.
        Review of Children of the Albatross. Nin is fascinated
    in a simple psychoanalytic way with waking fantasies and
    ego-ideals. She deletes objective observations and drama-
    tic development and records only subjective tensions and
    movement. Using abstractions and conventional metaphoric
    images, she offers insight into "the dance of generalities
    and types." The characters of Children of the Albatross
    are children of light, concerned only with egos, dreams,
    and relationships. They have no last names, titles which
    would imply worldly status or externality. Djuna is a
    dreamer who makes her dreams into a reality she cannot
    bear; Michael flees love; Paul is free enough to realize
    love.

6   HART, WILLIAM. "Analysis of the Antagonisms Inherent in the
    Human Struggle." Houston Post (16 November), Section 4,
    p. 21.
        Children of the Albatross analyzes relations between
    the sexes—the flight of men and women from each other,
    and from any situation which does not combine dream and
    reality. Nin's "subtle intelligence" produces a psycho-
    logically probing prose "sharpened by care for the value
    and meaning of words." The flaws in this work mostly stem
    from difficulty in ascertaining meaning; for example, we
    wonder if the problems of other characters in the story
    could be solved by developing Jay's love of the ordinary.
    Nin, however, rarely gives answers, certainly no placebos.
    What she does give is the "gift of literature"—prose "ex-
    quisitely fashioned."

7   McLAUGHLIN, RICHARD. "Shadow Dance." Saturday Review, 30
    (20 December), 16-17.
        Review of Children of the Albatross. Ostensibly con-
    cerned with the fears and dreams of youth, the novel is
    actually a journey into the subconscious where the spirit
    "dances between light and shadow" to avoid the obstacles
    in its path. The tensions of relationships are occasion-
    ally rendered but usually Nin avoids such exposure. Djuna
    is a dancer whose house represents her many-faceted

personality, including the dark, locked room where she
keeps the childhood fears and terrors stemming from the
desertion of her father. For this reason, she seeks man
as child, not man the father, and finds the adolescents
Paul, Michael, and Donald, who are searching for new challenges. As quickly as they alight, these "children of the
albatross," ascend and leave Djuna to travel the city's
interior passageways alone with the dream as her only form
of reality. Notes the lushness of the novel, the tonal
quality of the symbolic language Nin uses. The psychological problems explored in the book demand characters of
"paper mache," more puppet-like than flesh and blood.
Their transparency creates a "fragile, remote spell" in
which one reads their thoughts and seeks to create unity
from the situation and their actions.

1948 A BOOKS - NONE

1948 B SHORTER WRITINGS

1   ANON. Review of <u>Under a Glass Bell and Other Stories</u>. New
York <u>Herald Tribune Weekly Book Review</u> (21 November), p. 33.
"Fact and fantasy mingle continually and the world appears as a subjective vision, bathed in private emotion."
The stories "reflect Nin's preoccupation with the suffering, restless ego." Most of the characters are Bohemians,
but some of the most successful have no "artistic preten-
sions."

2   DAVIS, ROBERT GORHAM. "The Fantastic World of Anaïs Nin."
<u>The New York Times Book Review</u> (28 March), p. 24.
The early stories Nin wrote and included in <u>Under a
Glass Bell</u> are preoccupied with fantasy, yet reality is
still very evident as in "Birth." The dreams of the characters both effect and are affected by the events of their
daily life. Later work illustrates Nin's total absorption
in the dream world. The novelette "Winter of Artifice"
discusses a young girl's love for her father and how she
begins a diary to lure him to return. It is a reflection
of Nin's own life and her diary, which was highly praised by
Henry Miller. This may account for the total self-absorp-
tion evident in her later work, as well as the importance
she places on all her behavior, both trivial and significant.

3   GAROFFOLO, VINCENT. "Under the Glass Bell and Other Stories."
     The New Mexico Quarterly Review, 18 (Summer), 247-249.
         Edmund Wilson has described Nin's stories and novels as
     "a world of feminine perception and fancy," a description
     which accurately marks "the limits" of the stories in this
     collection. The stories offer intense and revealing per-
     ceptions but are also "monotonous and vapid." The diffi-
     culty of creating her characters' drives and obsessions
     does not absolve Nin for the incompleteness of her work.
     Sometimes she gives the impression of straining to provide
     new insights into the human spirit. The sincerity of the
     book prompts hope that her future work will be less labored.

4   HARDWICK, ELIZABETH. "Fiction Chronicle." Partisan Review,
     15 (June), 705-711.
         Review of Under a Glass Bell. Nin persists in perpe-
     trating her "desperate youth" in her writing, although now
     it seems old-fashioned. A literary child of the 1920s, she
     is "dreary and pretentious," avoiding reality in order to
     glory in images of a "psychological underworld." Some of
     the stories in Under a Glass Bell are very effective, but
     the writing is too mystical and abstract. All the tales
     revolve around the "eternal feminine," yet Nin obscures
     more than reveals the inner development of woman's soul and
     passion. "One soon becomes bored" with her indirect lan-
     guage. Nin's frequent references to her unpublished diary
     as the key to understanding the stories are also frustrat-
     ing.

5   KINGERY, ROBERT E. "New Books Appraised--Fiction." Library
     Journal, 73 (1 January), 40.
         Brief review of Under a Glass Bell. These short stories
     of sensation and states of consciousness are intensely fem-
     inine. "All reiterate the themes and gain some signifi-
     cance in relation to Children of the Albatross," yet their
     "felicity of language" seems largely wasted.

6   YOUNG, VERNON. "Five Novels, Three Sexes, and Death." The
     Hudson Review, 1 (Autumn), 421-432.
         Review of Under a Glass Bell. Nin's ability to reveal
     the essence of femininity is flawed because it is obsessive.
     She is too solicitous of women and portrays men as the nat-
     ural enemy. The best illustration of this theme is found
     in the story "Hejda." Stories like "Djuna" and "Hejda"
     show that women do not want men; this is understandable,
     since Nin is incapable of creating whole, believable male
     characters. The "agonized privacy" of Nin's women generates
     no sympathy. These women are too self-satisfied, believing

1948

that their uniqueness has been ignored by men unable to understand them; they are cowards caught in infantile regression. At Nin's best, she is equalled only by D. H. Lawrence; her style can capture the fragmentation of urban life. Occasionally, however, Nin becomes "ludicrous" in her inability to separate judgment from intuition; and in abandoning conventional forms "she risks losing herself down tunnels of artifice."

1949 A BOOKS - NONE

1949 B SHORTER WRITINGS

1   ANON. "The Four-Chambered Heart." The Virginia Kirkus Service, 17 (15 November), 633.
    In Nin's typical "undulant" prose The Four-Chambered Heart depicts a "hothouse world of psychosexual emotions." It is recommended for those who enjoy Nin's decadent, Freudian, "almost foetal imagery" and exotic surnames.

2   NICHOLS, ELIZABETH P. "New Books Appraised--Fiction." Library Journal, 74 (1 December), 1818.
    Brief review of The Four-Chambered Heart. Nin's writing is fascinating because of her stimulating language and zest for psychoanalyzing her characters. This novel deals with humanity's dual nature of destruction and construction. Characterization is fuller than in Nin's previous work and the story is more unified. Nin's fluid movement and rhythm remain unchanged.

1950 A BOOKS - NONE

1950 B SHORTER WRITINGS

1   ANON. "Books Briefly Noted--Fiction." The New Yorker, 25 (28 January), 85.
    Brief review of The Four-Chambered Heart. Nin's "feverish female writing" effectively conveys the complicated love triangle in the novel. However, she does too much musing on love, death, guilt, sacrifice and so on.

2   ANON. "Love on a Barge." Time, 55 (6 February), 90.
    This novel "piles a mountainous icing of surrealist imagery and rubberly aphorisms on a little cake of plot no bigger than a thumb." Reviews Nin's life, noting that she was recognized among the avant-garde and acclaimed by

writers like Henry Miller before her work was published
commercially. Having privately published three books, she
arrived in New York in 1944, wanting to convert her diary
volumes into a long novel. The Four-Chambered Heart, like
her two previous works, Ladders to Fire and Children of the
Albatross, "reads more like a diary than a novel - but a
diary in which nothing actually happens."

3   ANON. "Bookshelf: From the Crop of New Winter Novels." The
    Christian Science Monitor (9 February), p. 15.
        Review of The Four-Chambered Heart. Djuna is a "mask"
    for Nin herself. Djuna is "all female"; Rango, "the superb
    male animal." Summarizes the plot. The "originality" is
    "entirely of external effect." "Strip this tale of its
    trappings, pierce through the much touted prose (which
    turns out to be ordinary, even trite phraseology set to
    self-conscious rhythm), and there is left only sterility."
    There is "nothing enduring about a story in which the high-
    est common denominator is a self-centered, thinly ration-
    alized animalism."

4   ANON. "Fiction Notes." Saturday Review, 33 (18 March), 28.
        Review of The Four-Chambered Heart. The character of
    Rango engenders "a queer sort of fascination about his
    story." Rango is the dreamer, the mountain man, for whose
    attention his sickly wife and young mistress avidly vie.
    Rango becomes whatever these two "ecstatically sacrificial
    slaves" desire to see, yet he would never belong completely
    to either because he exists in more than one world. Nin
    may refer to love as "the great narcotic," but in this nov-
    el the characters are in no way drugged.

5   CARRUTH, HAYDEN. "The Four-Chambered Heart." The Providence
    Sunday Journal (29 January), p. 10.
        The Four-Chambered Heart shows a very "feminine writer."
    It focuses on one girl with clarity of emotional detail and
    language that is more accurate poetically than Nin has used
    before. This is "some of the finest writing of our time."

6   D., E. "'Feminine Touch' in Literature." Chicago Sun Times
    (16 April), Section 2, p. 9.
        Review of The Four-Chambered Heart. Readers with a
    taste for what William Carlos Williams calls "a feminine
    touch in the arts" will find it in Nin's novel of a Paris
    art colony. But the book shows "a rather peculiar heart--
    even for a woman."

1950

7   De VILLA FRANCA, SUZANNE. "The Bookworm Turns." New Haven
Register (12 February), Magazine Section, p. 9.
       In The Four-Chambered Heart, Nin uses exotic materials--
artistic characters, Paris as a setting, an impressionistic
style--to create "home truth" in depicting the inner feelings of her central character, Djuna, whose major tragedy
is ours: the failure of relationships or circumstances to
call forth our complete selves. Nin's subject matter is
"the warm and the near." It is most absorbing for women,
who are attracted to Djuna's awareness and sensibility as
she explores her needs and desires.

8   FULOP-MILLER, RENE. "Freudian Noah's Ark." The New York
Times (29 January), p. 4.
       Review of The Four-Chambered Heart. The novel shows a
mature artist who has translated a series of psychic fantasies into a narrative. Rango is the primitive, natural
man from Guatemala making his way through the decadent
Parisian night life. His wife binds him to her with attacks of illness and hysteria. Djuna, Rango's mistress,
tries to give him the healing power of love. He is torn
between the positive and the negative and escapes through
political action. Expelled from the party for his visionary personality, he returns to his women. Djuna has realized that the romantic love she envisioned with him is
impossible, so she sinks the houseboat. One wonders if the
boat has preserved these people for a new beginning or for
a continuation of their hell. A world of dream unites with
the world of waking. Action is converted into inner experience; "the River Seine and the flowing Seine of the
psyche" become one. In drawing upon the insights of Freud
and Jung, Nin presents insight into the human psyche.

9   K[AY], K[EITH]. "The Four-Chambered Heart." San Francisco
Chronicle (19 February), "This World" Section, pp. 14, 16.
       Review of The Four-Chambered Heart. Nin has been called
a genius by Henry Miller, "who obviously says that to all
the girls." Nin's works are "little more than 200-page
soap operas." The prose is so pretentious, "detergent"
would be a better word than "soap." Djuna "is growing up
faster than the writer." Criticizes Rango's pompous language. Nin doesn't allow her characters to convey the
story. She explains instead of using action and dialogue.
She "has obviously never realized that, especially in a
novel, three's a crowd."

10   MORRIS, LLOYD. "Anaïs Nin's Special Art." New York <u>Herald</u>
      <u>Tribune Book Review</u> (12 March), p. 17.
           Review of <u>The Four-Chambered Heart</u>. Praise from Rebecca
      West and Edmund Wilson and the admiration of many younger
      writers have made Nin a celebrity. <u>The Four-Chambered</u>
      <u>Heart</u> continues Nin's "spiritual biography." The narrative
      method demonstrates her belief that realistic narrative
      forms have been exhausted. Her aim is to reveal the love
      experience directly by immersing readers in a sensibility
      that is feeling and suffering. Djuna, central to all the
      novels, asserts a "peculiarly feminine prejudice"; she
      exalts love as the goal of living and aims at a total union
      which her intellect knows to be impossible. Man in Nin's
      novels is "the obstacle to woman's fulfillment," a creature
      of "chaos, disorder, caprice, destruction."

11   ROLO, CHARLES J. "The Life of the Heart." <u>The Atlantic</u>, 185
      (February), 86-87.
           Nin's work breaks down the wall between the ego and the
      unconscious. Evoking "the feeling of dance," the novel re-
      lates the love between Djuna, the dancer, and Rango, who
      plays the guitar. Rango's natural jealousy and childish-
      ness shatter their happiness until Djuna realizes her love
      is created by his love for all the things she stifled in
      herself during childhood. Struggling to save their rela-
      tionship, Djuna tries to create "a world of two." Nin ex-
      plores the intricacies of the male/female relationship and
      tells the reader that nothing is more difficult than the
      fusion of two people in a relationship.

<u>1951 A BOOKS - NONE</u>

<u>1951 B SHORTER WRITINGS</u>

1   WARFEL, HARRY R. "Anaïs Nin," in <u>American Novelists of Today</u>.
      New York: American Book, pp. 321-322.
           Biography. Nin married Ian Hugo, an engraver. Quotes
      Nin: "I intend the greater part of my writing to be re-
      ceived directly through the senses, as one apprehends
      painting and music." Discusses the subject matter of the
      novels. <u>Winter of Artifice</u> "was the first novel written
      on the theme of psychoanalysis."

1954

1954 A BOOKS - NONE

1954 B SHORTER WRITINGS

1　GEISMAR, MAXWELL. "Temperament vs. Conscience." The Nation,
　　179 (24 July), 75-76.
　　　　A Spy in the House of Love is a perceptive story of the
　　rewards and punishments of a woman's passions. Humor
　　raises the novel to the level of "artistic tragi-comedy."
　　The story traces the exploits of Sabina, who is pursued by
　　the lie-detector, a figure from psychoanalysis and conven-
　　tional morality. Nin affirms female biological impulses
　　as equal in importance to those of male characters created
　　by other writers. With complete honesty reminiscent of
　　D. H. Lawrence, Nin tells of Sabina's impetuous emotions
　　and the power of conquest she feels. Sabina knows she must
　　hurt before she is hurt, escape before her lover escapes,
　　and so the price she pays is endless anxiety. The novel is
　　composed of a series of scenes in which masculine figures
　　demand Sabina play the roles she believes a woman is forced
　　to play. Eventually, she turns to Djuna, a female friend
　　created in an earlier Nin novel, for solace and advice.
　　Hence "friendship is the solace for passion perhaps, as art
　　is the crystallization of imperfect human desire."

2　ROLO, CHARLES. "Potpourri." The Atlantic, 194 (August), 86.
　　　　Review of A Spy in the House of Love. The novel's
　　structure suggests a ballet in which the dancer, Sabina,
　　seeks the reason for her need for mobility in love. She
　　does not know what she wants from her husband and three
　　other men or why she eventually rejects them. Criticizes
　　Nin for the easy self-knowledge Sabina is given at the end
　　of the novel. The reader should view the conclusion as
　　ending only one more chapter in Sabina's life, since all of
　　Nin's work can be considered a continual examination of
　　Sabina's inner spirit.

3　STONE, JEROME. "Fiction Note: The Psyche of the Huntress."
　　Saturday Review, 37 (15 May), 32.
　　　　Review of A Spy in the House of Love. Once again, Nin
　　has attempted to "illuminate the sub-cellars of the female
　　psyche," this time using her dreamy literary style to ex-
　　plore a woman's sexual encounters. Sabina is the woman who
　　is torn between filling her life with a multiplicity of ex-
　　periences and hoping to discover a relationship that will
　　"integrate" her personality and end her torture. This is
　　not Nin's best work since it is neither "poetically

imaginative" nor "psychologically profound." It conjures
up the image of a beautiful bird beating its wings against
the walls of its cage.

1955 A BOOKS - NONE

1955 B SHORTER WRITINGS

1   ANON. "Artist's Experiment in Films, Anaïs Nin to Appear at
     N.U." Evanston Review (19 May), p. 99.
         Announces a discussion on "The Poetic Film" to be given
     by Nin on the campus of Northwestern University following
     a showing of experimental films by Ian Hugo. Nin was also
     scheduled to give a lecture on writing, with readings from
     her own works. One of the films, "Bells of Atlantis," was
     based on Nin's work.

2   KUNITZ, STANLEY J. and HOWARD HAYCRAFT, eds. "Nin, Anaïs,"
     in Twentieth Century Authors: A Biographical Dictionary of
     Modern Literature. New York: H. W. Wilson, p. 720.
         Prints a biographical sketch supplied by Nin. At twen-
     ty, she married American banker and artist Hugh Guiler, who
     later became known as engraver and film maker Ian Hugo.
     Her "strange chronicles of the subconscious, written in
     esoteric and imaginative prose, have brought her the atten-
     tion of a small but highly literate public." Her published
     novels center on a dancer named Djuna, who acts as a "sen-
     sitive register" to human experience. Nin is "pale and
     slender, with brown-red hair and green eyes."

3   MUDRICK, MARVIN. "Humanity is the Principle." The Hudson
     Review, 7 (Winter), 610-619.
         Calls A Spy in the House of Love a "touchingly battered
     innocent survival of the 'twenties.'" Criticizes the char-
     acterization, dialogue, and setting. "Breathtakingly
     trite" characters discuss their problems with dialogue out
     of John's Other Wife. In the Village, lovers sit on studio
     couches listening to Debussy as if "nothing has changed
     since Coolidge." The central character, Sabina, is merely
     "a girl in search of an ideal mate" and the five men whom
     she encounters are stereotypes. Stops just short of ac-
     cusing Nin of "straightforward inanities."

4   PERLÈS, ALFRED. My Friend Henry Miller: An Intimate Biogra-
     phy. London: Neville Spearman, pp. 37-39, 106-108.
         Nin recognized the essential Henry Miller at a glance,
     and they became as close as Castor and Pollux. Nin began

1955

her diary in French and Spanish and continued it in English. She had a kind of supra-lingual language that Miller loved; one could only understand Nin by appreciating her language. Miller was the kind of man Nin had been looking for, because she felt let down by the other men in her life. She lapped up Miller's praise and criticism. Miller felt that guarding her diary caused Nin to live a marginal existence, and that the solution would be to publish the book.

1959 A BOOKS - NONE

1959 B SHORTER WRITINGS

1   DURRELL, LAWRENCE. "Preface," in <u>Children of the Albatross</u>. London: Peter Owen, pp. 9-10.
     Nin is a "writer of real force who has established her own private kingdom in contemporary literature." Nin belongs to "the great subjective-feminine tradition (Virginia Woolf, Djuna Barnes, Anna Kavan)." The common factor of this tradition is a focus on the changing experiences of each second, rather than on objective reality. Nin's "highly distilled prose...has the accent and rhythm of poetry." Her books are concerned with "poetic truth and the human personality," delivered through symbols. The subjectivity of Nin's books "demands complete surrender in the reader, without which the spell would not have a chance to work." Recommends the books "for finely-wrought musical writing shot through with clear insights into the inner world." Reprinted in 1974.B32.

2   FANCHER, EDWIN. "Anaïs Nin: Avant-Gardist with a Loyal Underground." <u>The Village Voice</u> (27 May), pp. 4-5.
     Praises <u>Under a Glass Bell</u>. Nin has been praised by some critics but she is not known to general readers. Recounts a visit to Nin as "a major figure in the avant-garde literary movement of the past twenty-five years." Surprised to meet "a quite beautiful and vibrant blonde." The five novels of <u>Cities of the Interior</u> "depict the interferences to life, the blocks and distortions to growth, and try to go to the neurotic core of their characters." The final book deals with the creation of health out of neurosis. Nin is "perhaps the most feminine of all modern writers and she deals with the deepest crisis of feminine character." Nin says Greenwich Village has the only community of arts in America.

3   FANCHETTE, JEAN. "Notes pour une Préface." Two Cities: La
    Revue Bilingue de Paris (15 April), pp. 56-60. [French.]
        Nin's unusual and dense work occupies a distinctive
    place in American literature. Nin is known in France for
    her preface to Tropic of Cancer, but her own work has not
    been translated into French. A key word to understanding
    Nin is "awareness." Nin knows. She projects a blinding
    light on that which generations of writers conveyed only in
    literary periphrases. Nin's art is in her knowing how to
    explain the chemistry between the body and the soul, in
    defining so many troubling biological instincts. Nin has
    never deviated from the search for classic self-control,
    the search for the perfect work. Only Virginia Woolf among
    previous women writers achieved this goal. House of Incest
    is a kind of "visceral evangelism whose prophet would have
    associated with surrealists." Nin's work gives off "an in-
    dividual scream in feminine literature." A Spy in the
    House of Love is Nin's best work. Sabina, face to face
    with her lies, finds herself at the end of the novel, so
    the inevitable game of light and shadow can be terminated.
    A Spy in the House of Love concentrates Nin's themes and
    energy more forcefully than previous books. Nin is also a
    moralist. Pity in Nin's books is directed at women who do
    not fully assume their feminine role. The language and
    form of Nin's novels are as important as her themes. She
    is searching for a new romantic period; the theme which
    preoccupies her most is the necessity for the modern person
    to find himself in the forest of new symbols produced by
    our age. Nin is gradually producing great work which al-
    ready makes her one of the most original of American novel-
    ists.

1960 A BOOKS - NONE

1960 B SHORTER WRITINGS

1   [CHASE, KATHLEEN.] "Cities of the Interior, by Anaïs Nin."
    Two Cities: La Revue Bilingue de Paris (15 May), pp. 100-
    103.
        Nin's observations in D. H. Lawrence: An Unprofessional
    Study apply to herself. She focuses on Lawrence's philoso-
    phy that literature and life should be composed of passion-
    ate blood-experience. Her own work has one main idea:
    "imprisoned in the flesh is the body's own genie." Other
    comments about Lawrence's work also describe her own: 1)
    the personnages are symbolical; 2) people who want a sane
    world limit their lives defensively; 3) the characters

1960

reveal themselves by involvement in the color, rhythm, and complexity of their physical surroundings. Nin goes further than Lawrence to reveal feelings and thoughts never owned by women, especially in print, and for this she has been accused of "going too far." Thus the acclaim she "so rightly deserves" is just now beginning to come to her.

2   ELLSWORTH, RAY. "Half Stories, Half Dreams." The American Record Guide (January), pp. 381-382.
    Review of two recordings put out by Contemporary Classics: Anaïs Nin Reading "House of Incest" and Anaïs Nin Reading from "Under a Glass Bell." Biography and physical description of Nin. Discussion of Nin's use of dreams; praise of her ability to "bring the reader (in this case the listener) up short." The covers of the records suggest Nin is a surrealist, but she "has no 'ism.'" Nin is an exquisite poetic stylist; House of Incest is not a novel but poetry. "Miss Nin speaks with a firm, clear voice. She does not dramatize but simply reads, letting the words carry the tale."

3   RAES, HUGO. "On volprezen Anaïs Nin" [Anaïs Nin: Not praised Enough]. Vlaamse Gids, 44 (August), 520-525. [Flemish.]
    Nin is one of the rare women of genius who have acquired recognition in the literary world while keeping fine feminine modesty. House of Incest is a prose poem in which she searches for herself in a tormented and rapturous manner. Nin works with images, dreams, and symbols. With her intuitive feminine antenna, she sounds the unknown dimensions of the human heart. Already in her first book, her pure imagery, subtle rhythm, which will make jewels of her further publications, can be found. Under a Glass Bell contains thirteen stories which are some of the loveliest ever published. In all these stories we are touched by her very fine and typically feminine feeling of compassion. Nin searches for the truth of the heart with love. Nin is good at drawing personalities. Her analysis of human relationships is the result of her own internal turmoils and difficulties and also of her study of psychoanalysis. In the largest part of her literary work, especially in Solar Barque, initial difficulties develop into a philosophy of life, vitality, and acceptance. Nin is actually a moralist. In 1959 Nin helped with the publication of Two Cities, a bilingual international literary magazine.

1961 A BOOKS - NONE

1961 B SHORTER WRITINGS

1   ANON. "Stuff of Dreams." <u>The Times Literary Supplement</u> (16
     June), p. 369.
          Review of <u>Seduction of the Minotaur</u>. Against a "moonlit"
     background, Nin expresses the difficult truth that the
     repetitive pattern of life comes from within oneself. She
     thoroughly understands the human striving for "wholeness
     and integration" and communicates this need to the reader
     through symbolic parables. The warmth of the tropics and
     the sensuousness of color are clearly described, but the
     dreamy atmosphere of the novel disappears in the last thirty
     pages of the story.

2   BRADBURY, MALCOLM. "New Novels." <u>Punch</u>, 240 (21 June),
     953-954.
          <u>Seduction of the Minotaur</u> is more of a "psychoanalyti-
     cal" than a "psychological" novel. The setting recalls
     D. H. Lawrence's use of Mexico. The tone is private; its
     "feminine sensitivity" is reminiscent of the work of Ger-
     trude Stein and Virginia Woolf. Lillian sees her spirit
     reflected in the characters, the landscape, and the images
     around her. The novel is both "self-conscious" and "very
     intelligent."

3   HODGART, PATRICIA. "Fire of Exile." <u>The Spectator</u>, 206
     (26 May), 771.
          Review of <u>Seduction of the Minotaur</u>. Voluntary or im-
     posed exile is a popular theme in literature today. The
     voluntary exile like Lillian in <u>Seduction of the Minotaur</u>
     returns with new insights. The sun and the intense physi-
     cal sensations of the tropics absorb Lillian so that she
     moves through the story in a trance, the surrealist's sur-
     render to dreams. The novel is full of surrealist images,
     and Nin's finally controlled prose makes a new and poig-
     nant story until the flashbacks to Lillian's past life.

4   MURRAY, COLIN. "Review of <u>Seduction of the Minotaur</u>." <u>Time</u>
     <u>and Tide</u> (1 June), p. 915.
          <u>Seduction of the Minotaur</u> deserves respect, but the book
     is "a bit of a bore." The unconventional characters en-
     deavoring to escape reality are absorbed in their own im-
     mature personalities much as American expatriates in <u>Tender</u>
     <u>Is the Night</u>. Fitzgerald, however, "communicates" whereas
     Nin, using such techniques as baffling flash-backs in the
     last third of the book, does not seem to care about commu-
     nication.

1962

1962 B SHORTER WRITINGS

1   ANON. "Private View." The Times Literary Supplement
         (16 March), p. 186.
             Nin's study of D. H. Lawrence deserves recognition for
         its perception and "sincerity." This "almost breathless"
         survey of Lawrence's themes and attitudes focuses on Kan-
         garoo, Women in Love, and Lady Chatterly. The style is
         without pretense. Nin stresses Lawrence's ability to write
         with almost feminine sensitivity.

2   BALDANZA, FRANK. "Anaïs Nin." The Minnesota Review, 2 (Win-
         ter), 263-271.
             Cities of the Interior is a collection of "pointless,
         rambling explorations" of the fears and relationships among
         characters traveling in the world's Bohemian spots. These
         characters reveal their past in sudden, long monologues
         which center on a childhood trauma that drove them into the
         mistakes of the present. Nin's writing style is frag-
         mented; her abstractions show a "reluctance to render ex-
         perience in fictional terms." She is insensitive to good
         usage and syntax. The "opulent effects" of her imagery are
         actually "gilt and paste." In House of Incest, surrealist
         images alternate with abstract sentimentalizing. A Spy in
         the House of Love has a "cloying eroticism." The banality
         of Nin's symbolism becomes obvious in Solar Barque, with
         its land-locked boats and "stratified cities." Winter of
         Artifice closely parallels Nin's life, yet the story turns
         into a soap opera declaring life in a dream world prefer-
         able to reality. Nin's undisciplined writing fails to
         counterbalance the madness of the inner worlds of her
         Bohemian-type characters in Under a Glass Bell. Only the
         short story "Birth" is a well-crafted tale. Some of the
         failure of Nin's fiction undoubtedly comes from her habit
         of keeping a diary. The inclusiveness and total self-
         absorption of the diary appear as "a lack of standards."
         Her "honesty becomes vulgarity." The diary is a record of
         the "folkways of bohemia," rather than a work of litera-
         ture.

3   BAY, ANDRÉ. "Introduction," in Les miroirs dans le Jardin.
         Paris: Éditions Stock, pp. 7-12. [French.]
             Introduction to Anne Laurel's translation of Ladders to
         Fire. In the 1930s Nin was not given the homage she de-
         served and her work is still not well known. Nin, Miller,
         and Durrell were three vagabonds of genius, whose works

were influenced by the same sources; but their works are
very different because the common goal of their work was
to discover their own identities. The instrument for revealing these identities was the same: love in its multiple manifestations. As a woman, Nin was in the most vulnerable position and she was least visible. She was more
delicate, but at least as rich a writer, and she is more
truly a pioneer. The same quest for identity that caused
Miller to proclaim his virility caused Nin to affirm her
femininity. Her novels have a woman character at their
center. Analyzes Ladders to Fire. Lillian is not satis-
fied by marriage and maternity; marriage excludes the dream
and she must pursue her ideal dream. Ladders to Fire, like
the work of Joyce or Proust, cannot be exhausted at first
sight.

4   EVANS, OLIVER. "Anaïs Nin and the Discovery of Inner Space."
     Prairie Schooner, 36 (Fall), 217-231.
          Nin rejects her characters' outer masks and concentrates
     on exposing "the ultimate motive" and "the genuine self" by
     means of her characters' dreams and fantasies. Like Sar-
     tre, Nin is a pioneer in the search for identity. Nin's
     male characters involve themselves in causes and mass move-
     ments, but her women pursue the harder goal of learning
     their true nature and living on the level of personal re-
     lationships. Nin favors flexible interpretations of sym-
     bols, and uses rhythmic words to induce aural trance. Her
     style blends symbolism, psychoanalysis, and occasional ab-
     stract statement. The publication of Cities of the Inte-
     rior by Swallow Press should focus attention on the impact
     and complexity of Nin's style. No other writer has so
     relentlessly pursued "the ultimate sources of character"
     and the "nuances of personal relationship."

5   MARGOSHES, ADAM. "Seduction of the Minotaur." The Village
     Voice (10 May), pp. 5-6.
          Today women are writing "AS WOMEN for the first time, in
     an idiom that expresses--and discovers--the feminine sen-
     sibility from within: something brand new, startling and
     altogether wonderful to see." In her latest book, Nin
     "intensifies and purifies her style into an instrument of
     almost supernatural sensibility." The book evokes the
     Mexican landscape with original imagery. Characterization
     is finely done. The real subject is the heroine and women
     today. Nin "breaks the silence" about what happens to
     women after their emancipation. The heroine is "the eman-
     ciapted woman who has found herself, but so far only her-
     self, not yet the world." "All sensitive women today are

1962

expatriates of a sort." Hopes that women will listen to
Nin's voice--for it is their own voice. In a few words
Nin says much about what's wrong with marriage. Nin "pen-
etrates to the very center of homosexuality" which is "an
attraction to the body surface, that is, to the superficial." Nin's writing is "about life today, everybody's
life."

6   OUELLETTE, FERNAND. "Notice sur Anaïs Nin." [Montreal]
     Liberté (May), 359-361. [French.]
        Two of Nin's novels are appearing in French, published
     by Stock. Gives Nin's biography and history of her diary,
     which testifies to her "evolution." Lists her critical
     prose and fiction. Describes her friendship with Miller.
     Quotes from the praise Miller and Durrell gave to Nin.
     Jean Fanchette's article (1959.B3) was the first article
     in French on Nin's work. The French-Canadian reader who
     makes contact with Nin's work is likely to take a profound
     liking to it.

1963 A BOOKS - NONE

1963 B SHORTER WRITINGS

1   ANON. "Symphony of Existence." The Times Literary Supple-
     ment (21 June), p. 465.
        Ladders to Fire was conceived as the first in a series
     of novels describing the relationships between four women
     and their environment. Nin says that the correct critical
     approach to her work will judge the essense, not the facts.
     This novel must be viewed as part of the whole series in
     order to understand the "total design." Nin writes with
     insight about the subconscious of her characters; but she
     does not present surface realism as effectively. Some-
     times the novel seems "a frosted bowl in which one may
     glimpse the X-ray photographs of gold-fish."

2   BROOKE, JOCELYN. "New Novels." The Listener, 69 (6 June),
     973.
        Review of Ladders to Fire. Judging by Ladders to Fire,
     Nin's famous diary will not deserve comparison with St.
     Augustine's revelations but instead with Henry Miller's
     work. Nin has little feeling for words and nothing of in-
     terest to say. Attacks the novel as a "tangled chronicle
     of erotic attachments (mainly lesbian)." Perhaps these
     negative judgments about Nin's work are wrong, for she has
     been highly praised not only by Miller but also by Edmund
     Wilson, Lawrence Durrell, and Rebecca West.

1963

3   CABAU, JACQUES. "Traduction: Une bonne femme." Paris
      L'Express (28 February), pp. 33-34. [French.]
         Review of French translation of Ladders to Fire. The
      book is in direct contradiction to what Anaïs Nin admires
      in Miller: It is as pure as Miller is erotic, as intro-
      spective and retired as Miller is open and cosmic. Ladders
      to Fire is as romantic as Miller's work but the lyricism
      comes from the nerves and not the blood. It is the com-
      plaint of the frustrated woman in search of her self. It
      is the education of a woman who wants to be woman, "a suf-
      fragette of love" who wants passionately to live her fate
      without knowing exactly what it is, who searches from page
      to page and from love to love. There is something genuine
      in Nin's effort to understand the soul of solitary woman,
      overly conscious of herself and preferring the dream to the
      real. But the book remains too vague and too uncertain to
      be a real novel; it is only "the confession of a narcissus
      who refuses to let herself go to her reflection in the
      water."

4   OUELLETTE, FERNAND. "La femme en quête d'elle-même." [Mon-
      treal] Liberté (January-February), pp. 69-72. [French.]
         For the first time, a novel by Nin has been translated
      into French, Ladders to Fire (Les miroirs dans le Jardin).
      Nin is a great writer and this is a great novel. Nin's
      art has clarity, shrewdness, acuteness, cunning artfulness,
      poetry; her characters mirror our own labyrinth. In fact,
      these characters are more alive than the pseudo-alive that
      we meet every day. Lillian is in an anguished, distressed
      state, hungry for passion. Her entire being is violence,
      guilt, sensitivity, ardor and unconsciousness. Sabina's
      past, Djuna's future, Jay's present cannot help Lillian.
      Anguish, fear of being by herself, leads Lillian to mental
      suicide. If Lillian could have lived her present, she
      would have realized the truth which is basic to a passion
      for life: the importance of being oneself. Through these
      characters, we live the thirst for love and conscience
      which consumes human beings, the cry of despair and the
      scream of solitude. Lillian is not lost; she could start
      to become herself. Sabina could search for love beyond
      passion. Djuna could accept the present.

5   PRICE, R. G. G. "New Novels." Punch, 244 (12 June), 865-866.
         Calls the characters of Ladders to Fire "Mrs. Dalloways
      under mescalin," characters who reject the world of
      "structures" for the personal relationships which shape
      their lives. The novel is less a "female labyrinth of
      oblique perceptions" than the result of "the over-ripe
      fruit of leisure."

1963

6   ROSS, ALAN. "Special Notices." The London Magazine, 3 (July),
     90-91.
           Review of Ladders to Fire. Nin belongs to the pre-war
     circle of Miller and his admirers. Although Miller places
     her reputation alongside those of Abelard and Augustine,
     her reputation continues to survive on a very flimsy base.
     Lillian's lust is never resolved in this novel, despite a
     series of infatuations with both men and women who are in
     turn involved with each other. This is an ambiguous, very
     amateur story. Nin lacks the ear for dialog and her prose
     is an "American translation of brute insensibility." Wit,
     characterization and ideas have no place in the "dreamy,
     girlish world" she creates.

7   ZINNES, HARRIET. "Anaïs Nin's World Reissued." Books Abroad,
     37 (Summer), 283-286.
           Nin inspires the same "syndrome of attack and adoration"
     as D. H. Lawrence. Like Lawrence, Nin is "tremendously in
     tune with life and has that indestructible passion of one
     who loves and knows life fearlessly." She "conceals noth-
     ing...knows no taboos." Like Lawrence, she is "one of the
     few writers to understand modern woman's striving" to ex-
     press her frustrations. "It is extraordinarily fresh in
     Anglo-American writing to have the description come through
     a woman's senses." Like Lawrence, Nin approaches fiction
     as a poet; another reason for the strong reaction to her.
     "The real theme" of Nin's work "is the most poetic of all
     themes: what is the self, or put another way, what is
     freedom?" House of Incest is "over-rich." But despite
     occasional failures, Nin achieves noteworthy success be-
     cause she "exults in life and in being a woman." Reprinted
     1974.B87.

1964 A BOOKS - NONE

1964 B SHORTER WRITINGS

1   ANON. "The Way In to Way Out." The Times Literary Supplement
     (30 April), p. 381.
           Collages is an "evocative" yet "mysteriously idiosyn-
     cratic" novel about Renate the painter and the people she
     meets. One suspects the characters are sketches of people
     Nin has met in her life, and the book is an insider's view
     of colorful moments in the literary world she has traveled.
     The prose is elaborate and the fables interesting. Per-
     haps the key to the story is not in Nin's vision of the
     ideal life but in the thoughts recorded in her diary.

1964

2 ANON. "Books Briefly Noted--General." The New Yorker, 40
(30 May), 136.
D. H. Lawrence: An Unprofessional Study is a reissue of
Nin's first book, originally published in Paris in 1932.
Its inaccuracy is best exemplified by the three different
titles given to Studies in Classic American Literature.

3 ANON. "Collages by Anaïs Nin." Los Angeles Free Press (26
November), p. 8.
Collages is based on the observation that there is a
symbolic relationship between a person's inner life and
his gestures. The secret thoughts and dreams of the characters spill out through their fingers and define them.
The reader has to recognize this is true of himself too.
"He sees himself defenseless against the world." It is a
"frightening book." The characters and the reader "stand
naked." Then they are "caressed with words." They are
brought far closer to their sensual nature than is custom-
ary. Nin does not transform reality into the dream; she
proves the reality of the dream. The language is not
merely a matter of style. "The meaning of the book is
contained in the manner of the words." "Reading Collages
is like seeing the world through a Kaleidoscope."

4 ANON. "Briefly Noted--Fiction." The New Yorker, 40 (12 December), 244.
Review of Collages. Like an anachronism, this novel
speaks of a generation trapped by its youth, and so always
appearing younger than the generation which follows it.
Autobiographical sketches are told in the third person, and
real persons meet fictional characters with no explanations
from Nin. The backdrop is the confusion and "fakery" gen-
erated by the Dada movement. The writing appears "com-
pletely pointless," yet there are some very descriptive
passages. The scene in which artists gather to watch
Tinguely's self-destroying machine can be considered either
a "superb short story or a brilliant piece of reporting."

5 BRODIN, PIERRE. "Anaïs Nin," in Présences Contemporaines:
Écrivains Américains D'Aujourd' Hui. Paris: N.E.D.,
pp. 105-122. [French.]
Nin has been known internationally more than twenty
years but she is now gaining a wider audience. Brief introduction to the novels and diary; the latter gives her
a claim to be considered among the most important writers
of her time. Her work has a common theme--exploring the
inner life of women. Lillian, Djuna, and Sabina from
Cities of the Interior are always seeking a climate

1964

favorable to love. Nin shows that love is a product of the
imagination. The three women discover themselves and "liberate themselves from fatality." The men are less developed because they generally exist as satellites of the
women. Briefly discusses Jay, Rango, Varda, the father in
Winter of Artifice. All these characters are extremely complex. Compares them to characters created by Virginia Woolf.
In order to construct the interior world, Nin uses a style
that is both spontaneous and ornate and uses rich, rhythmic
language. She discards realism and the imitation of ordinary speech. She experiments with words and images in a
form parallel to modern painting. Analyzes some of her
images; they always show striking workmanship. The symbols
she borrows from the arts are admirably adapted to the
psychology of the people described. Nin has a very strong
sense of sincerity and great compassion, but Nin is not
essentially a moralist. Nin's writing departs from the
main literary movements of the United States. Praises the
"Japanese" delicacy of her style.

6   FULLER, JOHN. "In the Truck." New Statesman, 67 (1 May),
     688.
          Reviews Collages. Criticizes Nin for refusing to devel-
     op her characters fully. The novel is a "fictionalized
     hash" of memories from Nin's early bohemian life among
     artists. Although there are some interesting scenes, the
     tone of the novel is too private, "all impasto and pos-
     ture."

7   FUSON, BEN W. "New Books Appraised: Literature." Library
     Journal, 89 (1 June), 2347.
          Nin's book on D. H. Lawrence, first published thirty-
     two years ago, is now being published for the first time
     in America by Swallow Press. It was the first book issued
     after Lawrence's death that concentrated on the texture
     of his work. Today, it still is "one of the most valuable
     books on Lawrence." Academic libraries and all Lawrentians
     are urged to acquire this work.

8   GOYEN, WILLIAM. "Bits and Images of Life." The New York
     Times Book Review (29 November), pp. 5, 24.
          Review of Collages, with biographical note on Nin.
     Critics complain that Nin writes about dreams and fantasies,
     not life; Nin replies, "the quest of the self through the
     intricate maze of modern confusion is the central theme of
     my work." Each person in her roman fleuve is a collage of
     reality and dream. Her characters are in constant motion,
     pulling behind them a train of objects and memories.

1964

Character is defined by "wish-action," not surface action.
Nin's major characters are women, whose situation she defines in "sparse parable," then expands. Male-female relationships are characterized by the woman seeking her self-
definition in a partner. The narrative is not cumulative,
for Nin does not "build" the story; details are added and
others fall away, and the total character emerges from the
collage-like description. Collages itself is less a novel
than a chain of descriptive portraits revolving around the
young painter Renate. The characters seem weightless, but
they project size. Nin's reputation continues to grow,
yet she retains a unique feminine vision and "a certain
vital artistry."

9   HORDER, JOHN. "Experiments." The Spectator, 213 (21 August),
     248.
         Review of Collages. Despite its book-jacket blurbs,
     this is only a minor work about an insubstantial relation-
     ship. The work is avant-garde writing at its worst, with
     psychology thrown in. However, some individual sentences
     give the reader a fleeting pleasure, and certain scenes
     are particularly pleasing. The book is only "a collection
     of bits and pieces," but the writing does have a quality
     all its own.

10   JENNINGS, ELIZABETH. "New Novels." The Listener, 71 (7 May),
     769.
         Collages deals solely with the inner world. Nin effec-
     tively sustains its intensity but is so obsessed with de-
     tail, atmosphere, and minute changes of emotions that the
     reader questions the book's genuineness. Everything is
     delicacy, sensitivity, and subtlety, and yet Nin lacks the
     toughness of writers like Virginia Woolf and Elizabeth
     Bowen. Yet Nin has succeeded in the difficult job of
     creating an artist, Renate, who is a convincing character.

11   MOORE, HARRY T. "Introduction," in D. H. Lawrence: An Un-
     professional Study. Denver: Alan Swallow, pp. 7-12.
         Welcomes reprints of Nin's sensitive critical study.
     At the time it was written, only Nin and Horace Gregory
     offered serious criticism of Lawrence's works. Nin's
     study is valuable for its discussion of the texture of
     Lawrence's writing and Lawrence's forceful expression.
     Nin does not make the mistake of detaching qualities of
     style from Lawrence's ideas. "The peculiar kind of
     intuition--emotional knowledge...in Nin's later fiction,
     she first applied to her explication of Lawrence."

1965

1965 A BOOKS - NONE

1965 B SHORTER WRITINGS

1   ANON. Review of <u>Collages</u>. <u>Choice</u>, 1 (February), 556-557.
      <u>Collages</u> is actually a series of sketches of flamboyant
artists and their friends. Although the novel appears
realistic, the chief development is in the inner life of
the characters. There is little plot, while unity is
achieved through the tone and the central character,
Renate. Nin uses a highly poetic style to imitate what she
sees as D. H. Lawrence's philosophy of "vision and the
primal consciousness." Some readers may find her "vision"
too static, but she does have a small group of devoted admirers. In general, Nin's work has not been widely read
nor has it been easily available in the United States until
1960, when Swallow Press started publishing more of it.

2   ARTAUD, ANTONIN. "Onze lettres à Anaïs Nin." <u>Tel Quel</u> (Winter), pp. 3-11. [French.]
      Prints eleven letters written by Antonin Artaud to Nin
between February and July, 1933. Artaud is pleased by
Nin's concern for him. <u>House of Incest</u> has psychological
tension and ideas that he agrees with. The manuscript Nin
gave him shows knowledge of subtle and secret psychological
states which he didn't feel until he had suffered greatly.
Because of Nin's interest in his work, he wants to dedicate
a book to her. Describes Nin's reaction to a painting as
artistic and emotional and as intense as love. Nin's body
and spirit are closely linked; she reacts powerfully to
spiritual things. Many things in her are asking to be born
if she finds a guide. Nin and Artaud are alike, especially
because of their silence.

3   FAVERTY, FREDERIC E. "For D. H. Lawrence, 1964 was a Year of
Reparation for His Reputation." <u>Chicago Sunday Tribune</u>
(10 January), "Books Today" Section, p. 8.
      Nin's book on Lawrence is full of valuable insights into
his thought and style. She focuses on his reliance on intuition and reveals his essential message (which is similar
to her own): "Emptiness in life is more unbearable than
death."

4   KORGES, JAMES. "Curiosities: Nin and Miller, Hemingway and
Seager." <u>Critique: Studies in Modern Fiction</u>, 7 (Spring -
Summer), 66-81.
      Nin is not a good novelist. Attacks <u>Collages</u> for
"verbal inaccuracy," "blemished prose," "puppet-like"

characters. The theme (women allow men to impose their
wills on them but men make women feel guilty when they impose their wills on men) is potentially powerful but "remains an abstraction." The women are all variations on
the same character; all are searching for love. Nin's
works "are perhaps our finest fiction of solipsism without
irony." The Four-Chambered Heart is Nin's best book:
"for the first time...Nin was close to rendering the relationship between two people, rather than reporting mono-
logues and actions...." "Nin is dealing in the clichés of
women's magazines and of soap opera; but in this novel she
controls the clichés." Djuna is a "remarkably stupid woman
who only pretends herself wise." It is not a great novel
but "a fine achievement by a minor, flawed novelist." The
best of Nin's writing has been her "intense, feminine insights (as in some short stories, such as "Birth")."

5   LERMAN, LEO. "Catch up with...." Mademoiselle, 60 (March),
    80.
        Collages is "a roman à clef by the world's most persist-
    ent vanguard writer." Nin's characters are people you
    "want very much to know," artists who live "intense, hot,
    sensitive, and sensitized lives." They "make believe for
    real," and their lives are "triumphant disaster or disas-
    trous triumph." Nin sees magically, creates fairy tales;
    everything in her books is "tangential, refracted...
    through prisms of gorgeous emotional (but superbly con-
    trolled) light." "The reader must swim with the tides
    created by the author." Compares Collages with John Stew-
    art Carter's Full Fathom Five, another plotless evocation
    of love.

6   STUHLMANN, GUNTHER. "Introduction," in Henry Miller: Letters
    to Anaïs Nin. Edited by Gunther Stuhlmann. New York:
    Putnam's Sons, pp. v-xxvi.
        This is a collection of letters by Miller to Nin from
    1931 to 1946. Brief outline of Nin's early life and the
    origins of the diary. Nin and Miller were opposites--she
    responded to things intuitively rather than intellectually,
    and sought the harmonious and beautiful, the motive behind
    the apparent one, inner space, and the reality of the
    dream. However, she recognized Miller's talent and ac-
    knowledged in him a "vital new quality," the embodiment of
    American energy and enthusiasm. Both were "uncommercial"
    writers, with no literary school or movement to back them.
    When June Miller, Henry's first wife, arrived in Paris in
    1931, she and Nin were mutually fascinated by the oppo-
    siteness of their personalities. Nin eventually backed

1965

publication of Miller's Tropic of Cancer, and wrote a
three-page preface which remains one of the most perceptive
evaluations of Miller's first book. Throughout Nin's later
travels, the two continued to correspond.

7   THIRLWALL, JOHN C. Review of Collages. Chelsea, no. 17
     (August), pp. 151-154.
         Throughout her career, Nin has explored the unconscious,
     believing it the source of creativity. She doesn't merely
     transform the concrete to the dreamlike, she actually gives
     "form and reality to the dream." Collages is an attack on
     the traditional novel, whose characters are developed in an
     orderly fashion as products of forces affecting them. Like
     Fellini's film "8 1/2," the book trusts that chance will
     cause meaning to emerge. The central character, Renate,
     and her friends try to express their feelings and relate to
     each other, but will not take the time to discover each
     other's inner worlds. Like these characters, the tradi-
     tional writer sees only exteriors and therefore is engaged
     in destruction, similar to "Tinguely's Machine that De-
     stroys Itself" at the end of the book.

8   WEST, PAUL. "D. H. Lawrence: Mystical Critic." The Southern
     Review, NS 1 (January), 218-222.
         D. H. Lawrence: An Unprofessional Study shows a critic
     who analyzes on the basis of intuition or feeling. Nin
     successfully describes "the feel of Lawrence's language."
     She emphasizes Lawrence's belief that thought is concrete
     and passes through the senses. For Nin, Lawrence is an
     example of the "female intellect," an intellect which drove
     him to write about the subconscious communications between
     people. In her study, Nin also makes a less impression-
     istic effort to study the effects of Lawrence's "'neutral,'
     undynamic Christianity," his manner of reasoning, and his
     technique of creating intimacy between his characters and
     the reader by casting them as artists. Nin expertly ex-
     plores Lawrence's belief in the depth of male friendship
     and Lawrence's "Whitman" side that believed in the Diony-
     sian beauty of nature. Nin offered correct opinions on
     the personality types of Lawrence's female characters, his
     views on the relativity of love, and his technique of in-
     tentional imprecision. Berates Nin for occasional lapses
     such as her belief Lawrence was not interested in the cos-
     mos.

9   ZINNES, HARRIET. Review of D. H. Lawrence: An Unprofessional
     Study and Collages. Books Abroad, 39 (Spring), 213-214.

In 1932, when D. H. Lawrence was receiving little praise, Nin published this very professional "unprofessional study" of Lawrence's creative aims. With the simultaneous issuing of Nin's book on Lawrence and Collages, one can observe the influence of Lawrence on Nin's own works. Like Lawrence, Nin is preoccupied with the subconscious as expressed in daily actions; all her characters have "single motivations stemming from and elucidating a complex of desires and re- pressions." Each story is both a complete symbol and a part of the collage. Motion takes place within the symbol, but the symbol is static as a canvas. Each character makes an inner voyage to learn who he is, what he wants--like Bruce the sailor, who can travel only through time, or the true poet aiming to know his own soul.

1966 A BOOKS - NONE

1966 B SHORTER WRITINGS

1   ANON. Review of The Diary of Anaïs Nin, Volume One. The Vir- ginia Kirkus Service, 34 (15 February), 225.
Diary I is a selection from 150 volumes. Considered both an "opium habit" as well as "revelations" by her friends, Nin's diary is more a compulsive confessional. "Along with the intoxication of words, there is a narcissistic self- indulgence." Perhaps Nin does have the ability to speak for all women as she claims. In addition to those interested in Nin the writer, there are readers interested in her re- lationship with Miller. A coterie of her friends can bear this "person turned inside out" more than the general read- er.

2   ANON. "Traffic Island: The Diary of Anaïs Nin." Newsweek, 67 (2 May), 104.
Diary I is a mixture of precise vignettes and poetic manifestations of the soul, a private record of the inter- actions among Nin's famous group of associates. With the Millers and Artaud, Nin was a curious blend of "Muse and mother hen"; with Allendy and Rank she experienced detach- ment--the reverse of her draining friendships. Rank was the first to note that Nin used the diary as a defensive, "traffic island" from which to analyze and survey the ana- lyst. His attempt to separate Nin from the diary failed. She went on to assert a new value for it, believing that what she has to say is the woman speaking for all women past and present who are speechless or are copies of men.

1966

3   ANON. "Books Briefly Noted--General." <u>The New Yorker</u>, 42
     (4 June), 166.
         <u>Diary</u> I is an edited work drawn from ten of Nin's manu-
     script volumes. In it, Nin records her struggles to de-
     cide, with the help of friends Miller, Artaud, and Rank,
     what kind of writer and woman she should become. Nin was
     no more self-preoccupied than her friends, for a conversa-
     tion in the diary reads like two monologues. However, the
     book shows Nin's talent.

4   ANON. "Opium of a Rare Spirit." <u>The Times Literary Supple-
     ment</u> (21 July), p. 633.
         Review of <u>Diary</u> I. Henry Miller compared Nin's diary to
     writings of St. Augustine, Petronius, Abelard, Rousseau and
     Proust, but it is closer to the work of Marie Bashkirtseff.
     Bashkirtseff also kept a journal, and her parents separated
     when she was young. Bashkirtseff used a <u>nom de plume</u> for
     her correspondence with Maupassant, but Nin reveled in her
     role as muse for aspiring writers like Miller and Artaud.
     The reader's interest in Nin and her friends wanes when
     Nin begins to reveal an infinite number of "real selves,"
     each described in the serious tone of one explaining a
     "cult." Rank and Nin's friends tried to dissuade her from
     continuing her diary entries, but the habit from childhood
     survived with noteworthy persistence. The diary's egocen-
     tricity may pall, but the work does have a "strange fasci-
     nation" for the reader.

5   BUCKMASTER, HENRIETTA. "What Is the Sum of Her Words?" <u>The
     Christian Science Monitor</u> (16 June), p. 5.
         Review of <u>Diary</u> I. Nin's mystique centers around her
     diary. Stuhlmann's introduction finds profundity in this
     published volume, but Nin considers art only in its ego-
     centric and narcotic aspects, and her repeated talk of com-
     passion is mere "attitudinizing." The other characters in
     the book are actually copies of Nin's personality. She
     presents clearly her relationships with the Millers and
     Artaud, but her view of herself vacillates between objec-
     tivity and delusive self-dramatization. It is hard to
     separate reality from illusion in the diary. Nothing
     exists but the self, and sensations are collected until
     they lose all meaning. Her fantasy world becomes a drug
     and she takes no corrective action.

6   BUTCHER, FANNY. "A Long Awaited Literary Flight." <u>Chicago
     Tribune</u> (22 May), Section 9, p. 7.
         Review of <u>Diary</u> I. Nin's admirers believe that publica-
     tion of this diary will allow readers to know the real Nin.

1966

Nin uses words as the Japanese use flowers, to create a
sense of grace and movement. One feels she sees too deeply
and her probings are never finished. Nin's fascination
with Miller's unhappy marriage and his urge to explore all
kinds of sex lead to too-lengthy analysis of his "devious-
ness." Equally intensive but briefer are her analyses of
her father, Rank, Allendy, and Artaud; but she is most absorbed in herself. The diary can be terrifyingly revealing, repelling, and even occasionally boring; "a long
awaited literary flight to the moon has missed its promised
rendezvous."

7   CADE, WARE. "The Diary of Anaïs Nin." The Village Voice
    (26 May), pp. 5-6, 30-31.
        Review of Diary I. Summarizes Nin's life up to Diary I.
    Nin's diary is "as close a touchstone of a woman's inner
    life" as can be found. Nin shows herself "a strange mix-
    ture of the helpless, clairvoyant, and the creative." She
    became a symbol of understanding and freedom to her friends.
    The crucial encounter in volume one was her meeting with
    her father. With Rank's help, she realized the need to be
    perfect could be turned only into art, not life. A "new"
    Nin was born; "a stronger-minded, even harsh woman" with
    "an air of independence, of selfish anger and sharp new
    perception." The diary is "a story of grace and of growing
    awareness" and is a "singularly potent book."

8   CHASE, KATHLEEN. "The Extraordinary Life of Anaïs Nin." The
    Chapel Hill Weekly (5 June), p. 4.
        Review of Diary I. The long awaited book "exceeds all
    expectations." High praise for all aspects of it: as lit-
    erature, revelation of self and others, aid for understand-
    ing Nin's work and life, picture of life in Paris in the
    1930s. Surveys the contents of volume one. The diary is
    Nin's "self-portrait par excellance," written "with scrupu-
    lous honesty, searching humbly for answers to her ques-
    tions." Nin does speak for many women. "She wrote
    obliquely-- 'From the dream outward'--in a unique style,
    combining the terseness of dream language with the flow of
    poetry." The diary is a "moving and great book."

9   CHASE, KATHLEEN. "The Diary of Anaïs Nin, 1931-34." Books
    Abroad, 40 (Autumn), 471-472.
        Nin's writing expresses her concept of "an expanded
    world, a limitless world containing all." She skips mean-
    ingless detail in the diary, and concentrates on probing
    her many roles and masks. The diary is also a valuable
    record of her literary struggles, the life of Paris in the

1966

1930s, and the development of Miller's Tropic of Cancer, for which Nin wrote the preface. Publication of the diary should increase and enhance the study of Nin's fiction. In the diary, one sees that the key to all Nin's work is compassion.

10   CORODIMAS, PETER. Review of The Diary of Anais Nin, Volume One. Best Sellers, 26 (15 May), 66.
      Review of Diary I. One approaches Nin's diary with pre-conceived admiration because of her struggle for a "multi-level existence," her sensitive introspection, and her literary independence. She began her own printing press when American publishers would not accept her work; gradu-ally, her surrealistic experimentation received recogni-tion. This volume concentrates on Nin's friendship with Henry Miller. With Rank's help, Nin broke free from total bondage to the diary and was able to face her father's de-sertion. Nin herself is the most interesting aspect of the book; both impressionistic and realistic scenes express her preoccupation with self-awareness and psychological growth. This work is not so much a diary as a "mildly surrealistic bildungsroman."

11   EDEL, LEON. "Life without Father." Saturday Review, 49 (7 May), 91.
      Review of Diary I. A "record of self-contemplation in many mirrors," the diary fulfilled three needs for Nin: creating a concrete self, substituting for the father who deserted her mother, and creating a life pleasing to her father. In volume one, Nin is a cultured blue-stocking visiting Parisian bistros and entertaining the "literary anarchists" of the period. She projects the image of a child trying to please Daddy, an adolescent hoping to re-unite her parents and obtain her father's love (a role also underlying Nin's attempts to make peace between Henry Mil-ler and his wife June). The psychoanalysts, Rank and Al-lendy, become Nin's symbolic lovers and fathers, introduc-ing symbolic incest. Nin is a disciple of Lawrence and the surrealists in a period when literature probed the "dis-tortions of the dream." Hopefully, future volumes of the diary will not overwhelm "the petite, meticulous form of Nin herself."

12   FURBANK, P. N. "Dressing for Father." The Listener, 76 (14 July), 63-64.
      Review of Diary I. This volume is basically a descrip-tion of Nin's four sets of relationships: with Henry and June Miller; with Rank and Allendy; with Artaud; and with

1966

her father. This is the masterpiece Nin's friends have
hailed; it is "strange, interesting, and yet unsatisfac-
tory." The diary reflects its origins in "dressing up an
ideal self" that would lure her father back; Nin culti-
vates intense relationships to carry off her new finery.
The diary "does not live," except for an occasional vivid
image, because nothing is described for its own sake.
Nin unfairly sees herself as Cinderella, since she has been
beautiful and appreciated from the start.

13 GARRIGUE, JEAN. "The Self behind the Selves." The New York
Times Book Review (24 April), p. 1.
Review of Diary I. Nin's voluminous diary established
her literary reputation years before it was published. The
first published volume describes her associates and friends
as if they were characters in a novel, covering all "the
modalities and irregularities of experience." The immediacy of the diary entries are reflections of the fact it was
her constant companion. From accounts of introspections
and intimacies, emerges the figure of Nin as daughter,
sister, mistress, friend, and protector. The diary
strengthens her self-confidence and allows her to express
what she believes is her true self, the woman artist. Few
people are willing to accept this "adventurous, independent
figure"; thus the search for her self-image is dangerous.
Nin's diary illustrates that she is "neither moralizer nor
judge but a witness"; it captures the essence of her con-
stantly evolving spirit.

14 GRIFFIN, LLOYD W. Review of The Diary of Anaïs Nin, Volume
One. Library Journal, 91 (1 April), 1884.
The section of the diary covering the years 1931-1934
presents extensive portraits of a variety of people Nin
knew, from Antonin Artaud and Otto Rank to Rebecca West and
St. Exupery. In this volume, Nin relates her attraction
to June, Henry Miller's wife; ideas on her relationship
with her father; and discusses her ability to write. The
backgrounds in the journal, ranging from Parisian bordellos
to the hospital where she gave birth to her dead child, all
receive detailed consideration.

15 HEPPENSTALL, RAYNER. "The Journals of Anaïs Nin, 1931-4."
London Magazine (July), p. 105.
Review of Diary I. Gunther Stuhlmann is "half-educated,"
"flatfooted" and "uninformed" in his introduction. The
first two hundred and fifty pages of the diary have too
much analysis and too little anecdote. There is too much
on Miller, even for addicts. However, Nin's writing is

1966

"cool, lucid, shrewd"; "she was not a fool" in judging
Miller. Nin enlivens her diary by erotic descriptions.
The best part of the diary is the account of the still
birth. The total omission of people such as Nin's husband
is "silly."

16 JONES, JACK. "The Lady of Paris." The Denver Quarterly, 1
    (Summer), 102-105.
        Review of Diary I. Nin was the contemporary Lady Mura-
    saki. Notes how Rank and Miller were influenced by the
    Zeitgeist of the 1930s while Nin recorded the exchanges
    between Henry, his wife June, and herself in her diary.
    The fantasy world in which June dwelt and ensnared Henry is
    an epitome of the whole diary. The first published volume
    of the diary represents Nin's efforts to cling to sensibil-
    ity while Europe was ensnared in the "fascinating illusions"
    of Hitler and Stalin.

17 KITCHING, JESSIE. "Non Fiction." Publishers Weekly, 189
    (7 February), 89.
        Diary I shows Nin's frank, deeply emotional, and self-
    analytical personality. She has the artist-writer's vision
    of life. Miller and his wife June are of major concern in
    this volume. Nin works through her relationship with her
    father with the aid of a psychiatrist.

18 LIPTON, VICTOR. "The Little Straw Basket." Prairie Schooner,
    40 (Fall), 266-272.
        Review of Diary I. Nin's "pure artistic talent" is out-
    standing "in a world whose humans are cyborgian and whose
    art is pop." Ironically, the diary is a justification of
    surrealism and symbolism, currently unpopular techniques
    among writers. The diary becomes a tale of Nin's striving
    for a "feminine creative principle" which will not be at
    war with the "male ideology" Miller represents. Only Rank
    could have provided the theory that Nin used to live crea-
    tively both as woman and artist. June Miller's struggle
    is the other side of Nin's: her fight is without "creativ-
    ity" so her "wiles become negative"; she is the "embodiment
    of every feminine escape without the assistance of civili-
    zation." Miller is humbled by Nin's beautiful writing,
    while Nin "feels her creative self with Miller." One won-
    ders which image was created first: Nin with her charm and
    insight, or Miller who awakened those charms within her.

19 MacADAM, ALFRED J. "The Private World of Artistry." The New
    Leader, 49 (18 July), 17-18.

1966

Review of <u>Diary</u> I. Nin's diary is a memoir of life
among the artists of the 1930s, and an examination of her
own personality. Nin feels a need, rooted in her concept
of her father, to overthrow the authority of the dominat-
ing men in her life by finding fault with them. In analysis with Rank, Nin rejects Rank's stereotype of women and
begins to form her own self-concept; rather than center
her life around one man, she decides upon "enlightened
solipsism." Then, in 1934, she is able to confront her
father with his faults and resist his domination. The
diary is disappointing because it makes no reference to
Nin's husband or her sexual experiences; abstractions are
substituted for actual life experiences. Stuhlmann only
rarely indicates an omission, and the reader does not know
which names are pseudonyms. However, the diary is a "definitive statement" on the life of the twentieth-century
artist, and provides a key to Nin's fiction. It is an ex-
cellent example of "life turning itself into fiction."

20 MAZZOCCO, ROBERT. "To Tell You the Truth." <u>New York Review
    of Books</u> (8 September), pp. 6, 8.
    Review of <u>Diary</u> I. Nin is the abandoned child suffering
the eternal desire for return; she has the traditionally
unsatisfied nature of the injured romantic which is itself
a satisfaction. In this solemnly awaited and piously acclaimed memoir, she fantasizes about her friends and her
life, and lives a life of the senses that is frightening
because she lacks both stamina and spontaneity. All in the
book admire her "as she waits to be uplifted." The two
gaudy figures in the book are June Miller and Joaquin Nin.
Nin is "the failed visionary, struggling to be born"; yet
she is still something "genuine," which gives "inescapable
lyric dignity to so much of her monumental gush."

21 METZGER, DEENA. "The Diary of Anaïs Nin, 1931-1934." <u>Los
    Angeles Free Press</u> (29 April), p. 7.
    <u>Diary</u> I is a "great book," warring against the restraint,
callousness, and petty intellectuality of modern literature;
it reaffirms the life of imagination and feeling. Nin says
the diary voices the arena of personal "feminine overful-
ness," where life is enjoyed, not manipulated and transformed as in disciplined art. With extraordinary sensitivity, Nin seeks out the rare, unique, colorful--the
"essence" of those famous people she presents, not just
their actions. Using synaesthetic imagery, she seeks to en-
compass and fuse intimacy and intuitive experience with the
details of the physical world and thus gain real understanding of persons, feelings, events in their complexity. The

1966

diary is one of the few works of art that goes both into
the self and into the world.

22 MILLER, HENRY. "Between Freud & Henry Miller." The Village
Voice (26 May), pp. 5-6.
Nin is "one of those exceptionally balanced persons" who
gives the "illusion of doing everything without effort."
There is scarcely a correction in the whole manuscript of
the diary. The diary is "tumultuous, almost unbearably
naked." "No woman has ever written in like manner" and
few men have had the courage to reveal the truth this hon-
estly. Her Spanish blood is responsible for "the direct,
realistic, and violent aspects of her work." Nin's harmony and stability is the result of "slow organic growth."
Nin "lives entirely in the imagination" but also "nourishes" life. "She gives the illusion of acting always from
a movable center" so that "she seems not to have any problems." "If she has no moral scruples, it is because she
has arrived at a state of grace." The diary shows "the
struggle for supremacy between the old world and the new."
Nin resembles an Oriental but is not limited to one nationality or group. She is one of the people who "remove the
stench which usually accompanies the word 'human.'"

23 MOORE, HARRY T. "A Poetic Authenticity of Being." Chicago
Daily News (23 April), "Panorama" Section, p. 7.
Review of Diary I. Discusses Nin's family background
and the origin of the diary. Interest in Nin developed
slowly but "today her reputation as a novelist is well established." Nin's fiction presents "the feminine experience...a special kind of sensitivity which a man can know
only by indirection, guesswork and an extremely sympathetic
understanding--the kind of sensitivity that is not just
feminine but intrinsically female." The diary is the
source of the fiction, "a profound female confessional,"
and an "exciting investigation of the very processes of
life." Paris of 1931-1934 comes alive in Diary I.

24 MOORE, HARRY T. "A Long-Awaited Diary." St. Louis Post Dis-
patch (1 May), B, p. 4.
Presents a brief history of Nin's life and friends in
Diary I. "The diary is, like Nin's fiction, an intense
revelation of female experience--the word feminine suggests
too many frills and laces on the surface, while this journal really goes to the heart of existence." Nin does not
present superficial gossip but "prolonged searching and
intimate conversations." The book is "true" but also has

the power of an imaginative work. Praises the portraits
and story as absorbing and intense. The prose is "both
poetic and aphoristic."

25 PERLEY, MARIE E. "A Mammoth Confessional." Louisville
Courier-Journal (15 May), D, p. 6.
Review of Diary I. Less a crutch or opiate than a
faithful mirror of Nin's alter ego, Diary I allures with
its "highly polished distillation" of "high moments," its
portrait of the psyche, and portraits of public figures.
With "unadulterated narcissism," Nin sees herself as fragile, delicate and given only to supporting others' needs.
But she is a "scorpion lurking in the foliage," a mistress
of "shock tactics"; with "word-perfect timing," she can
shatter "passages of superb lyricism" with a lurid phrase
or a description of sexual perversion. This work, with
its Proustian depth and immediacy, should stimulate lively
discussions in literary circles.

26 PORTEUS, HUGH GORDON. "The Journals of Anaïs Nin." London
Observer (14 August), p. 19.
Nin's "fastidiously written" Diary I provides a welcome
change from the "heavy scents" of her fiction--which resembles the other "overwritten" works of the "pocket an-
archists (Durrell, Miller, Fraenkel, Perlés)" of the
thirties. Her relations with others, until Otto Rank helps
end her father-fixation, show strange fluctuations. Nin
supplies many "disjointed but perfect" passages of description, particularly the poignant account of the delivery of
her child.

27 RAVEN, SIMON. "Writing on the Wall." The Spectator, 47
(8 July), 49.
Diary I recounts Nin's friendship with Henry and June
Miller. The narrative is "leaden and humorless," inter-
rupted with long passages of introspection and moralizing.
Nin is too busy "producing herself in the role of the wise
woman." Her self-esteem is founded on her claim to have
acquired compassion through understanding.

28 SAYRE, NORA. "Miss Nin." New Statesman, 72 (16 September),
402.
Review of Diary I. Notes that it is odd that women are
always considered experts on women, a misconception Nin
expresses in her novels about female characters who are always searching for their true identity. Their sexual drive
impels them towards male stereotypes like the "Heathcliff"
or sensual "island man." Eventually, these women reject

1966

the flesh and attempt to find themselves through divination
and intuition. "Mythinformation" is dispensed by the diary
in its descriptions of Nin's involvement with Henry Miller,
his wife, Antonin Artaud, and the birth of her dead child.
Themes in Nin's works are captured in platitudes: "realism
is ugly, symbols are good...men are children..., women are
superior." Accords Nin the ability to make all her friends
sound foolish in the diary, yet wise enough to recognize
her as their mother, muse, and inspiration. Despite the
backdrop of the Parisian art circle of the 1930s, the diary
projects only the personal problems of one woman whose
writing lacks the ability to keep the reader interested.

29   SHAPIRO, KARL. "The Charmed Circle of Anaïs Nin." Book Week,
     3 (1 May), 3.
        Review of Diary I. Publication of the first volume of
     Nin's diary vindicates its claims to greatness. It shows
     qualities of the novel as well as the journal, and tran-
     scends both. Praises Nin's clear personal style, imagery,
     and perceptiveness. Discusses the contents of the diary:
     relationship with Henry and June Miller, psychoanalysis
     under Allendy and Rank. The diary volume closes with a
     "neo-zolaesque horror of an aborted birth." The diary is
     a "great book" because of "style, perspicuity, and natural
     organization, but more because it is unclassifiable as a
     book at all."

*30 SHERMAN, JOHN K. "Nin Diary is a Transmitter of Experience."
     Minneapolis Tribune (8 June).
        Unlocatable. Cited in Zee, Nancy Scholar. "Anaïs Nin:
     Beyond the Mask." Ph.D. dissertation, Brown University,
     1973, p. 264.

31   SIMON, MARION. "From Out of a Brooklyn Bank Vault, The In-
     credible Diary of Miss Nin." The National Observer (2 May),
     p. 19.
        Review of Diary I. Diary I depicts a woman's troubled
     quest for self-knowledge. Nin seeks the "high moments...
     to be fully alive" by living "instinctively in all direc-
     tions." Nin refers to the two women she is: one woman
     "drowning" and desperate and the other woman leaping into
     a scene concealing her weaknesses and presenting to the
     world a helpful, eager smile. "A remarkable picture of
     contemporary woman as writer. Readers should discover its
     poetry and imagery for themselves."

32   STUHLMANN, GUNTHER. "Introduction," in The Diary of Anaïs
      Nin, Volume One: 1931-1934. Edited by Gunther Stuhlmann.
      New York: The Swallow Press and Harcourt, Brace, and
      World, pp. v-xii.
          Nin's diary has been the object of speculation for more
      than thirty years. The primary significance of the diary
      is its articulate record of "a modern woman's journey to-
      ward self-discovery." Nin believes people despair when
      they cannot find cosmic meaning in life, but that the only
      real meaning is the individual meaning we give to life.
      The diary was begun as a letter to Nin's father; later it
      became her refuge as she grew up in America. It became
      her "filter" for her experiences, and she attempted to
      make it into a meaningful pattern. At times, her diary was
      a source of worry, perhaps a waste of her life, but she
      hung on to it. The natural flow of her writing comes from
      the freshness of immediacy and the enrichment of reflec-
      tion. She explores her self to the core, looking for truth,
      and she fears an ultimate exposure. Despite the problems
      of protecting some personal privacy, the quantity of manu-
      scripts, and legal hurdles, an edited version of the diary
      was deemed publishable. Character deletions and name
      changes are basically unimportant because Nin's truth is
      primarily psychological.

33   TROTTER, WILLIAM R. "The Paris Scene in Dazzling Prose." The
      Charlotte Observer (24 April), F, p. 6.
          Review of Diary I. It will not appeal to everyone. The
      style is "frequently dazzling, warmly vital, musical in its
      rhythms...incisive...sensuous...but revelatory, and always
      as honest as a human being can be." The style is "essen-
      tially feminine but very strong." Remarkable characters
      are brought to life as in no other work. Nin sees June
      Miller "as only a woman sees a woman." The pages on Miller
      and his wife are "wildly, colorfully, passionately alive,"
      bringing Miller to us as "a 3-dimensional and rather beau-
      tiful human being." Perhaps the highlight is the delivery
      of the child. "Only a woman could have written this way
      of the commingled joy and agony of childbirth." "One of
      the finest works of its type in modern literature."

34   WHITTINGTON-EGAN, RICHARD. "Biography." Books and Bookmen,
      11 (August), 30-31.
          Review of Diary I. Nin is not well known to British
      readers. She has produced "a dozen lyrical impressionis-
      tic novels in a taut, tense style which should be colour-
      ful and evocative, but somehow...is too intelligent to be
      really sensuous." The diary has all the sensuousness that

1966

the fiction lacks. It combines "the wistfulness of Marie
Bashkirtseff, the robustness of Simone de Beauvoir, the
vision of Virginia Woolf and the pathos of Colette." Nin's
diary shows the influence of Lawrence, Miller, and Rank,
but the best work is uniquely hers.

35 ZINNES, HARRIET. "No Mystery Lost." The American Scholar,
36 (Winter), 150-154.
Review of Diary I. With the publication of the diary,
the feminine mystique of "woman, giver and goddess" which
surrounds Nin was diffused to a wide audience. The diary
is an obsession "which imposes a discipline on her as a
writer by its focus on the active and the momentary." In
the daily task of writing diary entries, Nin has the op-
portunity to face the world's sordidness. Nin knew she
needed to reject her natural inclination towards elegance,
the "static" world, in order to comprehend the "common,"
as another aspect of art. Through analysis with Allendy
and Rank, Nin sought to eliminate her compassion, but this
characteristic shaped her conception of women. She expresses it in her writing as a vision of woman as the
giver and the goddess. For Nin, her work is one more
voice which speaks for all women; hence she believes she
must define the word "woman." Nin found her femininity
both a strength and a weakness.

1967 A BOOKS - NONE

1967 B SHORTER WRITINGS

*1 ANON. Washington Post (21 March), D, p. 2.
Unlocatable. Cited in Mority, Charles, ed. Current
Biography, Yearbook, 1975. New York: H. W. Wilson,
p. 301.

2 ANON. "Nonfiction." Publishers Weekly, 191 (10 April), 79.
Review of Diary II. Nin is a gifted writer who expresses herself in personal, "very feminine" terms. Nin
explores herself and her well-known artist friends while
living in New York and Paris in the 1930s. The diary is
not complete and the reader senses the gaps. But it does
provide some "remarkable insights" and observations with
a rather "fey charm."

3 ANON. Review of The Diary of Anaïs Nin, Volume Two. The
Virginia Kirkus Service, 35 (15 April), 545.

Review of <u>Diary</u> II. Nin is probably one of the last of
"the literary divas." If one judges by her diary, her life
seems to be little more than a dramatic landscape for her
arias. Nin's self-interest is the cement of this second
volume as she tries to become the mother of us all. The
themes of love, friendship, and art "throb in the pages"
and Nin displays her "shopworn images." A dazzling cast
of writers and friends--Miller, Rank, Durrell--assemble to
pay tribute to Nin's talents and virtues.

4   ANON. "Diary of Anaïs Nin, Playing Mother to All." <u>The Na-
    tional Observer</u>, 6 (3 July), 17.
        Short introduction to excerpt from <u>Diary</u> II. Rank once
    told Nin her diary was "invaluable as a study of a woman's
    point of view...a document by a woman who thinks as a
    woman, not like a man." The subject of woman as creator
    dominates many of the entries of volume two, "a remarkable
    volume."

5   ANON. "Books Briefly Noted--General." <u>The New Yorker</u>, 43
    (5 August), 83.
        <u>Diary</u> II continues themes expressed in the first volume:
    friendship with Miller and Rank; a new friendship with
    Durrell; Nin's femininity exhibited both abstractly and
    concretely; her work in psychoanalysis and her role as
    artistic muse to friends. Nin became self-sacrificing
    virtually to the point of self-destruction. The diary
    shows Nin's self-absorption.

6   BALAKIAN, ANNA. "Sponge for the World's Tears." <u>Saturday
    Review</u>, 50 (22 July), 38-39.
        Review of <u>Diary</u> II. The years 1934-1939 marked "the end
    of our romantic life," said Nin, "while her spirit floated,
    rootless, without destination" on her houseboat anchored
    on the Seine in Paris as war grew close. "Nin's attempts
    to spiritually steer the boat in which she placed her
    spirit symbolize the ability of the artist to overcome the
    duality between material vision and metaphysical vision."
    As one of the non-national artists who express themselves
    in several languages and through several cultures, Nin's
    inward self surpassed national boundaries. This background
    assisted her in recording human contacts from the bohemia
    of artists to the salon of Baron Rothschild. Nin prefers
    the creativity possible through the diary, a "feminine
    medium," as opposed to "masculine alchemy" where personal
    experiences are converted into novels. Nin's perceptions
    developed through her exploration of self; men should learn
    from her discoveries about such things as male/female

attraction. Nin's writing is informal yet has literary
style. Her honesty is an illusion because of the incom-
plete descriptions of personalities and events, perhaps to
preserve such memories as personal. The narcissism in the
first volume of the diary is "transformed by Nin's capa-
bility to love." Unlike the usual introspective writer,
Nin uses her ability to dream to give her characters "a
universal dimension," rather than to withdraw.

7   CENTING, RICHARD. "The Diary of Anaïs Nin: Vol. I (1931-
    1934) and Vol. II (1934-1939)." Detroit The Fifth Estate
    (15-31 July), p. 6.
        The diaries are "revolutionary, destined to take their
    place with the great transcendental works." Nin offers
    "the dream" as the humanistic alternative to modern anxi-
    ety. Nin stands as a model of one who saved herself
    through faith in creativity. The diary also supplies ma-
    terial for the fiction, such as "Birth," "one of the
    greatest short stories of our time." "Hopefully this
    diary is the predecessor of a female literature that can
    unveil the mystery of the womb, and retrieve man from the
    folly of his self-imposed alienation from nature."

8   CORODIMAS, PETER. Review of The Diary of Anaïs Nin, Volume
    Two. Best Sellers, 27 (1 August), 181.
        Review of Diary II. This second volume fulfills the
    expectations generated by the first. It is filled with
    portraits of Nin's artist friends written with the close,
    personal style of her writing. This volume enlarges upon
    Nin's creative technique--her ease in rejecting, accept-
    ing, altering, and returning to ideas that are handled in
    her fluid style. "Woman's art must be nourished by her as
    a human creation, not a creature like man's abstractions";
    man creates in solitude, but woman must be absorbed in
    life and connect man with his human self. Nin expresses
    her role in creating art not only in her written ideas but
    also in her constant generosity with time, money and ad-
    vice to those around her. Nin's readers will occasionally
    be puzzled but will also be stimulated by Nin's theories
    and comments. Nin arrests time and space for the reader;
    in learning about Nin, one learns "how to take oneself
    seriously."

9   DICK, KENNETH C. "Anaïs Nin," in Henry Miller, Colossus of
    One. The Netherlands: Alberts-Sittard, pp. 107-158.
        Biography of Nin, emphasizing her hypocrisy and faults.
    Quotes extensively from the diary to paint a portrait of
    Nin's relations with June Miller. Nin wanted to marry

Henry Miller during the time Miller was writing <u>Tropic of Cancer</u>; she was then married to French banker Hugh Guiler. Describes unpleasant meetings with Nin after she became popular in America. Nin-Miller letters are cited to provide insights into Miller's naiveté. Nin's prose has an almost hypnotic cadence, but she destroys her truths with sentimental outpourings. All her fiction is merely thinly veiled biography and autobiography and of interest only to those who are depicted in it. Her surrealistic writing has neither clarity nor force. Dismisses the praise of critics such as Henry Miller and Oliver Evans, but concurs in Miller's occasional criticisms of Nin's style. Outlines Miller's letters in praise of Nin. Nin is less an enigma than a woman who has created her own tight little world. Her continual references to her father become maudlin. Despite all her seemingly "hot" experiences in Paris, she shies away from sex in the diary, enticing the reader "to the fringes of Lesbos and then pulling down the shade." Many people are still trying to untangle the semi-historical picture Nin gives of the Anaïs, June, Henry triangle.

10 ELLMANN, MARY. "Growing up Sublime." <u>Chicago Review</u>, 19:125-128.
    Review of <u>Diary</u> II. According to Nin, the diary exists in a conflicting state between life and literature, since she is obliged to lie in order to maintain the illusions of her friends while she records the truth in her diary. Descriptions of the male relationships she shared are sometimes distorted, but there are interesting revelations about Miller and Joaquin Nin. Rank diagnosed Nin's conflict as the problem of the artist who feels she is not truly an ordinary person. Nin rejected Rank's sexually discriminating idea that a man cured of neurosis becomes an artist and a woman cured becomes a woman; she attempted to become an artist as well as a woman. Nin exercises "a tight control on experience." She limits herself to exploring responses to the "elevated commonplace" and does so determinedly rather than skillfully. Words have one meaning; she avoids ambiguities and favors the list, which creates a feeling of "grace and sublimity" but also threatens an "ungovernable lust" for inappropriate words.

11 FRANKLIN, BENJAMIN V. "Resemblance to Novel in Anaïs Nin Diaries." <u>Columbus Dispatch</u> (2 July), "Entertainment Section," p. 14.
    Review of <u>Diary</u> II. The diary resembles a novel; it has "interesting characters who interact and build suspense" and carefully constructed plots. At times it

1967

resembles stream of consciousness, which makes for immediacy. By the outbreak of World War II, "all major personalities have been logically accounted for and all crucial
conflicts have been satisfactorily resolved." Nin's journal is "an intense apologia and a totally aware and almost
overbearingly candid account of her relationships." She
is the dominant character; "never falsely modest," she
"appears in her diary as a goddess, as a saint, as an all-
seeing and all-knowing seer."

12   GARRIGUE, JEAN. "Second Installment." The New York Times
     Book Review (16 July), pp. 4-5.
          Review of Diary II. Nin ignores the threats of the out-
     side world and concentrates on recording the "in-and-out
     weave between scene, portrait, and conversation," and the
     inward changes of her psyche. Nin refuses political views;
     she believes the world cannot be reformed so one must cre-
     ate an individually perfect world. This volume describes
     Nin's efforts to have her personal world reveal the "truth
     of the moment," the significance of the incidental, and
     "the whirl of fantasies." Nin successfully links incident
     with imagination and permits events "to grow." She keeps
     the diary to establish her identity and preserve and pro-
     tect her ideas, but in arguing that the diary is more
     truthful than the novel she gets caught in self-justifica-
     tion and idealization. This volume lacks economy and
     drive; the "dialog of the self" is often lost, and Nin
     loses contact with reality. At the end of the volume,
     however, the pace quickens and details reappear.

13   HALPERIN, ELAINE P. "The Diary of Anaïs Nin." Chicago Sunday
     Tribune (9 July), "Books Today" Section, p. 6.
          Review of Diary II. The two volumes of the diary show
     "more narcissism than genius," but from their outpourings
     came Nin's "roman fleuve," Cities of the Interior. Volume
     two is less preoccupied with self as Nin becomes a Loyalist
     and explores the role of the artist in the modern world.
     It is "a day-to-day account of a personal life that attempts
     to distill experience into truths reaching beyond the self";
     the attempt is not altogether successful, but there is nev-
     ertheless "lyricism of distinction."

14   HANDLIN, OSCAR. "Readers Choice." Atlantic Monthly, 220
     (September), 131.
          Review of Diary II. As Nin moved through the avant-
     garde of Paris and New York, she recorded her thoughts in
     a diary that exposed her own doubts and weaknesses as well
     as those of her friends. Volume two presents Nin's

exploration of herself as a woman and as an artist. Although she seemed self-confident to others, this volume shows the lack of fulfillment in her life. She notes that the uproar about the Spanish Civil War among her friends collapsed into talk. Thus it is significant that she chose the diary to create her own world, "conceding the inability to help build the world outside."

15 HASPRAY, RICHARD. "Transmutations." The Minnesota Review, 7:168-169.
Collages has a beginning which suggests several rereadings. Conventions common to the plotted novel are discarded in favor of a chain of character portraits and situations; Nin continually changes the images and relationships to illustrate the variety of her characters. Superficially, the portraits can be seen as thinly disguised sketches of the people Nin writes about in her diary, but, in this novel they represent unconscious motivations of the personality.

16 MacNAMARA, DESMOND. "Nin Et Al." New Statesman, 74 (1 December), 778.
Diary II traces Nin's steps as she leaves Rank in New York and returns to Paris' Left Bank to share the friendship of writers like Miller and Durrell. A "perceptive critic of people," Nin describes Miller as ready to destroy what he has created the previous day. The clue to his work, she believes, is his burlesque of sex or anything considered to be sacred or significant in life. In studying the problem of neurosis, Nin holds that it is a "modern form of romanticism" or search for perfection, the inability to act out the imagined. The volume's one flaw is its lack of humor.

17 MALOFF, SAUL. "The Seven Veils." Newsweek, 70 (3 July), 76.
Review of Diary II. Volume two is only a small part of Nin's diary, but it shows her self absorption. Nin only occasionally steps "through the seven veils" and re-enters the world. For her friends, Nin was the "high priestess" of art, which brings salvation. This is the theme that monotonously controls the volume. But Nin is seductive in her "relentless" femininity, and the rhythms of the book cause the reader to forget the "tedium" and "fatuities" and be won over by Nin.

18 METZGER, DEENA. "Anaïs Nin Volume II: The Spanish Revolution." Los Angeles Free Press (28 July), "Living Arts Supplement," p. 15.

1967

> Nin constructs a "great book" which recreates worlds--
> worlds within a world: conscious and unconscious, dream-
> ing, voyages into selves. Fez, the labyrinthine city,
> serves the book with a metaphor for the inner life. Rela-
> tionships act as keys to Nin's life and as central con-
> cerns of the diary; she embraces all types: Miller, Rank,
> Gonzalo the revolutionary, Helba, Durrell, others. Nin
> seeks what she defines as a woman's way to fight evil in
> man--intuitively with "a core of gentleness," to minister
> to and observe the dark, vital needs with creative games
> of poetry, costumes, music, guitars, watercolors, words.
> "To a destroyed world she whispers 'creation, creation,
> creation....'"

*19   PORTEUS, H[UGH] G[ORDON]. Review of The Diary of Anaïs Nin,
      Volume Two. Observer (October), p. 27.
           Unlocatable. Cited in Book Review Index, 1967 Cumula-
      tion. Detroit: Gale Research, unpaged.

20   SCHNEIDER, DUANE B. "The Book Review--Biography and Personal
      Narrative." Library Journal, 92 (1 June), 2150.
           Review of Diary II. It is as good as the first volume.
      Interior and exterior worlds are considered in detail,
      analyzed, and fused. The interior shows introspection and
      self-examination aided by the diary and psychoanalysis.
      The exterior includes all the relationships with Nin's
      friends. One sees Nin's world of dream and reality and the
      progress of her expanding consciousness. Nin expresses
      her "love to create," her inclination to form constructive
      relationships.

21   SHAPIRO, KARL. "The Diary of Anaïs Nin: Vol. II." New York
      Herald-Tribune (18 June), "Book Week," pp. 4, 12.
           Diary I and II show the ten terrible years (1930-1939)
      which form a "debacle of disaffiliation"--the last time an
      artist could pretend to be free. The editorial omissions
      are disturbing because the journal "demands a total expo-
      sure." This journal is different from ordinary diaries
      because Nin directs the lives of her associates. It was a
      "life raft" to her, but it reveals the actress and the
      dancer rather than the novelist. Together with those fa-
      mous artists around her, Nin persistently believes in "dis-
      engagement": "The monster I have to kill everyday is real-
      ism." The diary "is its own excuse for being. It could
      not have taken any other form; and its influence on her
      characters is every where evident." Reprinted 1967.B22.

22 SHAPIRO, KARL. "The Novel of Her Life." Book World, 4
    (18 June), 4.
    Reprint of 1967.B21.

23 STERN, DANIEL. "The Woman Novelist--Up from the Male Pseudo-
    nym." Commonweal, 87 (27 October), 123-126.
    Nin's work, when well done, shows a particular sensibil-
    ity not commonly achieved by the male writer, and so in
    her work the reader can enjoy the best of both sexes. Her
    poetic novels have been enjoyed by the underground reader
    for many years. The first volume of her diary was a "pow-
    erful statement of the creative consciousness." The diary
    is art in which the reports of actual people's activities
    create their personalities. The second volume, just pub-
    lished, is as good as the first. It is part of a long
    "narrative poem" written by Nin, who was a friend to some
    of the great writers of the times. She acts as a "mirror,
    reflecting...her perceptions of these men while remaining
    herself."

24 STUHLMANN, GUNTHER. "Preface," in The Diary of Anaïs Nin,
    Volume Two: 1934-1939. Edited by Gunther Stuhlmann.
    New York: The Swallow Press and Harcourt, Brace and World,
    pp. v-ix.
    The reception for Diary I was enthusiastic. Summarizes
    contents of volume one. The text of volume two represents
    about one-half of the original diary manuscripts--volumes
    40 to 60, covering 1934 to 1939. Nin's husband and mem-
    bers of her family were eliminated, and the names of some
    of her analytical patients had to be changed or omitted;
    the dates provided by the editor merely summarize the
    specific and sometimes confusing dates in the original.
    Volume two shows "perhaps, a move away from introspection."
    Nin still focuses on herself and "she still is caught in
    the web of her different personae, but the world, somehow,
    is becoming more real...." The "selective eye of the
    earlier diary...is becoming more and more a conscious ar-
    tistic principle: the captured moment of intense emotional
    reality." The shift in emphasis perhaps also stems from
    the political turmoil of the age. Nin's choice of the
    private world is not retreat: "It is an act of defiance,
    an optimistic staking out of a corner that is 'livable' in
    her own terms."

25 WHITMAN, ALDEN. "Books of the Times." The New York Times
    (22 July), p. 23.
    Review of Diary II. Nin wrote down everything that was
    of importance to her, especially the compliments she re-
    ceived from men. Already believing she was quite special

1967

and a writer of extraordinary sensitivity, Nin wrote about "soulmates" Miller, Rank, Durrell, Stuart Gilbert, and the rest of the Parisian crowd and what they said to her. "Now thirty years later, it has been bowdlerized and published and is all very profound or is it?"

26   WICKES, GEORGE. "An Astral Being." Shenandoah, 18 (Spring), 74-78.
      Review of Diary I. Miller maintains the diary is a work of art, and Stuhlmann and Nin's selection and shaping carry the art a step further. The resulting volume is "a well-delineated tale," digressing from its "plot" only to illustrate the source material for Nin's novels. Like Nin's fiction, this volume reflects Nin's study of narcissism and of the relationship between her life and her art. It was Miller rather than Allendy or Rank who finally rescued Nin from total introspection. Nin constantly portrays triangular relationships—some real and some imagined. She has a need to invent and dramatize romantic intrigues, to pit one person against another. Despite this technique, the volume eventually becomes static and repetitive because of her constant introspection, the same fault that hurts her other work; her "cold, dispassionate tone" is also a flaw.

27   WISPERLAERE, PAUL DE. "Het dagboek van Anaïs Nin" [The Diary of Anaïs Nin]. De Gids, 130, 350-353. [Dutch.]
      Review of Diary I. The book is captivating as a document, as personal testimony of a very intelligent and at the same time mysterious and fascinating woman. Moreover, it has a great literary value because of its portraits, confessions, stories, interpretations. Discusses Nin's relationships with Henry and June Miller and with Artaud. Nin's work is important for an accurate interpretation of Miller's writing. Nin experiences life as an inexhaustible series of experiments, characters, disguises, and metamorphoses.

28   YOUNG, MARGUERITE. "Marguerite Young on Anaïs Nin." Voyages: A National Literary Magazine, 1:63-67.
      Praises Diary II. Nin's diaries are unusual because they "convey the artistic feelings of distillation, rarification, arrangement—as if she is the disciplined writer even when setting down her impressions of the day." The "formality" of art is found in Nin's diaries as well as in her fiction, perhaps because Nin's work is "dedicated to the ideal of the artist's quest for the one security a turbulent life may give, the one peace of the soul which is art." In spite of its intimacy, the diary shows aesthetic

distance. Quotes Nin on the special creative role of women,
who should not imitate men by creating in isolation or separated from nature. All of Nin's work is "one vast prose
poem," best compared to the mysterious Eastern city of Fez:
a city which illuminates "the dark corners of the human
heart." Nin "belongs as a writer with men of great gifts--
with those who view the metaphysics of mechanisms" (Haw-
thorne and Poe) and with others who achieve elegance--
(Lafcadio Hearn and Ronald Firbank).

1968 A BOOKS

1 EVANS, OLIVER. Anaïs Nin. Crosscurrents, Modern Critiques,
   edited by Harry T. Moore. Carbondale and Edwardsville,
   Ill.: Southern Illinois University Press, 226 pp.
       Introduction: Traces Evans' first discovery of Nin's
   writings in 1945 and his meeting with her in 1950. Chapter
   one: Discusses the diary as "the genesis" of Nin's fiction.
   Ideas basic to both include the theory of separate selves,
   supplanted by the idea of a basic or "real" self; Nin's
   intense "subjectivism"; the use of dreams. Chapter two:
   Analyzes House of Incest; the general intention is "to depict a series of psychological tortures" resulting from
   the self-engrossment or "incest" that results in the incapacity to love. Chapter three: Examines Winter of Artifice, Nin's most successful work in depicting emotional
   influences of characters upon each other; the "Djuna" part
   has the moral that "it is fatal for the lover to invent an
   a priori image of the beloved." Chapter four: Studies
   Under a Glass Bell, comparing it to Joyce's Dubliners because of the "extreme simplicity" of the style and the an-
   nouncement of themes later developed in the novels. Divides
   the stories into fantasies, realistic sketches, portraits.
   Chapter five: Explains Nin's theory of fiction and her
   techniques; for Nin, fiction is primarily characterization.
   Also analyzes Ladders to Fire, which has the theme of
   "woman's search for completion" but is confusing in its
   overlapping women characters. Chapter six: Describes
   Children of the Albatross as a celebration of "youthful
   idealism and innocence"; the three women in the novel are
   archetypes of the destructive woman, the earth mother, and
   the feminine friend. Chapter seven: Studies The Four-
   Chambered Heart; this novel teaches that Djuna must give
   up the romantic idealism which led her to expect the impossible. Chapter eight: Discusses A Spy in the House of
   Love; the most "experimental" of Nin's longer narratives is
   her most successful work in depicting the "anxieties of
   self division." Chapter nine: Analyzes The Seduction of

1968

the Minotaur; all the major characters are defined in terms
of their commitment either to the principle of life or
death. Chapter ten: Judges Collages as a collection of
short stories rather than a novel, an uneven book that lacks
unity. Chapter eleven: Describes Nin's theories of fiction and declares she is very important because of what
she has contributed to the form of the novel. "She writes
best about women." Her scope is "very narrow" but her
achievement is important.

1968 B SHORTER WRITINGS

1   ANON. "Priestess of the Diary." The Times Literary Supple-
     ment (11 January), p. 41.
         Review of Diary II. It is difficult to evaluate the
     praise given Nin's diary since the published version has
     been heavily edited for legal and personal reasons. Mar-
     riage must have had a deep effect on Nin, but the published
     volumes make little reference to her husband. Volume two
     shows a more mature, extroverted Nin. The odd grammars
     and metaphors of the diary can reflect confusion which the
     discipline of the novel would have eliminated. The diary
     is "a kind of blackmail," for "the shadow of Nin the re-
     corder" falls across all her relationships. Nin believed
     a diary exploring the self would become a work of art.
     Occasionally, her emotions appear directly through her cul-
     tivated style. Yet Nin's picture of life as a dream
     causes the events of the diary to disappear the way dreams
     do. She is unaware of her narcissism and her diary remains
     only a pursuit of self.

2   ANON. Review of The Diary of Anaïs Nin, Volume One. Anti-
     quarian Bookman, 41 (22 January), 282.
         Volume one of the legendary diary is important not only
     as a revelation of Nin but also for its full and frank
     portraits of Miller and Rank. This is an important work
     for literary life in Paris in the early 1930s.

3   ANON. "Muse of the Dream." MD Medical Newsmagazine, 12
     (May), 193-198.
         Nin is a sensitive explorer of inner space who tries to
     write "from the dream outward." The major influences on
     her diary and fiction were her father's desertion, her
     sympathy for D. H. Lawrence's work, her friendships with
     Miller and bohemia, and with Rank and the world of psycho-
     analysis. From her early years to middle age, the diary
     presents direct emotional impressions of her world, some-
     times factual and analytic, but always artistic and poetic.

1968

Currently, she spends mornings editing the older diaries, giving lectures, and consulting with young writers, and evenings writing in the ongoing diary. Her primary concern is to make the workings of the unconscious as clear and meaningful as conscious activity.

4   ANON. "Anaïs Nin in Japan." Open City: Weekly Review of the Los Angeles Renaissance, no. 53 (22-30 May), p. 6.
A talk between Japanese critic Jun Eto, novelist Kenzaboro Oe, and Nin in Tokyo, 1967, with a translator. Nin says Japanese and American literature have "dual" aspects: delicacy and violence, toughness and sensitivity. She says she has read all the Japanese writers available to her in translation and declares she "has an affinity with them." Jun Eto says it must be reciprocal because they are translating all her books. Nin is interested in Japanese novels because they try to express the ambiguous and subtle with clarity. She says American literature has subtle, poetic and psychological writers, but they are less well known than realists. Jun Eto says the Japanese understand the meaning of tragedy. Nin says Americans repudiate it; American writers do not resign themselves to suffering, they take revenge on it.

5   ANON. Review of The Novel of the Future. The Virginia Kirkus Service, 36 (15 September), 1096.
Nin is in love with the "flux" of the universe, the "flow" of men and nature. She believes the novelist has the duty to create a new synthesis to include these movements. Her ideas are not logical structures but "incantatory sound-patterns." She insists forcefully on even the banal. With much self-righteousness, she believes she is advocating something new, adventurous, and profound, yet her ideas merely echo the century-old battle of the poetic novel versus the naturalistic one. She is more useful when speaking about her own fiction and the aesthetic discoveries she made or rejected.

6   ANON. "Non Fiction." Publishers Weekly, 192 (7 October), 51.
Review of The Novel of the Future. Although Nin earnestly believes she is writing about the novel of the future, she only succeeds in creating a sense of déjà vu. Nin must still live in Paris of the 1920s, for she rejoices in the invention of "symbolism" and "stream of consciousness." Nin's book is a literary polemic endorsing "free association" in the novel.

7   BENSTOCK, BERNARD. "The Present Recaptured: D. H. Lawrence
    and Others." <u>The Southern Review</u>, NS 4 (July), 802–
    816.
        Nin's audience has grown, and her diary is no longer
    considered even mildly shocking. Although her experiences
    are honestly recorded, Nin lacks the ability to elevate
    her diary from confession to self-analysis and thus to
    bridge the canyon between reality and poetry. She retreats
    from life to create a "dream prose" of symbolism and myth-
    ology without the substance or realism of daily language.
    The political and economic conditions of the 1930s marked
    the end of the view of art as an "aesthetic movement" and
    coincided with the death of one example of this movement,
    D. H. Lawrence. In her diary, Nin records her awareness
    of the change to a literature of realism. She refused to
    accept the pessimism and torpor that was gripping the world
    and attempted to reconcile the conflicting literary philos-
    ophies presented by her favorites, Lawrence and Miller.

8   BRADBURY, MALCOLM. "Aesthetic Decadence." <u>Manchester Guard-
    ian Weekly</u>, 99 (12 September), 14.
        Brief review. <u>Under a Glass Bell</u> mixes Nin's strengths
    and weaknesses. "Her clarity of prose, and its power to
    offer a distinct if limited vision, make her one of the
    minor yet important expatriate voices, and the reissue is
    a welcome event."

9   CHASE, KATHLEEN. "The Marvelous World and Art of Anaïs Nin."
    <u>The Chapel Hill Weekly</u> (5 May), p. 4.
        Review of <u>Diary</u> II. The best clue to Nin's work and
    world is the "Dream." <u>Diary</u> I tells of her efforts to
    get in with her dream of writing; <u>Diary</u> II, her progress
    as a writer. The "Dream" has determined her style; she
    skips meaningless details. This style is "clear, original,
    and enchanting." Earlier, it looked as though it would
    take a century for Nin to win recognition, but now she is
    appreciated. Discusses Evans' book on Nin (1968.A1) and
    praises it as "indispensable" for readers of Nin.

10 COLE, BARRY. "Soothsayers." <u>The Spectator</u>, 221 (13 Septem-
    ber), 364.
        Review of <u>Under a Glass Bell</u>. Though Nin has an inter-
    national reputation, her writing is more a matter of prac-
    tice than inspiration. This collection of stories is a
    waste of time and money, since the small, expensive book
    is a rehash of facts published in the cheaper volume of
    the diary. Nin uses the modish style of the 1930s and can
    say very little in a great many words.

1968

11 ELLMANN, MARY. Thinking About Women. New York: Harcourt,
    Brace, and World, pp. 187-191.
        Nin seems to endorse prevailing stereotypes of women,
    and it is difficult to decide whether she is pretending or
    deceiving herself. She associates the worst, most unde-
    sirable "female" traits with other women; she is not speak-
    ing of herself when she says "man attacks the vital cen-
    ter" and "woman fills out the circumference." In her
    diary she confuses pregnancy with copulation and repeats
    the stereotyped erotic image of woman "bathing in a wave
    of sensuality." Her observation that women are more honest
    than men is only a reply to the question: "Which sex is
    more dishonest?" No group who are constantly scrutinized
    can be open. When Nin wearies of her ability to be a
    source of harmony, she cashes in on the reputed female dis-
    like of abstraction and touts the warm, human, glowing ad-
    vantages of being a woman. Nin succumbs to the temptation
    of personally displaying the ideals imposed on the female
    sex.

12 GRAHAM, KENNETH. "Ruined Raj." The Listener, 80 (5 Septem-
    ber), 313.
        Review of Under a Glass Bell. This is a reissue of a
    collection of stories dating from the 1930s and 1940s,
    but the "mild, elegant surrealism" still appeals. There
    is a feeling of pathos about these dreams of submarine
    foliage, labyrinths, mandolins, and objects trouvés. The
    sensuous character sketches make "pretty performances,"
    but the tradition is "too obvious and the appeal to fancy
    too trivial."

13 HAUSER, MARIANNE. "Anaïs Nin: Myth and Reality." Studies
    in the 20th Century, 1 (Fall), 45-50.
        Praises Diary I and II as "a solid work of art, pain-
    staking in its accuracy, profound as well as witty, and
    illuminated by poetic vision." Nin's genius "resists
    classification." Praises her prose, "whose energy springs
    from lingual discoveries." More than most diaries, Nin's
    is a "purgatory" or a "confessional" search for the self.
    The diary is the record of a working writer showing that
    writing is hard work. Discusses the large number of per-
    sonalities in the diary. Nin sees through to the inner
    person, hence producing portraits of true intimacy. "Her
    gossip is cosmic, not social." The portrait she draws of
    her father is "perhaps one of the finest in literature."
    The need to come to terms with him as her obsession gives
    the diary its basic tension.

1968

14   McEVILLY, WAYNE. "Portrait of Anaïs Nin as a Bodhisattva:
     Reflections on the Diary, 1934-1939." Studies in the 20th
     Century, 1 (Fall), 51-60.
          Discusses Diary I and II. The diaries resemble a fugue,
     because they are "weavings of basic themes or subjects,
     themes which although worked through many variations of
     mood, tempo, structure, are yet always discernable as them-
     selves." Identifies three permutations on the central
     theme: the bodhisattva theme, or the strand of compassion
     and giving (The bodhisattva and writer know the world is
     illusion yet they urge others to live the dream fully.);
     the weaving theme, or the strand of belief in the possi-
     bility of transforming all events and experiences into the
     rich and strange; the music theme, the conscious insist-
     ence on the fact that all that is humanly important, in-
     cluding writing, "comes to us in the mode of music." There
     is also the dream of perfection, the insistence that the
     dream is not to escape reality but to create it. Nin's re-
     fusal to accept the reality of facts makes her more of a
     true existentialist than the writers known by this label.

15   MOORE, HARRY T. "Preface," in Anaïs Nin, by Oliver Evans.
     Crosscurrents, Modern Critiques, edited by Harry T. Moore.
     Carbondale and Edwardsville, Ill.: Southern Illinois Uni-
     versity Press, pp. v-vi.
          Nin "virtually invented a type of novel" and "virtually
     invented a language." Stresses Nin's "uniqueness." Nin is
     "a pronouncedly feminine type of woman"; "the elemental
     word female" best characterizes her work. The diary is as
     unique as her fiction. Describes a personal meeting with
     Nin at Ben Abramson's Argus Book Shop. Evans' book
     (1968.A1) is timely because Nin is now established and
     popular. Praises the quality and value of Evans' study of
     Nin.

16   SCHNEIDER, DUANE. "Fusion of Two Worlds." The Kenyon Review,
     30:137-140.
          Review of Diary II. Nin continues to describe the fu-
     sion of the objective world with the interior world. When
     forced to choose between writing and psychoanalysis, Nin
     chooses writing. Against Europe's dominant consciousness
     of war, Nin retains the "human vision" which enhances the
     value of the diary. Nin believes the world can be changed
     by individuals trying to live out their dreams, but the
     struggle between her dream world and reality creates ten-
     sion. Nin is forced to seek respite in the "absolute."
     Her life is ruled by "love of creation and expansion" and
     rejection of restriction; thus, she stays free of the

1968

"panacea" of political systems. The success of the diary
will stimulate critical recognition of Nin's artistry.
Nin's diary "symbolizes every man's attempt to know himself and to see into human nature."

17 SCHNEIDER, DUANE. "The Book Review--Literature." Library
    Journal, 93 (15 November), 4300.
        Brief review of The Novel of the Future. Although it
    is supposed to be a volume of literary criticism, it goes
    beyond such limits. Nin surveys the key ideas and methods
    behind her diary and fiction. It is a clear expression of
    her vision and the values she seeks to express in her work,
    including the importance of the dream and the subconscious
    in art. "Modern fiction has seldom been so incisively and
    sensitively analyzed."

18 STERN, DANIEL. "Princess of the Underground." The Nation,
    206 (4 March), 311-313.
        Review of Diary I and II. Since the nineteenth century,
    writers have produced both the "nonfiction novel" and the
    surrealistic story which rejects reality. Nin's diary re-
    flects this development. "Night versus day, inner versus
    outer," are expressed by the contrast between her "free-
    flowing lyric mood" and her "taut, detailed scenes."
    Nin's descriptions are not distorted from fact, yet they
    are created according to the time and place Nin chooses
    and appear as "stylistic set pieces in the volume." As an
    artist, Nin discusses the problem of what makes reality
    concrete, and how to treat the "surreal" side of life.
    The diary shares in today's obsessive drive towards con-
    tinual creation. Nin's obsession with recording reality
    has given her the freedom to create new worlds. The reader
    discovers that both fantasy and reality must be accepted to
    have the "imaginative courage" expressed so well in Nin's
    diary.

19 STERN, DANIEL. "The Diary of Anaïs Nin." Studies in the
    20th Century, 1 (Fall), 39-43.
        Since the nineteenth century, the main question about
    the artist's method has been realism vs. anti-realism.
    Cities of the Interior shows "a feminine vision raised to
    the highest power." The word "modern" applies to the diary
    because Nin is breaking down walls between the reader and
    herself and because the diary is involved with the most
    modern of drives--"obsession." The obsession is the diary
    itself. In spite of Nin's preference for the dream world
    of night, she has created a clear and specific sense of
    time and place and created "one of the most magnificent

set of characters to appear in any contemporary work of art." Both volumes have many "superb set-pieces." Both volumes show the struggle of two styles: "night versus day, inner versus outer." At her best, Nin merges the two, and her best is characteristic of most of the diary. She has solved some of the most crucial problems of the modern artist: "How real must reality be--how does one deal with the dark side, the surreal side of living...." The diary teaches that the way to the dream world "may be approached by the artistic manipulation of our day-time language" and teaches that "reality is never as real as we think."

20   TINDALL, GILLIAN. "Doldrums." New Statesman, 76 (6 September), 292.
     Review of Under a Glass Bell. Before "hippy" became a common label, Nin projected the image of an international artist who studied with Rank, made friends with writers like Henry Miller, and learned the meditational values of the East. Nin actually embodies the familiar "Paris-New York-West Coast circuit," but she was truly a pioneer in earlier times. Although her refined writing style describes places of interest to the reader, her egotism reduces them to "a common sameness." She has the ability to occasionally draw "definitive" portraits of acquaintances, but the reader should not be forced to hunt through her works to read these sketches.

1969 A BOOKS - NONE

1969 B SHORTER WRITINGS

1   ANON. "Herself Surprised." The Times Literary Supplement (24 July), p. 829.
     Review of The Novel of the Future. In this study, Nin examines the work of writers close to her sympathies: John Hawkes, William Goyen, Marguerite Young, and especially herself. The book will please Nin fans with its repetitious flow of the unconscious. Those who view Nin as possessing a "narrow, flawed talent" will find themselves agreeing with many of her ideas but will take offense at her patronizing manner, especially when she claims her limitations to be her virtues. She fails to mention Jane Austen, "whose Emma is the archetype of the subjective-presentation novel," or Tolstoy, who also studied the war between the sexes. The index is inadequate. Nin is merely a "cultural waif" clutching her

diaries and hoping their publication will earn her immor-
tality--though it is unlikely they have more stature than
Marie Bashkirtseff's anonymous letters to Guy de Maupassant.

2   ANON. "Non-Fiction." Publishers Weekly, 196 (1 September),
     50.
          Review of Diary III. Nin is poet, novelist, and lay-
     analyst, but she is best known for her diary. In this
     volume, Nin returns to New York and becomes the center of
     a group of returned expatriates and refugee artists. The
     diary also records the private publication of Under a
     Glass Bell and the role of Edmund Wilson in bringing Nin
     recognition.

3   ANON. Review of The Diary of Anaïs Nin, Volume Three. The
     Virginia Kirkus Service, 37 (1 September), 980.
          Review of Diary III. Nin is "flowing and flying; it
     is difficult to think she could be more airborne now than
     before since her sensibilities are already stippling the
     pages." She records contact with celebrities and the
     coldness and lack of intimacy of New York City. The reader
     will not question Nin's desire to "heighten and create
     life all around me" but will question the "solipsistic
     'me.'"

4   ANON. "L'admiratrice admirée." Paris Le Figaro Littéraire
     (15-21 September), p. 14. [French.]
          Review of Diary I. Nin's diary has finally been pub-
     lished. Since the 1930s, rumor has called it one of the
     literary documents of the century. In 1937, Miller said
     the diary would rank with the confessions of Saint Augus-
     tine, Petronius, Abelard, Rousseau, and Proust. By virtue
     of the literary principle "let us admire each other,"
     Henry's admiration has its award, for he is often mentioned
     in the diary. Nin's description of Miller's first appear-
     ance is memorable.

5   ATLAS, JAMES. "Nostalgia: The Diary of Anaïs Nin." The
     Harvard Crimson (4 December), p. 2.
          Review of Diary III. Praises Nin's "gift" for recording
     the years before and during World War II. The diary is
     most remarkable for evoking an age; famous people "move
     like ghosts through the long years of the War, animated,
     prodded back into life." "All the stylish arguments which
     plagued that generation are talked out." The diary goes
     beyond biography to achieve "the unearthing of a sensibil-
     ity diminished by the wracking crisis...and yet able to go
     on."

1969

6   BALAKIAN, ANNA. Review of <u>Anaïs Nin</u>, by Oliver Evans. <u>Ameri-</u>
    <u>can Literature</u>, 41 (March), 130-133.
        Evans' work (1968.A1) is the first comprehensive book on
    Nin's writings. Although he says he will not use value judg-
    ments, Evans uses superlatives to express his enthusiasm.
    Many earlier critics inappropriately applied the standards
    of the traditional novel to her work, which is currently
    identified with the <u>nouveau roman</u>. Evans carefully analy-
    zes each Nin novel and explores the symbols which link the
    books: the minotaur, albatross, glass bell, etc. Nin uses
    symbolism and the techniques of surrealism. She has the
    courage to reject logical patterns and craft her novels
    "along analogical lines heretofore associated with poetry."
    Nin attempts to form an individual language that will ex-
    press universal truths. She creates only a limited number
    of characters in order to emphasize "the variation in the
    ego and its overflow into the collective self." Hopefully,
    Evans's book will lead to inclusion of Nin's works on col-
    lege reading lists.

7   BISHOP, THOMAS. "Pick of the Paperbacks." <u>Saturday Review</u>,
    52 (31 May), 29.
        Review of <u>Diary</u> I. Nin has always been an unusual lit-
    erary figure, spending her time among European writers or
    living in semi-seclusion in Greenwich Village. This first
    volume edited from her manuscript diary is a series of
    fragments, less revelations of the artistic world than ac-
    counts of her friendships, her psychoanalysis, and "her
    own awareness of the hypersensitive nature that left her
    always an observer rather than a participant in life."

8   CABAU, JACQUES. "Journal: Quand Anaïs Nin Se Droguait à
    l'Écriture." Paris <u>L'Express</u> (3-9 November), pp. 135-136.
    [French.]
        Review of <u>Diary</u> I. Discusses contents of this volume.
    The diary does not resemble the journal of Michelet or the
    the Goncourts. Nin does not have taste for the key-hole.
    When she causes a scandal, it is with the freedom of a
    militant woman. She has a lover and says so. She does
    not fear words. Muse and mother hen, Nin urges bohemian
    writers toward the discipline of the artist. The diary
    is about writing; love is only the pretext. The diary is
    not a history but a document about the solitary vice of
    literature. Nin is shut in the exile of words; her journal
    is a document about the universal schizophrenia of writers,
    for whom writing is a drug. Nin's journal is a laboratory
    where she reveals the transformation of life into writing.

9   CASEY, FLORENCE. "A Bird Does not Need to Study Aviation."
     The Christian Science Monitor (14 January), C, p. 1.
          Review of The Novel of the Future. Nin's novels and
     prose poems are "touching and elegant explorations of the
     unconscious." Attacks the prose and ideas in The Novel of
     the Future; Nin believes she can justify a nonlogical
     statement by repeating it. "Nobody seems to have taught
     her any logic," so that she does not know what a literary
     theory is. "She adores uncritically" what she likes in
     art and makes little effort to grasp intellectually what
     she dislikes. She has no notion of art as dialectical
     activity between two contrasting viewpoints. Hopes that
     Nin will go back to writing fiction and publishing the
     diary.

10   CHASE, KATHLEEN. "A Nin Fresh Print & on Record." The Chapel
     Hill Weekly (2 February), p. 4.
          Review of The Novel of the Future. Summarizes some of
     the chief ideas in the book on the relation between the
     dream and reality, on writers who integrate prose and
     poetry, on the contribution American writers have made to
     the rhythm of the poetic novel. The Novel of the Future
     is "a much needed book" for the general reader as well as
     the student and writer. It is an "important book" and
     "persuasive." Also praises the recordings of excerpts read
     by Nin from the diary for Spoken Arts, Inc. "I have not
     experienced in all literature the equal of Anaïs Nin's
     searing record of the [sic] birth of a still-born child."

11   CURLEY, DOROTHY NYREN and MAURICE KRAMER, eds. "Nin, Anaïs
     (1903-   )," in A Library of Literary Criticism. Fourth
     edition, Vol. 2. New York: Ungar Publishing, pp. 420-
     423.
          Quotes from eleven critical essays or reviews of Nin.

12   FEINANDEZ, DIANE. "L'arithmétique de l'inconscient." La
     Quinzaine Littéraire, no. 84 (1-15 December), pp. 8-9.
     [French.]
          Review of Diary I. The diary includes remarkable por-
     traits of Miller, Rank, Artaud, Allendy, which alone cap-
     tivate the reader. But the most interesting character is
     Nin. In the diary, needs and frustrations take on words.
     Like a human being, the diary plays different roles:
     sometimes it is the absent father, sometimes a confidant,
     sometimes a lover. The diary is dialogue and also auto-
     analysis. Nin's solidarity with women, her understanding
     of the feminine world, her desire to seduce men probably
     stem from a desire to revenge her abandoned mother.

1969

13   GARRIGUE, JEAN. "The Diary of Anaïs Nin." The New York Times
      Book Review (23 November), pp. 28, 30.
          Review of Diary III. Nin contrasts New York's speed and
      "cult of toughness" with the warm social milieu she left
      behind. The diary continues to be a "quilt of juxtaposi-
      tions": conversations, revelations, fragments of erotica,
      confessions, and oedipal hangups. Nin says she writes to
      an impersonal environment with sensitivity, openness, and
      liberating access to the unconscious. Speaking as woman
      artist, she realizes she has suffered guilt because wanting
      to write placed her in competition with men; women are too
      inclined to the sacrificial role of the "little mother."
      The volume ends affirmatively: Under a Glass Bell is being
      recognized; her technique has found readers. At times, Nin
      is "repetitive and obsessive," but she gives "a varied pic-
      ture of life and the soul." Her monologue is actually a
      dialogue about threats to the heart and the imagination,
      and it is important to all of us.

14   HAUTE, BARBARA and CAROLYN RILEY, eds. "Nin, Anaïs 1903-   ,"
      in 200 Contemporary Authors. Detroit: Gale, pp. 203-204.
          Biography. Nin "reportedly married Hugh Guiler (a
      banker, later, under the name Ian Hugo, a filmmaker and il-
      lustrator of Miss Nin's books) 1920, although Miss Nin told
      CA that, contrary to the information in other reference
      sources, she has never been married." Lists publications
      and work in progress (editing her journal). Nin's fiction
      always focuses on a woman character. She has been criti-
      cized for neglecting the outer world, but Nin's goal has
      been to remove barriers between the inner and outer.
      Quotes from reviews of Nin.

15   HICKS, GRANVILLE. Review of The Novel of the Future. Satur-
      day Review, 52 (25 January), 25-26.
          Nin uses The Novel of the Future to discuss the kind of
      poetic and surrealistic work she creates. She also con-
      siders the work of Henry Miller, Nathaniel West, John
      Hawkes, Marguerite Young, Djuna Barnes, and William Goyen.
      It is unlikely that any particular type of novel will be
      the only novel of the future, but Nin's type of novel is
      significant today and she does a good job of describing
      its strengths.

16   KANTERS, ROBERT. "Anaïs Nin par Anaïs Nin." Paris Le Figaro
      Littéraire (3-9 November), pp. 21-22. [French.]
          Review of Diary I. Nin's diary is a valuable biograph-
      ical document, but it also is a valuable key to her work.
      The personality of Nin and her relationship with her diary

is of chief interest. Nin is a very beautiful, thin woman
even at forty-five. Discusses her relationships with her
father and analysts. As an artist, Anaïs Nin knew the importance of men in a woman's life, of love and of sex.
Her obsession with houses is a pathetic key to her need
for protection and security. The second element of interest in the diary is the vivacious description of others.
The central character is, of course, Henry Miller, who is
depicted effectively. When Miller's wife, June, arrived
in Paris, the diary became a novel. Nin is caught between
the truth and the falsehood of June. She lives and analyzes the situation with the depth and intensity one can expect from Nin. The diary becomes almost the type of anti-
novel written by Miller.

17 KIRSCH, ROBERT. "Books: Studying Diary Masterwork of Noted
    Writer Anaïs Nin." Los Angeles Times (30 November), "Cal-
    endar" Section, p. 64.
        High praise for Diary III, which gives the "adventure
    of the emotions and intellect of one of the most penetrat-
    ing personages of our era." Nin is a fine writer, but her
    diary is her "masterwork." The "greatness" of the diary
    is that Nin accepts the challenge of demanding "nothing
    less than the truth about herself." The literature of the
    twentieth century rarely reveals much about the emancipa-
    tion of women, but Nin outdoes both Simone de Beauvoir and
    Mary McCarthy.

18 KNAPP, BETTINA. "The Novel of the Future." The Village Voice
    (10 April), pp. 6-7.
        Review that largely summarizes Nin's ideas. Nin sug-
    gests that writers follow Jung's dictum "proceed from the
    dream outward." For Nin, the dream "is the focal point
    from which all creativity radiates." The writer must cap-
    ture the changing images and reveal his "secret, tortured
    demoniac self." His self-knowledge gives the writer a link
    between himself and others. Nin says the writer needs
    fortitude and courage for his quest. The courage to shed
    tradition and structure as Nin has done in her works re-
    quires "extreme discipline." The creative artist must ex-
    perience conflict, struggle, confrontations. The writer
    is a visionary and uses symbols to express the inexpressi-
    ble. Impulses should be given free rein before discipline
    is imposed. The discovery of the unconscious put an end to
    the chronological novel. In The Novel of the Future Nin
    does "a remarkable job...of synthesizing the fruits of her
    experiences as novelist, poetess, diarist." The book is
    "a valuable guide."

1969

19   KYRIA, PIERRE. "Anaïs Nin et la Conquete du Moi." Paris Le
     Magazine Littéraire (December), pp. 28-30. [French.]
          Review of Diary I. Will Nin be known in American lit-
     erature as the author of the diary? Nin said that it was
     her most important work, and her friend Miller agrees. A
     legend has been created around it; in the United States,
     Great Britain, and Germany, Nin is, above all, the author
     of the diary. The first volume of this diary has just been
     published in France. It is the revelation of an exception-
     al personality and an important human document. Recounts
     Nin's life. Cities of the Interior explores the psychology
     of feminine characters from Nin's own experiences. The
     diary was a secure retreat for Nin. It has the style of
     intimate confession, of personal analysis. Discusses the
     content of Diary I. It is a valuable source for those in-
     terested in Miller or Artaud and in the literary discus-
     sions recorded. However, the chief value of the diary is
     its picture of a courageous woman who gives birth to the
     artist in herself.

20   LAS VERGNAS, RAYMOND. "Visages de l'Amour." Paris Les
     Nouvelles Littéraires, no. 1921 (25 June), p. 5. [French.]
          Nin's biography. A Spy in the House of Love is closer
     to a prose poem than to a romantic story. Nin denies hav-
     ing projected some aspects of herself unto her characters.
     But the colors "red and silver" that her heroines wear are
     her favorite colors. And there seems to be a close con-
     nection between Henry Miller and Jay, who plays a chief
     role in Ladders to Fire. Nin's style is poetic and "fem-
     ininely emotive." She explores the drama of the modern
     woman who, having challenged traditional taboos, feels
     overwhelmed by her freedom and more imprisoned by her in-
     dependence than she was by past restrictions.

21   LAS VERGNAS, RAYMOND. "Portraits d'Artistes." Paris Les
     Nouvelles Littéraires, no. 2197 (30 October), p. 7.
     [French.]
          Review of Diary I. Nin holds a special place in Ameri-
     can literature due to biographical facts that made her an
     American by accident. Biography. In Diary I, Nin de-
     scribes her Protean youth. The book focuses on her quest
     for herself (through her quest for her father) and her
     fascination with psychoanalysis. In the diary, Nin iden-
     tifies herself primarily as a woman. It is interesting to
     compare what she says about her relationship with Miller
     with the image Miller gives in his Letters to Anaïs Nin
     (1965), where he discusses only literature. Discusses the
     Nin, Henry and June Miller triangle. The book reaches its

1969

highest point with the description of the stillbirth. Nin departs from the major literary movements; her place in literary history is with and equal to Miller and Durrell.

22   McEVILLY, WAYNE. "Afterword," in Seduction of the Minotaur. Chicago: Swallow Press, pp. 137-152.
        Seduction of the Minotaur "has something to teach." Nin's "feminine touch" is a "rare gift"; it "urges toward openness, expansion, insight...the world of woman's wisdom...." "Perhaps never before has the anima been so conscious of itself as in the works of Anaïs Nin." Nin ranks with other "magicians" such as Goethe, Albertus Magnus, Paul Klee, Mozart. Nin's work "feeds the soul." Readers will encounter their own shadow selves at the center of the labyrinth. The death of Dr. Hernandez, "the modern Christ," brings Lillian as Lazarus back to life. Lillian's journey is "into Heraclitean fire," and she learns to accept "the gift of presence, the immensity of the persona...the astonishing, in the most humble, everyday reality." Reprinted 1969.B23; 1970.B56; 1974.B54.

23   McEVILLY, WAYNE. "The Two Faces of Death in Anaïs Nin's Seduction of the Minotaur." The New Mexico Quarterly, 38 (Winter-Spring), 179-192.
        Reprint of 1969.B22.

24   MÉRAS, PHYLLIS. Review of The Diary of Anaïs Nin, Volume Three. Book World, 3 (30 November), 20.
        Nin's long diary has been compared to the confessions of St. Augustine, but he wrote to save souls and Nin to praise herself. To enjoy the diary, the reader must approach it with liking for Nin. In this volume, Nin discovers black society, but the liberal views of the 1940s seem condescending today. As in other volumes, Nin details her largesse to others while lamenting her poverty. Nin has been called a superb stylist, but her writing suffers from preciosity and monotonous rhythms. Her belief that she writes as a poet within the framework of prose suggests a failure to understand how poetry differs from prose. She should have spent more time recording insights into literary personalities and less on her obsession with her feminine psyche. If the reader is not familiar with her work, it "is a taste that takes a good deal of acquiring."

*25   Minute (23 October).
        Unlocatable. Cited in Van Der Elst, Marie-Claire. "The Recognition of AN in France: a Selective Bibliography by Marie Claire Van Der Elst." Under the Sign of Pisces, 2 (Spring 1971), 11.

1969

26 PELOUX, JEAN. "Anaïs Nin ou le journal d'une Internationale."
Paris Le Figaro Littéraire (27 October - 2 November),
p. 22. [French.]
Interview with Nin. Nin is a very lively, enthusiasic,
warm, ardent, and harmonious lady. She is a writer without
a country. Americans do not include her in their literature because they view her as a French woman. In France,
she is thought of as American. Nin says she is international. Biography of Nin. She says the young in America
read her diary, but most Americans ignore their best authors (William Goyen, Marguerite Young, Daniel Stern).

27 ROWE, WILLIAM. "The Divided Novelist." Twentieth Century,
177:48-49.
Review of The Novel of the Future. Nin argues that her
literary peers have equated realism with ugliness and
violence and abandoned the study of unconscious reality.
Her pursuit of the dream places Nin in the category of
writers like John Hawkes, Djuna Barnes, and Nathaniel West
who were inspired by French surrealism. Nin seeks to jus-
tify the "psychoanalytic canon," but she does not answer
the question of how to get beyond Joycean fragmentation.
The two chapters on Nin's diary show insights relevant today: a "diary is true to becoming and continuum," for the
diarist does not know the future. The fiction of the
twentieth century has become aware of its limitations.

28 SCHLESINGER, MARIAN C. "Anaïs Nin: An Era Recalled." The
Boston Globe (8 December), p. 21.
Nin was in Boston to talk about Diary III and attend
Robert Snyder's film "The Henry Miller Odyssey." Biography
of Nin and history of the diary. Praises its "remarkably
perceptive insights and luminous prose." Nin is a woman
with "a gentle face with delicate features" and a good
listener. She shows the "same extraordinary precision of
language" in formulating her ideas in conversation as in
the diary. Nin says she allowed her diaries to be published because there is an affinity between the 1930s and
the 1960s. Her concern for individuality, self discipline,
and personal responsibility interests youths today.

29 SCHNEIDER, DUANE. Review of The Diary of Anaïs Nin, Volume
Three. Library Journal, 94 (1 December), 4437.
Nin's lasting appeal comes not only from her poetic
style and brilliant portraits but also from the complete-
ness with which she reveals her feelings about life. For
this reason, Diary III makes the reader feel emotional
pain as Nin describes her departure from a Europe in war

and her attempts to establish herself in New York where
she handles the challenges of new friendships and the de-
feats involved in trying to get her work published.

30   STEEN, MIKE. "Anaïs Nin," in A Look at Tennessee Williams.
      New York: Hawthorn Books, pp. 193-207.
          Interview of Nin by Steen, focusing on Nin's opinion of
      Tennessee Williams. Steen says Nin is perceptive, sensi-
      tive, and sincere and praises "the gentle and honest style"
      of her diary, her "natural talent for expressing her
      thoughts in a fluid and lucid matter-of-fact manner." Nin
      is "completely feminine and lyrical in her surrealist
      style." Nin praises Williams' sensitive pictures of women
      and close identification with them. She says Williams was
      "a great poet." Nin says that Williams entered into the
      nightmare and produced art from it but has perhaps become
      haunted by nightmare. Nin once was "engulfed" by her
      dreams and fantasies, but she later learned to avoid this.
      Nin says drugs wear off, but "when you create, you don't
      come back to the same point." Williams turned his many
      selves into literary characters, but Nin needed the diary
      to avoid fictionalizing the reality of relationships. Be-
      cause of the diary, she "can't lie" about the past or what
      she was. Williams has not been able to keep his life sep-
      arate from his plays, but Nin always knew the difference
      between what she was inventing and reality. Williams'
      solitude is very dangerous; Nin thinks of insanity as
      loneliness.

31   STUHLMANN, GUNTHER. "Preface," in The Diary of Anaïs Nin,
      Volume Three: 1939-1944. Edited by Gunther Stuhlmann.
      New York: Harcourt Brace Jovanovich, pp. v-xiv.
          Describes Nin's experiences as a child in the 1920s in
      New York. Diary II shows Nin in New York in 1934, where
      she had to choose between psychoanalysis and writing. In
      1939 Nin came to New York again; Diary III reflects the
      isolation she felt there. "Her introspection shifts from
      her own emotions to the emotions of her friends, to a
      clearer assessment of her craft." Two of the keynotes of
      Nin's lifework are "feminine perception and a true inter-
      nationality." Nin "employed, rather than rejected her
      strength as a woman." The volume omits certain persons
      and changes certain names.

32   TAX, MEREDITH. "Anaïs Nin: A Woman's Diary." Boston The
      Old Mole (9-22 May), pp. 12-13.
          Review of Diary I. "Every breakthrough in cultural
      analysis, such as this diary, changes our imaginative

1969

grasp of human possibilities and thus has political meaning." The diary records "one woman's struggle to consciousness." The omissions in the diary "have great
dignity" and prevent us from giving her life "the second-
class interest of scandal." Because Nin expresses needs
other than sexual ones, "her diary is an important one for
women to read."

33   VOITLE, ROBERT B.   "Nin, Anaïs," in Encyclopedia of World
Literature in the 20th Century. Edited by Wolfgang B.
Fleischmann.   Vol. 2.   New York: Ungar Publishing,
pp. 452-453.
Biography of Nin.   Introduction to her fiction and
diary.   Nin's fiction is "a long effort to convey the sig-
nificance of recurrent dreams, fantasies, and myths without destroying them by explication."   Her writing is "almost always moving, but it puzzles the reader who is not
able to hold in check for a while his appetite for immedi-
ate meaning."   In 1965 she was becoming more widely recog-
nized.   The diary is "a work of art in its own right."

34   WADDINGTON, MIRIAM.   "Review of The Novel of the Future."
Journal of the Otto Rank Association, 4 (June), 54-60.
Agrees with Nin's complaint against literary critics who
attack "the narrowness and subjectivity of women's writings."   Nin's study of the novel shows courage because it
discusses the novel "through image and illustration instead
of through critical argument."   Nin describes writing novels as "a directed dream...the pull of the conscious casting its nets into the unconscious."   Only the artist has
"Nin's gift of directing the dream."   Criticizes Nin for
not placing enough emphasis on social or economic factors.
But few writers have written "out of an authentic psychological experience" like Nin's.   Nin is among the few who
recognize the changes of the future.

35   WICKES, GEORGE.   Americans in Paris.   Garden City, N.Y.:
Doubleday, pp. 265-268.
Nin was a cultured cosmopolitan who presents herself as
a kind of Emma Bovary living in a village outside Paris.
She played the roles of gracious lady of Louveciennes,
bohemian writer, and psychoanalyst's apprentice.   She was
fond of June Miller, but she helped send Henry to England
when June's arrival in Paris made his life impossible.   Nin
frequently lent Henry Miller money and moral support; he,
in turn, admired her as a writer.   She became his chief
literary mentor and taught him as much as she learned from
him.   Miller was impressed with the work in Nin's own

diary: dreams and fantasies analyzed in light of surrealism, psychoanalysis, and astrology. His "Scenario" was
directly inspired by her House of Incest; both works are
adaptations of film techniques to written dream scenarios,
to form a sequence of surrealistic visions.

1970 A BOOKS

1 SCHNEIDER, DUANE. An Interview with Anaïs Nin. Athens, Ohio:
   The Duane Schneider Press, 35 pp.
   Nin answers questions, discussing the following: The
   relationship between characters in diary and fiction; the
   neglect of her novels because she was typed as a special
   coterie writer; the popularity she gained through the diary
   because she disobeyed the prohibition against introspection
   and the growth of the self; changes in the diary (the later
   volumes deal with other people); the diary as "a study of
   growth"; her methods of composition; her value for the unconscious in writing and the emotional life; the feminine
   as closer to nature in contrast to male "rationalization"
   of feelings; her interest in R. D. Laing; how she spends
   her work day; her best works of fiction (Under a Glass
   Bell and House of Incest, and shorter works like Collages);
   her interest in the filming of A Spy in the House of Love;
   her friendships with Miller and Durrell; differences between American and European culture (no intimacy in America); her identity as an international writer rather than
   local or regional; her close association with Marguerite
   Young. Reprinted 1973.A3.

1970 B SHORTER WRITINGS

1 ALDAN, DAISY. "AN Interviewed by Daisy Aldan." Under the
   Sign of Pisces, 1 (Spring), 7-9.
   Nin uses poetry as her medium of communication because
   it expresses the psyche. Her characters are taken from
   life, but they become archetypes and myths. The diary ful-
   fills Nin's interest in humans as human beings; the poetry
   expresses their place in the universe, their meaning. To
   Nin, everyone appears first as a person, and second as a
   symbol expressing the psychological level of our existence,
   "from which our acts stem." Journalism depicts life in one
   dimension; poetry shows life as metaphysics. Nin's recurring symbols are the labyrinth—the journey with an unknown outcome, and the possibility of getting lost; the
   ocean, representing the unconscious; precious stones and
   minerals, which come from reduction and compression and are

the equivalent of lines of poetry; the ship--a journey "to Night, to Day,--to the Moon, to the Sun"; and gold, for ecstasy and illumination.

2 AMOIA, ALBA. "The Novel of the Future, By Anaïs Nin." Studies in the 20th Century, no. 6 (Fall), pp. 109-117.
   Praises The Novel of the Future for describing not only "the possible reconstruction of an art form, but the possible reconstruction of a society...." It is "a sensitive and illuminating book that ought to be read by all who are interested in the future of the novel"; it exhibits "great perception and imagination" and discusses "in depth every aspect of the creative process." Summarizes the main points of Nin's discussion of the novel and the creative process.

*3 ANDERSON, JIM. [London], OZ, no. 29 (July).
   Unlocatable. Cited in Under the Sign of Pisces, 4 (Winter,1973), 16.

4 ANDERSON, PATRICK. "Secret Vice." The Spectator, 224 (20 June), 820.
   Review of Diary III. Nin has trouble adjusting to the U.S., which is too materialistic and impersonal for her "ultra-feminine private world." Her complaints seem to echo many who left Europe at the outbreak of war: relationships are all impersonal, and all conceal their secret lives. Tales of Nin's friends, lame duck writers, are all limited by her "claustrophobic egotism." Nin herself confesses the journals are a secret vice: a vice is not art, and pathos is not the victory of control. The diary lacks breadth and the common touch. However, Nin is an interesting woman and her diary can be enjoyed by the reader.

5 ANON. "An Afternoon with Anaïs Nin, An Evening with Henry Miller." The Harvard Advocate, 103 (February), 2-3.
   Nin attended the Eastern premier of "The Henry Miller Odyssey," Robert Snyder's documentary film, at Harvard. "Delicate and beautiful, she possessed the perfect poise of a bird." Nin discussed Diary III with "awareness about how much she was a living symbol of some magical hour in the century." The diary "grew out of the urgency of perception, out of a clarity which unceasingly renewed itself with each event recorded."

6 ANON. "Nin's Journals." London Times (28 May), p. 10.
   Review of Diary III. American youth are still fighting the same materialism and competitiveness Nin has been

battling since she settled in America thirty years ago.
She believes that her works feed youth's romantic idealism.
Nin says she has always supported rebels, noting her friendships with Artaud and Miller, but she does not support the
militant women's liberation movement because women are not
kept down by men, but keep themselves down. Daniele Suissa
plans to produce a film of A Spy in the House of Love,
starring Jeanne Moreau. Over the past 20 years, Nin has
been in several underground films produced by artists like
Maya Deren and Ian Hugo.

7 ANON. "Woman of Words." The Times Literary Supplement
   (11 June), p. 633.
      Review of Diary III. For this volume, Nin selects an
   internal confrontation with the U.S. and the resumption of
   her literary patronage of Miller, Gonzalo, Robert Duncan,
   and others. Her narrative is fresher than in the first
   two volumes because she was forced to leave many diary
   manuscripts in France and was unable to reread and ponder
   her previous entries. Her husband, briefly mentioned in
   volume two, has disappeared, and the reader soon realizes
   Nin is not revealing the whole truth. She allows herself
   to create character sketches of her literary friends that
   move into fancy, erasing the line between intuition and
   imagination. Edmund Wilson's review of Nin's work accu-
   rately notes her inability to conclude her elaborate descriptions. Perhaps the most "entertaining" entries in
   this volume are the examples of erotica she wrote for
   money; these stories have the necessary "beginnings, mid-
   dles, and ends" and are free of her incessant narcissism.

8 ANON. "Paperbacks--The Study of Literature." Best Sellers,
   30 (1 November), 331.
      Review of The Novel of the Future. "Anaïs Nin may not
   know just what 'The Novel of the Future' will be but her
   book under that title is worth anybody's while."

9 BLAKESTON, OSWELL. "Understanding by Osmosis." Books and
   Bookmen, 15 (August), 12.
      Review of Diary III. During the war years, Nin preached
   that "the artist alone can save us from leaders" who ex-
   ploit the masses' emotions with hysterical clichés. Artists who turned away from "the subjective life of direct
   action were traitors to the universal community." Since
   everyone lives by irrational impulses, artists must be
   "tutors of the soul" and doctors of the communal psyche.
   Laura Rider expressed this view before Nin did, but Nin
   urges acceptance of the belief that the revolution begins

within oneself. Almost ironically juxtapositioned with
these ideals is Nin's record of her ability in making a
living. Though a generous friend, she seems too eager to
elicit emotional responses and lead others into her games.
She is happiest dealing with "'uncomplicated' negroes,
unhappy homosexuals, ...ripe-for-analyst film stars." She
poetizes people, and some of her feminine sensitivity will
strike readers as self-indulgent. She is at her best when
recording quick, journalistic notes on the present. The
cult of Anaïs Nin is well established.

10   BRODERICK, CATHERINE VREELAND. "Chapter I: The Four-
      Chambered Heart," and "Chapter III: Comparative Thematic
      Analysis of The Four-Chambered Heart and Génitrix," in "A
      Comparative Thematic Study of François Mauriac's Génitrix
      and Anaïs Nin's The Four-Chambered Heart." Ph.D. disser-
      tation, University of North Carolina, pp. 11-93, 178-213.
          Uses the method for analyzing a literary work developed
      in Eugene H. Falk's Types of Thematic Structure. Chapter
      one: Studies linear coherence, the themes of the story
      (the conflict between the private world and the world out-
      side; the difficulty of human relationships; life as change
      and discovery through a realistic relationship to one's
      selves and other people; death in life versus a creative
      life; the evolution from childhood to maturity); causal
      coherence, the themes of the plot (the blind quest for
      childhood dreams; the need for human interdependence; the
      need for continual growth and development; the fear of
      failure; self-deception through playing roles; woman's
      negative will used wrongly to fulfill herself through oth-
      ers, contrasted with her giving warmth and creativity to
      men); generic coherence of themes, dominant linking images
      (the houseboat as refuge; the river Seine as flow and
      change; Djuna as water; Rango as fire; the four-chambered
      heart as opposites unified in a single person). Chapter
      three: Compares themes in The Four-Chambered Heart and
      Génetrix; similar themes include the need for human inter-
      dependence, the fear of failure, the themes of death in
      life and rebirth; themes carried by motifs occurring in
      both novels include the theme of adult attempts to live by
      childhood's values.

11   CARY, RICHARD. "Anaïs Nin." Colby Library Quarterly, S 9
      no. 2 (June), p. 120.
          Quotes the inscriptions to Bern Porter that Nin wrote
      in her books; she valued Porter for his commitment to both
      science and art. "The words 'friend' and 'friendship'

recur with unassumptive sincerity throughout her inscrip-
tions, leaving the impression that she does not bandy the
terms lightly."

12 CENTING, RICHARD. "Jerzy Kosinski." Under the Sign of
    Pisces, 1 (Winter), 9-11.
        Jerzy Kosinski's novel The Painted Bird (1965) is dis-
    cussed by Nin in The Novel of the Future. Reports on Ko-
    sinski's letters and conversations about Nin. Nin is a
    "cultural transplant" and hence has a foreigner's special
    awareness of language. Nin views people as individuals
    rather than as members of groups. Sexuality in her works
    is "a struggle between seeking the refuge in ourselves or
    seeking it in others."

13 C[ENTING], R[ICHARD]. "A Look at Tennessee Williams." Under
    the Sign of Pisces, 1 (Spring), 12-13.
        Mike Steen's book A Look at Tennessee Williams (1969)
    includes an interview with Nin in which she recounts her
    memories of Williams. She became interested in his work
    in 1940. She also points out the similarity between Wil-
    liams' work and D. H. Lawrence's, "especially in his iden-
    tification with women." Steen's introduction says Nin is
    "completely feminine and lyrical in her surrealist style."

14 C[ENTING], R[ICHARD]. "Spying on the Doors." Under the Sign
    of Pisces, 1 (Spring), 11.
        The lyrics of a song entitled "Spy" by the rock group
    Jim Morrison and the Doors are obviously taken from A Spy
    in the House of Love. Nin did not give approval for the
    use of her title.

15 C[ENTING], R[ICHARD]. "Affinities." Under the Sign of
    Pisces, 1 (Summer), 12.
        Nin says Affinities (1970), a short story anthology
    edited by John Tytell and Harold Jaffe, was the first an-
    thology to include any of her stories.

16 C[ENTING], R[ICHARD]. "AN Collection of Rochelle Holt."
    Under the Sign of Pisces, 1 (Summer), 9-10.
        Rochelle L. Holt won an award at the University of Iowa
    for her collection of books relating to Nin and the art of
    writing. For the contest, Holt wrote an essay which shows
    Nin's influence on her own character.

1970

17   C[ENTING], R[ICHARD]. "Anna Kavan's Shout of Red." <u>Under the</u>
<u>Sign of Pisces</u>, 1 (Summer), 1-8.
     Essay primarily on Anna Kavan. Nin's bibliography at
the end of <u>The Novel of the Future</u> includes six titles by
Anna Kavan, more books than for any other author in the
bibliography. Nin was attracted to Kavan because of her
exploration of dreams, the unconscious, and the symbolic
act.

18   C[ENTING], R[ICHARD]. "Matrix." <u>Under the Sign of Pisces</u>, 1
(Summer), 12.
     <u>Matrix: for she of the new aeon</u> is a new little maga-
zine. Excerpts from Nin's current diary illuminate the
work of Marguerite Young.

19   C[ENTING], R[ICHARD]. "Neglected Books." <u>Under the Sign of</u>
<u>Pisces</u>, 1 (Summer), 9.
     Nin contributed a list of eleven neglected writers to
<u>The American Scholar</u>: Marguerite Young, Maude Hutchins,
John Hawkes, Anna Kavan, Marianne Hauser and others.

20   C[ENTING], R[ICHARD]. "<u>Poverty Playhouse</u>." <u>Under the Sign</u>
<u>of Pisces</u>, 1 (Summer), 12-13.
     <u>The Voice of a Woman</u>, a play by John McLean and Sharon
Bunn based on Nin's <u>Diary</u> I, was produced May 28-June 13
by Poverty Playhouse, Dallas, Texas.

21   C[ENTING], R[ICHARD]. "<u>Ian Hugo and Anaïs Nin</u>." <u>Under the</u>
<u>Sign of Pisces</u>, 1 (Fall), 9-10.
     Hugo is a New York executive, engraver, and film maker;
many Nin publications include Hugo's engravings. Nin has
sometimes appeared in the cast of his films ("Through the
Magiscope," 1969, and "Apertura," 1970), and a spoken text
by Nin is used in "Bells of Atlantis," 1952.

22   C[ENTING], R[ICHARD]. "<u>News of Jean Varda</u>." <u>Under the Sign</u>
<u>of Pisces</u>, 1 (Fall), 10-11.
     Jean Varda, the California collage artist, appears in
<u>Diary</u> III, and there is a character named Varda in <u>Col</u>-
<u>lages</u>. Centing met Varda together with Nin and took a
photograph of the two; he offers a print to readers. Nin
said that because her publisher does not use color illustrations for the published diary, justice is not done to
illustrations such as Varda's work.

23   C[ENTING], R[ICHARD]. "<u>The Otto Rank Association</u>." <u>Under the</u>
<u>Sign of Pisces</u>, 1 (Fall), 8-9.

1970

The Journal of the Otto Rank Association contains material by and about Nin. Marianne Hauser's "Thoughts on The
Diary of Anaïs Nin" (1970.B50) is "among the best writing"
on Nin.

24 [CENTING, RICHARD and BENJAMIN FRANKLIN V.] "The Henry Miller
Odyssey." Under the Sign of Pisces, 1 (Winter), 3-6; 1
(Spring), 9-11.
Excerpts from the conversation between Nin and Miller in
the Robert Snyder film "The Henry Miller Odyssey" (1969).
Miller saw Nin as shy, yet her silent listening was "always
eloquent." Nin sees the dream as a blueprint for the future
and a key to the secret self. Miller sees Nin transforming
rather than fighting the world. Nin avoids repetition in
order to live out many patterns. Nin believes in love of
the individual and cosmic love. Miller asks if the sacri-
fices made in the name of art are worthwhile or an illusion
of the ego. Nin says the artist wants to have a relationship with the world, a love relationship with many. Men
seek the abstract and create ideas. Nin believes that
women have never lost the sense of the human as the most
important.

25 [CENTING, RICHARD and BENJAMIN FRANKLIN V.] Under the Sign
of Pisces, 1 (Winter), 1.

The editors of Under the Sign of Pisces are Richard
Centing and Benjamin Franklin V. The newsletter was established to publish articles on Nin's life and work, letters to and from her, a quarterly checklist of writings by
and about Nin, and news of her circle. The Nin circle includes the people given in the diaries but also will grow
with the newsletter. Nin enthusiastically endorsed the
newsletter and offered to help the editors.

26 [CENTING, RICHARD and BENJAMIN FRANKLIN V.] "AN: A Selected
Current Checklist." Under the Sign of Pisces, 1 (Spring),
15.
Annotates five articles from journals (1969-1970).

27 [CENTING, RICHARD and BENJAMIN FRANKLIN V.] "Phoenix Rising."
Under the Sign of Pisces, 1 (Spring), 14.
Quotes from the brochure announcing a reprint edition
and new edition of The Phoenix, a little magazine originally published from 1938 to 1940. In 1938, The Phoenix
printed Miller's "Un Être Étoilique," "the first major
essay" on Nin. Excerpts from Nin's diary were also first
printed in the magazine in 1939.

1970

28   [CENTING, RICHARD and BENJAMIN FRANKLIN V.] "Reception for
      Diary III." Under the Sign of Pisces, 1 (Spring), 12.
          Reports on "An Evening with Anaïs Nin" at a booksellers
      in Los Angeles in 1969.

29   [CENTING, RICHARD and BENJAMIN FRANKLIN V.] "The Swallow
      Press." Under the Sign of Pisces, 1 (Spring), 12.
          Swallow Press has reprinted Seduction of the Minotaur
      with an "Afterword" by Wayne McEvilly. The Swallow Press
      catalog includes ten in-print books by Nin.

30   [CENTING, RICHARD and BENJAMIN FRANKLIN V.] "AN: A Selected
      Current Checklist." Under the Sign of Pisces, 1 (Summer),
      15-16.
          Annotates six articles from journals (1968-1970).

31   [CENTING, RICHARD and BENJAMIN FRANKLIN V.] "AN Exhibit at
      Ohio State." Under the Sign of Pisces, 1 (Fall), 13.
          An exhibit in 1970 at Ohio State University on Nin was
      assembled by Richard Centing from his personal collection.

32   [CENTING, RICHARD and BENJAMIN FRANKLIN V.] "AN on Louis
      Gross." Under the Sign of Pisces, 1 (Fall), 14.
          An exhibit at the University of Santa Clara on the work
      of sculptor Louis Gross was described in a brochure with
      comment by Nin.

33   CHAPELAN, MAURICE. "Anaïs au pays des souvenirs." Paris Le
      Figaro Litteraire (28 December-3 January), p. 20. [French.]
          Review of Diary I. Early photographs show Nin a lovely
      delicate young woman, looking like a virgin by de Vinci.
      One photograph shows she is left-handed, a detail which has
      psychological importance. Her friends are bohemians but
      will later become famous; the principal friend is Henry
      Miller. Analysis was necessary to exorcize a sad child-
      hood with a sadistic father and a martyr mother. Nin is a
      vulnerable and generous woman who does her utmost for her
      friends. Her diary is exciting, thrilling reading for its
      literary quality, for its documentary value and for its
      introspection. Nin is a woman who searches for and finds
      herself.

34   CHASE, KATHLEEN. "WWI Years [sic] in New York, According to
      Nin." The Chapel Hill Weekly (8 February), p. 4.
          Review of Diary III. It is lauded as enthusiastically
      as previous volumes. Nin's portraits are "precise and
      penetrating," as usual. Quotes from Nin's portraits of
      characters in volume three. Nin visits Harlem and is

comfortable there; she feels lost in the United States but
opens her home to artists. She realizes she must stop being drained by others and concentrate on her own book.
When Under a Glass Bell was released in 1944, it won praise
from the artistic world.

35 CHASE, KATHLEEN. "Anaïs Nin--'The Freedom of the Artist.'"
The North Carolina Anvil (26 December), pp. 8-9.
Review of Diary III. Cites Nin's pitting the renuncia-
tory freedom of the artist against mass delusions based
on leaders' thrust for power and gain. Biographical material, including a discussion of Nin's astrological chart.
Nin's main themes are "the development of woman" and the
problem of giving without masochism. For Nin, dream and
action feed on one another.

36 CORODIMAS, PETER. Review of The Diary of Anaïs Nin, Volume
Three. Best Sellers, 29 (15 January), 404.
Review of Diary III. Nin's diary is more than vivid
picture of writers and artists from the 1930s to the pre-
sent--it also dramatizes the evolution of Nin's interior
life. The diary explores the artist and the creative
process, human relationships, and the importance of keeping contact with one's dream life. Nin's meditations are
transformed into personal action, and her action into further meditation, in the "beautiful cycle of daily existence." Nin sees truth as bound up with change, not something which can be extracted from one instance. The diary
is an organic, fluid art form able to express both truth
and change; but, paradoxically it is also a means for cap-
turing time and preserving the past. The reader shares
Nin's life as she lives it, on many levels. The diary has
unique qualities which make it a "major literary document"
of our time.

37 D., A.-M. "Anaïs Nin." Votre Beauté (September), pp. 66,
119. [French.]
Biography. Nin was one of the first women to be psycho-
analyzed. History of the diary. Stock has published volumes one and two in France. All women should read the
diary, which was written by a woman who creates herself.
In Diary I, Nin says that the purpose of the journal is to
speak to other women because she has become a symbol for
them. Nin is clear and warm, vulnerable and assured at the
same time. She immediately establishes sympathy with her
interviewer. She understands the role of women in modern
society. Interview of Nin on questions of interest to
women: she says psychoanalysis gave her a sense of self-

1970

confidence; she defines herself as a woman by saying there
is a fundamental difference between men and women (women
live in the subjective world of sensation and emotions);
she says that women in the United States are trying to
achieve liberation by work and professional activity but
society still imposes barriers; she does not approve of
women declaring war on men--it is necessary for women to
achieve harmony with themselves; she describes her love
for costume as a means of expressing her character; her
love of capes is almost a fetish.

38 DELACROIX, JEAN-JACQUES. "Un Roman Passionné: Le Journal
    D'Anaïs Nin." Elle (22 June), pp. 58-61. [French.]
       Diary II has no equivalent in literature. It shows an
    untiring quest of the self. Nin's diary is an invaluable
    document of the 1930s and 1940s. It is also about the men
    who loved Nin's large eyes, soft voice, beauty, sweetness,
    fragility, enthusiasm. Today Nin is still attractive and
    youthful. Interview of Nin by Delacroix. She discusses
    the origin of the diary. Her "fantastic memory for de-
    tails" developed with her work on the diary. She wrote
    freely; she has never erased anything. The diary became
    her own universe. She feared that if it were destroyed,
    her secret self would be destroyed. She no longer fears
    this. Before, she was shy and needed to be alone with the
    diary. Now she has learned to communicate with others.
    She says it is true that she has been the inspiration for
    other writers and helped them. She does not feel aging as
    a burden.

39 DURANTEAU, JOSANE. "Deux regards clairs sur le temps comme
    il va." L'Education (29 January), pp. 31-32. [French.]
       Nin has the temperament of an exceptional artist,
    strength of sincerity and femininity, sympathizes with and
    understands the solitude of the spirit and radical original-
    ity. The fiction is wonderful, but the journal takes one
    closer to Nin herself and to the radiance of words. Nin
    has called her journal a "journal of others"; it is pre-
    cisely because she is profoundly solitary that the pages
    she writes are full of friends, as if she tried to com-
    pletely preserve all the changes and passing emotions men-
    aced by dissolution. Nin's touching humility is one of
    her charms; she believes it is necessary to merit love.
    Praises the brilliant and profound anecdotes and portraits
    and self portrait in Diary I. The journal saves life as
    it passes. Nin's passion to understand and her indignation
    against suffering brought her to psychoanalysis. Describes
    a personal meeting with Nin. Nin appeared fragile and vul-
    nerable, answered questions sweetly and followed up the
    interview by writing to Duranteau in exquisite French.

1970

40   EDMISTON, SUSAN. "Portrait of Anaïs Nin." <u>Mademoiselle</u>, 71
      (October), 134-135, 222-225.
          Nin's works and appearances are in demand on college
      campuses; her appeal comes from the fact she has lived out
      the dreams of a beautiful woman who is an artist and a
      friend of the famous. Nin does not believe decorative
      clothing or decor should be eradicated because it is con-
      sidered feminine. Nin has expressed the universality of
      private events in her diary. Her diary shows role con-
      flicts generated by the sacrifices she made to fill the
      needs of men. "For all her faults, perhaps even <u>because</u>
      of them, she was the only woman who really spoke for wom-
      en." Although her work is aligned with the feminist move-
      ment, she approaches it with caution and a reserved judg-
      ment. All labels--including masculine and feminine--must
      be transcended. No one is to blame for the "female predi-
      cament." Women have to develop strength and help men
      realize they are not losing anything. Men must accept
      their emotional side while women must link emotion with
      reason. Nin strongly believes in the <u>couple</u>, regardless
      of its sexual composition. Two people complete each other
      and supply sensitive fluctuation. Women's liberation re-
      quires love and an end to hostility.

41   FICHTER, ROBERT. "Anaïs Nin Recalled." <u>Boston Herald Trav-</u>
      <u>eler</u> (4 January), "Book Guide Section," pp. 6-7.
          Ten years ago Nin was practically unknown when she read
      at Harvard. Rumor said "she detested other women." She
      was "the most fascinating woman," with "a doll's face."
      Harvard students exploited her for "private mythologies"
      as the men in the diary do. Then she was not known for her
      journal, which will some day be considered a classic. As
      the diary is better known, Miller may be referred to as the
      friend of Nin. Reports on a current Nin visit to Harvard.
      She is still "the beautiful woman...open, human, womanly,
      generous, sensitive...." Nin says she would like to meet
      women from the women's movement. If such women have mis-
      understood her, "it is clear they have also deeply under-
      stood her."

42   FRANKLIN, BENJAMIN V. "Reprint of <u>The Booster</u> Now Available."
      <u>Under the Sign of Pisces</u>, 1 (Winter), 11.
          Johnson Reprint has reissued <u>The Booster</u> and <u>Delta</u>, the
      little magazine edited by Alfred Perlès in Paris from 1937
      to 1939. Nin served on the editorial board. Nin's three
      contributions to <u>The Booster</u> constitute her first appear-
      ances in little magazines.

1970

43   F[RANKLIN], B[ENJAMIN, V]. "Caresse Crosby: 1892-1970."
      Under the Sign of Pisces, 1 (Spring), 1-3.
            Article on Caresse Crosby. Nin describes Crosby in her
      diary. Nin and Crosby worked together at least twice on
      publishing ventures.

44   F[RANKLIN], B[ENJAMIN, V]. "AN Radio Program." Under the
      Sign of Pisces, 1 (Summer), 11.
            Describes a University of Michigan radio program which
      includes readings by Nin, musical arrangements by her
      father, and an interview with her. Tapes for this inter-
      view and for Nin's lecture at Oakland University (Roches-
      ter, Michigan) are kept by the University of Michigan radio
      station.

45   F[RANKLIN], B[ENJAMIN, V]. "Voyages." Under the Sign of
      Pisces, 1 (Summer), 10-11.
            Voyages, a current little magazine, contains a number
      of items of interest to Nin readers: Marguerite Young's
      essay on Nin (1967.B28), excerpts from work by Nin, and a
      sketch of Nin by artist Don Bachardy.

46   F[RANKLIN], B[ENJAMIN, V]. "Frances Steloff." Under the
      Sign of Pisces, 1 (Fall), 1-8.
            Article primarily on Steloff and the Gotham Book Mart.
      Steloff has given receptions for the publication of Nin's
      books since 1942, when the Gotham Book Mart held a party
      for Winter of Artifice. Edmund Wilson procured his copy
      of Under a Glass Bell from the Gotham Book Mart in order
      to write the review that made Nin a celebrity. The Steloff
      papers include letters from Nin since 1939. The Gotham
      Book Mart "has always been the best source of AN's books."
      Steloff has sold rare copies of Nin's works at very low
      prices.

47   FREUSTIE, JEAN. "Le Complexe de Jocaste." Paris Le Nouvel
      Observateur (1 June), p. 43. [French.]
            Review of Diary II. The first volume could have been
      entitled "search for a father." We can assume that Anaïs
      Nin, after extensive psychological therapy, became mature.
      She moved away from introspection and learned to assert
      herself as a writer and a woman. In volume two, Nin deals
      with the bohemain lifestyle in Paris after the war. In
      spite of the friendship between Nin and Miller, there was
      conflict. Nin blamed Miller for his prosaic nature, in-
      difference towards others, and selfishness. Nin confines
      herself to generalities, letting us catch only a glimpse
      of a woman trying to create her work. The Anaïs-mother is

her good side; she has a generous and loving nature. In fact, Nin is interested, or wants to be interested, in all human beings. Perhaps the great lesson of the book is in her attachments. Immoderate taste for the picturesque and the magical finally became healthy from contact with realities.

48   FRIEDMAN, MELVIN J. "André Malraux and Anaïs Nin." Contemporary Literature, 11 (Winter), 104-113.
          Review of Oliver Evans' Anaïs Nin (1968.A1) and Denis Boak's André Malraux. Evans' study breaks new ground in scholarship on Nin. Malraux is an "adventurer-writer-politician"; Nin, an "intensely feminine spirit"--but both had careers which were "lessons in exotic myth-making," both were influenced by the surrealists, and both developed new literary idioms. Evans' review begins with a brief biography of Nin and great praise; he discusses the sources and influences on the diary and the novels, and outlines Nin's plots. Nin's novels are "fictions of characterization," concentrating on the emotional lives of the characters and using both symbolism and psychoanalysis. The contents of the novels derive from the diary, but the novels earn the right to be called literary. Evans believes the primary influences on Nin are Virginia Woolf, James Joyce, and D. H. Lawrence--not the Dostoyevsky and Nietzsche who inspired Malraux--and sees her technique as deriving from the nouveau roman, a type of lyrical novel. Malraux provides an epigraph for Nin's work in his preface to Lady Chatterly's Lover, where he speaks of the "integration of eroticism with life."

49   GRENIER, MECHTILT MEIJER. "Anaïs Nin." [Brussels] Synthesis (January-February), pp. 282-284. [French.]
          Nin's strength comes from love, a love that is present in all of her work. She is open-minded and shows her feelings but keeps part of herself private. Her work depicts the tension and antagonism in human relationships. The diary is basic to all her work. It is a documentary and search for the self. There is little Nin has not felt, seen, foreseen, assimilated. Nin is trying to stimulate and analyze the poetic novel. Reports on an interview of Nin by Greiner. Nin says she does not have any children because she distrusts the father figure. Her books make her appear to be a female Janus. She has been subject to violent criticism because it looks as though she is not involved with political or social issues. There was a time when she could not live without the diary. It is the young who read Nin in the United States. The Novel of the

1970

Future is one of Nin's last books. In it she tries to
stimulate the development of the poetic novel and to analyze its techniques. She studies a very diverse group of
writers, painters, movie-directors and psychologists in
order to aid the process of literary creation. Under her
ample violet cape, she disappears through one of the hotel
doors, going forth towards a thousand other works, leaving
behind "a chant in the dark street."

50   GRIFFITH, PAUL. "The 'Jewels' of Anaïs Nin: Cities of the
     Interior." Journal of the Otto Rank Association, 5 (Decem-
     ber), 82-91.
          Describes a personal encounter with Nin. Nin's major
     achievement--the novels in Cities of the Interior--has
     been neglected. Discusses the characters and themes of
     the novels. Lillian is "the modern unhappy woman";
     Sabina is "her opposite, the woman who dares to 'live like
     a man.'" One of the dominant themes of the series comes
     from Djuna's strength and sense of values--"her faith in
     the powers of intelligence to solve the quandries and dis-
     asters of human nature." None of the three women charac-
     ters finds as much satisfaction in being an artist as a
     man would. One of the achievements of Cities of the Inte-
     rior is its portrayal of psychoanalysis. Djuna, who plays
     the role of the analyst, is as much "a heroine as contem-
     porary life can create." Another theme of the novels is
     change. Seduction of the Minotaur resolves the woman's
     quest. Lillian "has accomplished the interplanetary voy-
     age" between herself and another person.

51   HAUSER, MARIANNE. "Thoughts on the Diary of Anaïs Nin."
     Journal of the Otto Rank Association, 5 (June), 61-67.
          Surveys major events of Nin's life, which resembles "a
     surrealist drama where the exception becomes the norm."
     A photograph of Nin's family in Diary I gives symbolic
     hints of Nin's childhood (with father absent) and Nin's
     character ("determination," eyes that "look both inward
     and outward," a mouth closed to guard a secret). Volumes
     one through three show "a mounting excitement, a rising
     curve" in the story of Nin's growth as artist and woman.
     Her manner of writing is "free," without self-conscious-
     ness. She is a "supreme artist," producing "a multi-faceted
     mirror on many levels." The diary is a "writer's workshop,"
     a source for Nin's fiction. The diary also shows the dif-
     ficulties and adversities facing writers. Nin's conflict
     is the classic love-hate relationship with her father. Both
     daughter and father have a hunger for perfection.

1970

52   JOSSELIN, JEAN-FRANÇOIS. "Journal 1931-1934." Paris <u>Le</u>
      <u>Nouvel Observateur</u> (12 January), p. 35. [French.]
          Review of <u>Diary</u> I. Nin appears like a fictional charac-
      ter. Her father was a famous musician, a selfish Don Juan
      who left his far "y. Her mother was authoritative and sol-
      emn. Nin has an obsessive recollection of a troubled
      childhood. Also consider the setting, the 1930s, and fi-
      nally the renowned friends: an American in Paris (Henry
      Miller), his "femme fatale" (June), a poet-actor (Antonin
      Artaud), psychiatrists (Allendy, Otto Rank). Nin is liter-
      ature "from top to toe." The fury of Miller's style as
      well as his life distressed her. Nin listened to him and
      went her own way. She felt free only while writing in the
      diary. When she sought her father and, at the same time,
      her childhood, she was in search of her present self, for
      her diary was a mirror in which she watched her attitudes.
      Memory and psychoanalysis become protagonists in her book.

53   KARANTANI, MASAKO. "An Introductory Essay on <u>A Spy in the</u>
      <u>House of Love</u>: A Note on Anaïs Nin." [Yokohama] <u>Ferris</u>
      <u>College Studies</u> (October), pp. 189-230. [Japanese.]
          <u>A Spy in the House of Love</u> is an experiment, a psycho-
      logical autobiography in which a woman's self-discovery and
      development are traced. Obstacles to a woman's maturity
      are dramatized through the story of a female Don Juan, a
      woman who cannot stop having affairs in spite of her love
      for her husband. The heroine discovers that her father
      caused her compulsive behavior and sense of guilt and that
      she had identified herself with her father in order to
      consummate an incestuous love. The heroine can identify
      herself with the international artist's community, but this
      community is destined to be destroyed by war. <u>A Spy in the</u>
      <u>House of Love</u> assumes that the more the heroine loses the
      reality of an outside community, the more she has to seek
      the reality of herself as an individual. The decision to
      live as an artist provides the basis for this novel.

54   LAS VERGNAS, RAYMOND. "Tricheurs au Coeur Tendre: Lettres
      Américaines: Anaïs Nin, Journal 1934-1939." <u>Les Nouvelles</u>
      <u>Littéraires</u>, no. 2236 (30 July), p. 5. [French.]
          Traces the events and characters in <u>Diary</u> I and II. Nin
      opposes the feminine conception of art to Miller's mascu-
      line egocentricity; the feminine artist is nourished by the
      world and conceives her work as the deliverance of a child.
      Nin cultivates courage, tenacity. She is interested in
      psychology as the archeology of the soul and becomes an
      apostle to aid others. The diary is not only a work of art

1970

being born, it has the rare merit of restoring urgency and
fluidity to a period of history. The diary shows sensibility, sincerity, authenticity; it is "an exemplary document."

55   LOEB, CLAIRE. "The Literary World of Anaïs Nin." Pacifica
      Tape Library, Los Angeles, [cassette] no. BB5233.
          Interview of Nin by Claire Loeb. Nin has been described
      as "the world's most emancipated woman." She responds to
      songs on the emancipated woman by saying the differences
      between men and women are exciting. Women think in a stage
      of pre-rationalization. Diary III has just been published
      and received much attention. Nin discusses Miller's and
      Rank's opposition to her diary, her feeling that American
      artists lacked a community, her allegiance to psychology,
      rather than politics or systems. Americans were not in-
      terested in Europe, one reason her work was neglected;
      moreover, there was a taboo on subjectivity and sensuous
      values in the novels. She always liked rebels, for in-
      stance, Rank. She never accepted dogmatic surrealism and
      she didn't like the refusal of surrealism to connect the
      dream to reality. The dream gives us the "plot" of our
      lives. She reads selections from the diary.

56   McEVILLY, WAYNE. "Dos rostos de la muerte en Seducción del
      minotauro, de Anaïs Nin." [Buenos Aires] Sur, no. 322-
      323 (January-April), pp. 233-247.
          Reprint of 1969.B22.

57   [McEVILLY, WAYNE.] "Wayne McEvilly." Under the Sign of
      Pisces, 1 (Winter), 2-3.
          Letter from McEvilly to Nin, discussing The Novel of the
      Future. There is a "mystical circle" between D. H. Law-
      rence: An Unprofessional Study and The Novel of the Future.
      The latter studies the theme of "conversion of insight
      (activity vs. passivity-expression vs. tourism-creation
      instead of sight-seeing in the depths of the psyche)."
      Nin's works speak directly to the youth who possesses a
      great deal of "passive insight" and is drawn to mind-
      opening substances. The book insists upon expansion of
      awareness and compassion and helps others grow by teaching
      the insight Nin has already gained.

58   McNAY, MICHAEL. "Non-belligerent in the Sex War." Manchester
      Guardian (30 May), "Arts Guardian" Section, p. 8.
          Reports on an interview with Nin. She has many young
      readers in the United States. She appears "fragile as a
      Chinese doll," is "a man's woman (which is why militant

feminists dislike her)." Miller tried to make her into a
female Miller, but she found her own way as a writer. She
"won freedom by cooperating" with husbands and lovers.
Nin says "a woman is responsible for her own freedom. She
can get it without declaring war on men." Her novels and
journals show belief in the individual. For today's students, Nin says, "the only good brave cause is the cause
of the individual."

59 METZGER, DEENA. "Insight, Intuition, Dreams." Los Angeles
    Free Press (30 January-4 February), pp. 34, 42, 47.
       Review of Diary III. Certain themes are in all of
    Nin's work: insight, intuition, dreams, harmony, fusion,
    diversity. The diary is "the connection between the life
    and art." To keep a diary like it is to show that crea-
    tion is not just transcribing or recording. Since the
    artist can create the world, he is responsible for it.
    Nin's objection to Kenneth Patchen is "political"--the
    objection of one who takes responsibility for her vision.
    The question of volume three is how to survive the night-
    mare, the war; Nin's choice is life, creation, and so she
    commits herself again to her work.

60 POCHODA, ELIZABETH. "Books." Glamour, 63 (March), 166.
       Review of Diary I-III. Nin polarizes the concepts of
    masculinity and femininity in the diary. In volume one,
    she reacts to her sense of abandonment by her father by
    defining her feminine role as totally compassionate and
    selfless, although her instincts impel her to a fuller
    life. Her creativity is expressed in fantasy, illusion,
    and dream, which her timidity forces her to channel into
    the diary. At first, analysis with Rank seems to offer
    a solution to Nin's fragmentation, but Rank believes fem-
    ininity and creativity are antithetical. Volume two is
    set in New York, and Nin's frustrations as a woman are
    identified with the confinements of a masculine world.
    In her diary, she remains free to affirm and negate, so she
    resolves to turn life into art. In volume three, the
    setting shifts to Paris, but Nin's internal struggle con-
    tinues. As the diary turns toward the outer world, Nin's
    portraits of her friends expand, and her relationships
    appear as vignettes for a novel. The ultra-feminine air
    of the diary creates an "asexual," often "cloying" tone.
    Nin retreats from the interplay of masculine and feminine
    that could characterize creativity without threatening sex-
    uality. However, no one else has so honestly described the
    internal lives of women who want to be more than the inven-
    tion of men.

1970

61   REGIS, DURAND. "Anaïs Nin et le 'Langage des Nerfs.'" <u>Les</u>
      <u>Langues Modernes</u>, 64 (July-August), 73-80, or 289-296.
      [French.]
          What strikes us on reading Nin's diary is the day-to-
      day report on a life and an era. The diary was a tool in
      the struggle against neurosis. It was a feverish search,
      a quest to understand the act of writing itself. Between
      1931 and 1939, the period of the two first volumes of the
      diary, Nin was torn between writing the diary or fiction.
      She valued the diary because it was "feminine" and "true";
      she was afraid of the process of creation involved in pro-
      ducing the fiction. At the same time, Nin was getting in
      touch with her neurosis, her fantasies, and obsessions,
      what she called "the language of nerves." Analysis with
      Rank was also important in reorienting her to creativity.
      The diary could be used "as a security lock somewhere be-
      tween the fragile work and the world." Analyzes <u>House of</u>
      <u>Incest</u>. The book aspires toward an ideal writing which
      would escape the principle of reality, a writing of pure
      desire. Everything in the poem refers to the labyrinth,
      which is a test one must overcome. The dance theme is an
      allegory of the discovery of writing.

62   RICHARDSON, MAURICE. "The Journals of Anaïs Nin, Vol. 3."
      London <u>The Observer</u> (2 August), p. 27.
          Review of <u>Diary</u> III. Feels Nin "deserves a wider pub-
      lic." Her writing is not difficult nor is she "far from
      the centre of the humanist beam." Volume three covers her
      arrival in New York, her producing "harmless, non-sadistic"
      pornography for pay, and her work with analyst Otto Rank.
      She makes perceptive comments on the "'boxed-in' quality"
      of America.

63   SCHNEIDER, DUANE. "The Art of Anaïs Nin." <u>The Southern Re-</u>
      <u>view</u>, 6 (Spring), 43-50.
          Unity is the chief characteristic of all Nin's work.
      In both her novels and diary, she achieves unity with the
      same three devices: recurring characters, symbols, and
      motifs; psychological analysis; and "the definition of a
      single primary character." The diary is more successful
      than the novels; it gives more scope for character develop-
      ment. In it, the "single, primary multifaceted character"
      is Nin herself, whose depiction "demonstrates explicitly
      that the love of growth, expansion, and life can transform
      a sizeable portion of the world." Sketches the contents of
      <u>Diary</u> I and II. Briefly analyzes the fiction. Lillian, of
      <u>Ladders to Fire</u>, is defined by movement. <u>A Spy in the</u>
      <u>House of Love</u> is the least successful of Nin's novels.

Children of the Albatross includes the complex symbol of the multifaceted house--less elusive than her later symbols. Nin is "usually quite explicit about which suggestions the reader ought to recognize." Reprinted 1974.B64.

64 SLOTNIKOFF, WILLIAM. "William Slotnikoff on Anaïs Nin and a Letter to Her from the Author." Trace, no. 17, pp. 235-240.
    Nin's works form one "vast prose poem" which seeks to discover the true self behind the mask she wears in daily life. She uses the artist as her character type in order to portray greater freedom of the spirit. The individual's search for a new reality is indistinguishable from the problems of false relationships and threatened institutions; Nin's work is part of a body of writing in which the audience identifies with the intense real personal daily life of the writer, and broadens his understanding of his own life. This literature is equipped with a new power to influence the history of events. Slotnikoff's 1953 letter to Nin records his experience in acquiring a copy of D. H. Lawrence: An Unprofessional Study. He is especially concerned with the needs of the inner soul for "new gestures, new embraces, new emotions," with the atrophy of the intuitive faculties, and with the search for the complement of self, the opposite half.

65 STERN, DANIEL. Review of The Diary of Anaïs Nin, Volume Three. Under the Sign of Pisces, 1 (Winter), 6-9.
    Diary III has a "prophetic quality"; Nin demands a "stronghold for cultural values" in opposition to the Marxist doctrine of the time. The consciousness expressed in the volume is that of a poet exiled in practical America. The volume is in the form of a novel, with comic relief from Nin's essays into pornography and a climax when she prints Under a Glass Bell. By printing her own works and insisting on being heard, Nin ends her own passivity. She wants her work to be taken as a whole. Dreams cannot be shared, but some writers can unite the dream and reality.

66 VAN CREVEL, LAURENS. "On Golconda Symbolism in Minotaur; a Translation from French by Anaïs Nin of Letter from Laurens Van Crevel." Under the Sign of Pisces, 1 (Winter), 3.
    The city of Golconda has appeared in other works besides Seduction of the Minotaur. Golconda is mentioned in "Ideas on the Novel" by Marquis de Sade, where he quotes from the charming Queen of Golconda and her beautiful tales of the century. The work de Sade refers to is Aline, Queen of

1970

> Golconda (1761) by Marquis Stanislas Boufflers, a friend of
> Voltaire--a story of libertinism mingling fantasy and real-
> ity.

67   VIDAL, GORE. Two Sisters: A Memoir in the Form of a Novel.
      Boston: Little, Brown, pp. 3-44, 162-256, passim.
         Includes a parody of Nin, who is represented by the
      character Marietta Donegal. Her favorite adjective is
      "ensorcelled"; she wants to be a "love goddess" and great
      artist. She is sixty-eight, yet still beautiful, "pre-
      served by an insatiable appetite for glory and sex." She
      is the author of memoirs in which Vidal is described and
      of fiction (The Archaic Smile). Describes an encounter
      between Vidal and Marietta in the present and also their
      relationship in 1947 when they were lovers. She claims
      that she wanted to release his inhibitions, to teach him
      to "flow." She declares "Woman" is "the first principle
      of the universe"; an admirer says "Marietta Donegal is the
      feminine principle." "There is nothing in Marietta but a
      hair-raising desire to be noticed at any cost."

68   VILLELAUR, ANNE. "Le feuilleton littéraire d'Anne Villelaur:
      Portraits." Paris Les Lettres Françaises, no. 1318 (21-
      27 January), p. 8. [French.]
         Review of Diary I. The diary is an interesting work for
      many reasons: It is a portrait of a woman who is searching
      for herself as woman and writer; it is a series of por-
      traits of other men and women. If Nin gives us only a
      limited number of portraits and not a gallery of famous
      people of the 1930s, it is because she prefers deep con-
      tacts born of continuous relationships. The reader is
      skeptical about the necessity for Nin to give up the diary,
      which has become a literary work in itself. The partici-
      pation of the reader seems to be one of the best guarantees
      of the quality of the book. The diary shows Nin "an essen-
      tially feminine being"; psychoanalysis helps her to iden-
      tify with her nature as a woman. Examines her relationships
      with June and Henry Miller and with Artaud.

1971 A BOOKS

1   HINZ, EVELYN J. The Mirror and the Garden: Realism and Real-
     ity in the Writings of Anaïs Nin. Columbus: The Ohio
     State University Libraries Publications Committee, 129 pp.
        Introduction: In contrast to the personal or political
     criticism usually given to Nin, the purpose of this book
     is to consider Nin's work from a literary point of view,

focusing on the "theme" of "realism and reality" in Nin's
criticism and fiction. Chapter one: Examines Nin's theory
of reality and her attack on "realists" in Realism and
Reality (1946). For Nin, the artist's role is to assert
the value of the personal and subjective. She uses the
symbol of the mirror for realism and neurosis, the symbol
of the garden for the natural and positive in life and
art. Chapter two: D. H. Lawrence: An Unprofessional
Study is a "creative" rather than a critical work. Nin's
purpose is to prove "the ultimate objectivity of the intuitive and poetic method" and its superiority to "realistic" knowing. Chapter three: Discusses the three "controlling ideas" in Nin's novels and analyzes the character
of Djuna in relationship to them. "Karma" refers to the
punishment fitting the crime; repetition of action until
awareness is reached; and the search for knowledge of the
real self. "Tropism" means that change and turning are
linked with creativity. "Fixation" says that stasis is
destructive. Chapter four: Studies the structure of Nin's
novels. The sense of flow is of primary importance. The
form is usually that of a journey. Metaphorical language,
abstraction, turning objects into symbols, and symphonic
structure are all important to organization. Examines
these techniques in A Spy in the House of Love. Chapter
five: Compares Nin's characters to those of the Psycho-
machia; in Nin's fiction "personifications of the basic
passions battle for supremacy in the female psyche." Examines the character of Lillian, "the libidinous and sensual 'Woman Agonistes.'" Chapter six: Studies the three
major poetic devices of Nin's fiction--poetic prose rhythm,
highly sensuous diction, imagery that is "original," "ac-
curate," and "concrete." Chapter seven: Compares The
Novel of the Future with Nin's earlier criticism. Her
basic theory of the difference between realism and reality
has not changed, but Nin clarifies her ideas and shows that
they apply to the present. Chapter eight: Discusses Diary
I-III. Like the fiction and criticism, these books also
focus on "the negative consequences of the mirror approach
to life and art and of the need and possibility of replac-
ing such a static and deterministic view with a positive
and organic one." Includes a bibliography of works by Nin
and secondary sources on her.

1971 B SHORTER WRITINGS

1   ANON. "Hothouse Crusader." The Times Literary Supplement
     (29 January), p. 113.
          Review of A Spy in the House of Love. Nin has become a
     writer with a "hothouse" image; but beneath the dreamlike,

1971

emotional writing of this novel is a passionate plea for
women's liberation. Nin deals with the obsessive guilt of
a woman trapped by living with one man in one home.
Sabina, the major character, will lie and cheat to retain
her sexual independence, yet she is appalled by her own
"desire for passion without responsibility, sex without
love." She appears to be a happy wife, hiding her deep
guilt, until the "Lie Detector" makes her face reality;
she is continually punishing herself by creating "fantasy
lovers" who could never serve as husbands. Nin mixes fantasy with exact detail, impressionism with clarity. It is
not necessarily odd to find this very feminine writer
championing liberation for women.

2   ANON. "A Conversation with Anaïs Nin." The Second Wave: A
     Magazine of the New Feminism, 1 (Summer), 10-16.
         Some feminists are hostile to Nin's work because they
     believe her emphasis on individual growth and change ex-
     cludes collective action. Her philosophy is "misinter-
     preted as an individualist philosophy and counterposed to
     the political or Marxist analysis which is construed as
     collective"; those who misinterpret Nin see her as an es-
     capist who builds her own little world while injustices
     continue. Reports on Nin's participation in a public dis-
     cussion with feminists and Nin's opinion on a number of
     topics: the role of introspection in liberation, the need
     for quality rather than jingoism in group thinking, the
     sexism of Rank and other psychoanalysts. Nin asks "What
     do you think I should do for the women's movement?" and is
     told that the group wants her to bridge differences and
     broaden the movement.

3   ANON. Review of The Diary of Anaïs Nin, Volume Four. The
     Virginia Kirkus Service, 39 (1 August), 858.
         Review of Diary IV. Nin continues "extracting essenses,"
     "distilling," and recording "total feeling" in the recrea-
     tion of her roman fleuve. Miller has left the scene and
     now young men flock around Nin. Edmund Wilson's friend-
     ship is too authoritative and severe, while Nin feels she
     can offer much to Gore Vidal. Nin is "the great Amphitrite
     in person." Her diary is "a sacralization of herself."

4   ANON. "Anaïs Nin Talks about Being a Woman." Vogue, 158
     (15 October), 98-99, 103.
         Interview of Nin. Nin's works appeal to the young be-
     cause she believes in living with the senses and the psyche.
     Her writing communicates with emotions, imagery, and myth.
     She tries not to imitate men but to strenthen and reveal

the pattern of women; as Rank told her, we do not yet understand woman's experience because her perceptions of life
have not yet been fully articulated. The male invention of
a taboo on women's sexuality is broken in Nin's works, because "eroticism is one of the basic means of self-knowledge." Miller tried to lessen men's puritanical supersti-
tions about women and make women more real to men; Nin
tries to show all the relationships and fluid connections
beyond sex. Men's feelings and women's feelings closely
resemble each other, and men should recognize their sensitive side. Through self-knowledge, Nin has learned the
importance of faith and the inner life for withstanding
outer pressures. She has achieved a sense of harmony and
self-integration since her period of great creativity when
she produced almost a book a year. She believes that increased awareness will cause internal changes. She is
fascinated by intuitive knowledge and believes in "achieving life on the poetic level."

5   BAIL, JOY and GEOFFREY COOK. "With Robert Bly." The San
    Francisco Book Review, no. 19, unpaged.
        An interview with Robert Bly, who recommends reading
    Diary III, especially because the father culture has col-
    lapsed and men don't understand what will happen next.
    "Women will have to write it."

6   BRODSLEY, LAUREL. "Anaïs Nin and The Novel of the Future."
    Delta: The Cambridge Literary Magazine, no. 48 (March),
    pp. 35-39.
        Throughout her fiction, Nin "minutely inspects a love
    which seeks only to multiply itself in others...love for
    a fictitious identity projected upon another as part of a
    search for oneself." Sabina of A Spy in the House of Love
    experiences a conflict between sanity and insanity, con-
    flict and serenity. "The central issue in Nin's work is
    "the relation between art and madness." Since the neurotic
    is a failed artist, Sabina might have been able to maintain
    all her roles if she had been an artist. Nin's diary and
    first stories attempt to "transcend and transmute madness"
    into communication through art. In the novels, however,
    the heroines are saved not by art but by personal relation-
    ships. They must "learn to feel and to weep." They have
    to learn that their private fantasies and projections are
    unreal. By the end of A Spy in the House of Love, Sabina
    has begun to face her self-deception. Nin seems to have
    resolved her own conflict over her multiple roles (shown
    consciously in the diary) and her characters become more
    free in her later works. In Seduction of the Minotaur,

95

1971

Lillian is prepared to see others as separate from herself.
Novel of the Future is a "manifesto" for the kind of contemporary novel written primarily by women, which probes
"more deeply into the nuances of human relationships and
intimate revelation" than male writers do.

7   BROYARD, ANATOLE. "Of Art, Ecstasy and Water." The New York
    Times (26 October), p. 39.
        Review of Diary IV. Edmund Wilson wants to teach Nin
    how to write, but she rebels; she may be full of genius or
    insanity, but "there is no self-doubt." Her faith in her-
    self and art attracts "lost souls" who find answers in her
    highly abstract messages. Nin's vocabulary is from a
    "Victorian antique shop of literature," and she philoso-
    phizes in the way others "preen." The mail Nin quotes at
    length in this volume is all alike—either because of the
    force of her character or the uniformity of her audience.
    Nin is not given to humor; the reader will have to supply
    it. "Turning her into a vogue may be the best solution to
    the ungallant task of evaluating her critically."

8   BUCKMASTER, HENRIETTA. "Incantations: for the Initiated
    Only." Christian Science Monitor (11 November), B, p. 7.
        Review of Diary IV. Nin is in New York, printing her
    own books and learning to live as "the Artist as Woman."
    The book should be read as the expression of a woman who
    is the best advocate of her own cult. Nin believes the
    poverty and struggle of the artist give him his magic and
    compel him to face the human condition; her language is
    comprehensible only to those who understand that pain is
    valuable. The two prominent figures in this volume are
    Edmund Wilson and Gore Vidal. Wilson wanted to marry Nin
    and teach her to write, but his "pragmatic hardness" re-
    pelled her; Vidal was spontaneous and a pleasure until he
    accused Nin of living in a fantasy world. The diary never
    undertakes much of the self-examination "implicit in great
    diaries," and it invites criticism from the reader since
    it disparages humanity. However, Nin "is on the side of
    the angels—though her angels do seem to be all mutations
    of herself."

9   CENTING, RICHARD. "Foreword: The Recognition of Anaïs Nin,"
    in The Mirror and the Garden by Evelyn J. Hinz. Columbus:
    The Ohio State University Libraries Publications Committee,
    pp. ix-x.
        Hinz' book is the first analysis of all of Nin's pub-
    lished work. (Diary III and The Novel of the Future were
    published after Evans' book came out in 1968.) Approves

of Hinz treating Nin as an American writer, for Nin has
been excluded from journals and writers' series because of
limitations on her nationality. This is not to deny Nin's
link with France, where her diary has sold well. In America, recognition of Nin is also growing and "an audience
for her work is established." However, serious criticism
of Nin is lacking. "The Mirror and the Garden now provides
such a critique through objective insights into the subjective world of Anaïs Nin and the milieu of modern art and
thought of which her work is a significant part."

10 C[ENTING], R[ICHARD]. "Kiss the Joy as It Flies." Under the
Sign of Pisces, 2 (Winter), 11-12.
     Review of John Pearson's book (1970); Pearson quotes Nin
and admits her strong influence.

11 C[ENTING], R[ICHARD]. "The Novel of the Future." Under the
Sign of Pisces, 2 (Winter), 12.
     The Novel of the Future is available in paperback.

12 C[ENTING], R[ICHARD]. "AN's Birthday." Under the Sign of
Pisces, 2 (Spring), 15.
     Nin's birthday was celebrated February 21, 1971. Sev-
eral poems were written for the occasion and an exhibit of
books by and about her was displayed in Sioux City.

13 C[ENTING], R[ICHARD]. "Course on AN: Summer 1971." Under
the Sign of Pisces, 2 (Spring), 8-9.
     Announces Wayne McEvilly's course "Anaïs Nin and Current
Fiction," and his talk on Nin and Lawrence for the University of New Mexico.

14 C[ENTING], R[ICHARD]. "Diary in Paperback." Under the Sign
of Pisces, 2 (Spring), 15.
     Volume three of The Diary of Anaïs Nin (1939-1944) has
been newly issued in paper.

15 C[ENTING], R[ICHARD]. "The Recognition of AN Abroad." Under
the Sign of Pisces, 2 (Spring), 9-10.
     Mentions French and Dutch bibliographies of Nin's work
forthcoming in Under the Sign of Pisces and translations
of her works into Czech, Spanish, and Japanese. Nin has
been gaining increased recognition in France.

16 C[ENTING], R[ICHARD]. "Reviews by Anaïs Nin." Under the Sign
of Pisces, 2 (Spring), 14.
     Nin does not often write reviews, but she reviewed
Jacque Henri Lartigue's Diary of a Century in 1921 and The
Notebooks for Crime and Punishment in 1967.

1971

17   C[ENTING], R[ICHARD]. "AN on Marianne Hauser." <u>Under the</u>
      <u>Sign of Pisces</u>, 2 (Summer), 1.
           Nin has written an essay on Hauser's <u>A Lesson in Music</u>
      for <u>Rediscoveries</u>, a collection of essays on neglected
      works of fiction (1971).

18   C[ENTING], R[ICHARD]. "Gilbert and Kathleen Chase." <u>Under</u>
      <u>the Sign of Pisces</u>, 2 (Summer), 5-6.
           Describes psychologist Gilbert Chase and wife Kath-
      leen's visit to Ohio State and lists their reviews of Nin
      (1960-1970).

19   C[ENTING], R[ICHARD]. "Teaching Anaïs Nin." <u>Under the Sign</u>
      <u>of Pisces</u>, 2 (Summer), 6-7.
           Lists courses featuring Nin (1969-1971).

20   C[ENTING], R[ICHARD]. "AN: Commencement Addresses, 1971."
      <u>Under the Sign of Pisces</u>, 2 (Fall), 12-13.
           Nin gave addresses at Reed College and at Bennington
      College.

21   C[ENTING], R[ICHARD]. "New Book of Criticism on AN." <u>Under</u>
      <u>the Sign of Pisces</u>, 2 (Fall), 6-7.
           Reviews Evelyn J. Hinz' book <u>The Mirror and the Garden:</u>
      <u>Realism in the Writings of Anaïs Nin</u> (1971). Hinz offers
      "the first analysis of Anaïs Nin's entire published work
      through <u>Diary</u> III," gives brilliant critiques, and relates
      Nin's work to her traditions and times.

22   C[ENTING], R[ICHARD]. "Second Wave: Interview with AN."
      <u>Under the Sign of Pisces</u>, 2 (Fall), 13-14.
           Discusses a Nin lecture sponsored by Female Liberation
      of Boston and cites a Nin interview in <u>The Second Wave</u>
      (1971).

23   C[ENTING], R[ICHARD]. "Stylus: W. S. Gray and AN." <u>Under</u>
      <u>the Sign of Pisces</u>, 2 (Fall), 14-15.
           Cites Dr. Gray's interview in <u>Stylus: The Magazine of</u>
      <u>the Washington Literary Society of Randolph-Macon College</u>
      (Spring, 1971), in which Dr. Gray mentions his friendship
      with Nin.

24   [CENTING, RICHARD and BENJAMIN FRANKLIN V]. "Nin Notes."
      <u>Under the Sign of Pisces</u>, 2 (Fall), 15-16.
           A bibliography that covers miscellaneous sources on Nin
      (1967-1971): reviews of Nin's books, articles on Nin, re-
      prints of excerpts from Nin's books, quotes from anecdotal
      references to Nin, and Benjamin Franklin V's descriptive
      bibliography of Nin (1973.A1).

25   CLARK, EVELYN, BARBARA REYES and NANCY WILLIAMSON. "A Mirror
      for Us All." The Second Wave, no. 2 (Summer), pp. 8-9.
          Nin's diary is "political in the most classic sense...
      working out solutions to the oldest political question:
      the woman question... She was the first to discover
      consciousness-raising." Rank and Miller were afraid of
      Nin's effort to convey the unadorned truth; critics "would
      like to believe that Anaïs is a delightful visitor from
      another world--that...irrational world that men have as-
      signed to the second sex--and that the diary is just a
      toy." Chronicles a group discussion of the diary. Bio-
      graphical material, emphasizing the role of analyst Martha
      Jaeger.

26   ENGLISH, PRISCILLA. "An Interview with Anaïs Nin (September,
      1971)." New Woman Magazine, no. 7 (December), pp. 26-31.
          Nin discusses the difficulties of writing as a woman
      during the 1930s and 1940s, when "feminine writing" was
      held in low esteem. She says the conflict for women be-
      tween pursuing a career and private life can be solved.
      "Since woman has had more self-doubt and less self-
      confidence and less time to make her own individuality she
      has been more dependent on the persona." Psychology helps
      us get rid of these "false selves." We don't know what
      women are capable of in art--their contribution has not
      been recorded. Nin is beginning to find women who are
      equivalent to the male artists who interested her in the
      past. Perhaps this generation of women is stronger. She
      approves of the bisexuality of the sexual revolution. The
      early reviews attacked her for devoting attention to women
      characters who demand freedom, but now critics are not
      shocked. Discusses her "x-ray" theory of art, depicting
      the inner drama, not realism of the surface. She went to
      a woman analyst whenever she was in a crisis. She doesn't
      have blocks to creative flow anymore: "I think that's the
      time when the conflict stops; your personal conflict no
      longer ties you up and paralyzes you." Reprinted 1974.B33.

27   F[RANKLIN], B[ENJAMIN, V]. "AN's Childhood Diary." Under the
      Sign of Pisces, 2 (Winter), 15-16.
          Small Voices: A Grownup's Treasury of Selections from
      the Diaries, Journals and Notebooks of Young Children
      (1966) includes selections from 11-year-old Nin. The
      entries "suggest a maturity beyond her years" and sensitiv-
      ity and perception. The selections were first published in
      Birth (1959).

1971

28   F[RANKLIN], B[ENJAMIN, V]. "New Nin Publication: <u>Nuances</u>."
     <u>Under the Sign of Pisces</u>, 2 (Winter), 13-14.
         A special limited edition of <u>Nuances</u> was published by
     San Souri Press (1970).

29   F[RANKLIN], B[ENJAMIN, V]. "Book that Includes Nin Circle."
     <u>Under the Sign of Pisces</u>, 2 (Spring), 12-13.
         In George Wickes' <u>Americans in Paris</u> (1969), Nin is
     "pictured as an exotic woman and as a writer more aware of
     Miller's early literary talents than he himself" in the
     Paris of the 1930s.

30   F[RANKLIN], B[ENJAMIN, V]. "Varda." <u>Under the Sign of Pis-
     ces</u>, 2 (Spring), 6-8.
         Discusses the late artist Jean Varda, friend of Henry
     Miller and Anaïs Nin, and describes Varda's jacket illus-
     trations for Nin's books.

31   F[RANKLIN], B[ENJAMIN, V]. "AN's Recordings, Editorship of
     Periodicals and Films." <u>Under the Sign of Pisces</u>, 2
     (Fall), 7-10.
         Lists Nin recordings (1948-1968); her editing of little
     magazines (1937-1971): <u>The Booster</u> and <u>Delta</u> (Paris), <u>Two
     Cities</u> (Paris), and <u>Voyages: A National Literary Magazine</u>
     and films by Kenneth Anger, Maya Deren, Ian Hugo, and
     Robert Snyder in which she appeared (1946-1970).

32   F[RANKLIN], B[ENJAMIN, V]. "The Nin Reviews." <u>Under the Sign
     of Pisces</u>, 2 (Fall), 11-12.
         Lists books reviewed by Nin (1965-1971).

33   JASON, PHILIP K. "Teaching <u>A Spy in the House of Love</u>."
     <u>Under the Sign of Pisces</u>, 2 (Summer), 7-16.
         Images of music and circularity predominate in <u>A Spy in
     the House of Love</u>. Between affairs with Philip and Mambo,
     Sabina's erotic dreams are described in terms of Debussy.
     She goes from the sound of "Ile Joyeuse" to Mambo's drum-
     ming. Stravinsky's "Firebird" suggests Sabina's multiple
     selves through polytonality and the release of the many
     beautiful women from Kastchei's castle. At the end of the
     novel, the Lie Detector scolds Sabina for seeking her
     wholeness in music; life should not have a "rigid unity,"
     but contain acceptance of change in order to perceive "the
     self's underlying continuities." The end of the novel
     nearly repeats the opening passages, describing a circle.
     Circularity is introduced through truck wheels, umbrellas,
     parasols, and Sabina's cape. Eventually, the umbrella be-
     comes the central image of the book: the umbrella both

protects Sabina and helps her keep her balance; its ribs
may be an endless circle, or "tributaries to a solid
core." Finally, Sabina's umbrella-like skirt collapses;
the false selves have deflated.

34   JOHNSON, ALBERT. "Non Fiction." Publishers Weekly, 200
      (30 August), 267.
          Review of Diary IV. Nin has won late praise for the
      first three volumes of her diary. Diary IV covers the
      period when she wrote Under a Glass Bell, Winter of Arti-
      fice, and Ladders to Fire. It is also a record of her
      reactions to the 1940s, and to men like Edmund Wilson and
      Gore Vidal who disappointed her, since she felt "hostility
      towards authority, money, and the organization of the
      world." This is a self-portrait of a "determinedly proud
      woman who was also oblivious to trivia and risked much to
      hold her own course in life."

35   KIRSCH, ROBERT. "Odyssey to an Outer Life." Los Angeles
      Times (22 October), IV, pp. 2, 6.
          Review of Diary IV. In its new form, the diary is a
      cross between diary and novel. The theme is writing it-
      self. The struggle is the same, "emancipation from the
      determinism of neurosis, from captivity by the ghosts of
      past experience." This is the job of the artist. America
      is recreated in Nin's best prose. She sees Edmund Wilson
      and Gore Vidal "in that special way she has of cutting
      through to the deepest terrain of personality." The empha-
      sis is on "an odyssey from inner to outer life." Nin is
      beginning to win recognition as a writer.

36   KYRIA, PIERRE. "Anaïs Nin." Les Nouvelles Littéraires, no.
      2291 (20 August), p. 7. [French.]
          Review of Diary III. Nin, who has written fifteen nov-
      els [sic] and an essay on D. H. Lawrence, gained the atten-
      tion of the French people only since the publication of
      her diary. Diary I showed the introspection of a young
      woman who undertook the task of learning about her true
      self. In Diary II the outer world became more important.
      Diary III is the record of Nin's third confrontation with
      the United States between 1939 and 1944. Europe contrasted
      sharply with a materialist, primitive America and Nin felt
      isolated in New York. She constantly searched for "the
      meaning of the inner life." She wrote about her well-known
      friends and sought out those who would nourish her vivid
      intellectual curiosity. From failure to hope, from doubt
      to certainty, Nin recorded everything offered to her. She

1971

tried at the same time, to accomplish her work of novelist, perhaps ignoring the fact that one day this diary would be her revenge.

37 LHOSTE, PIERRE. "Anaïs Nin: Mes amis et leurs démons." Les Nouvelles Littéraires, no. 2259 (7 January), p. 6. [French.]
    Interview between Nin and Lhoste. Nin says sections have been deleted from Diary II but nothing essential is missing. She believes that we do not know what women feel because they do not know how to articulate the irrational. Nin suffered greatly when Dr. Martin Luther King was assassinated because she supported his ideas of non-violence. She loves the poetic novels of Pierre-Jean Jouve because he gives emotional truth and excludes prosaic detail. Everyone has his devil; she exorcised hers by writing in the diary. She described Miller's work habits. Men are afraid of women. The blending of novel and diary may become important in current literature.

38 LOCKE, RAYMOND FRIDAY. "Anaïs Nin and the Paintings of D. H. Lawrence." Mankind, 3 (August), 18-21.
    Praises Nin's D. H. Lawrence: An Unprofessional Study, "the only truly professional critical study of Lawrence's work" of all the books written in the first years after Lawrence's death. Reading this book in the 1950s led Locke to read Nin's fiction. Recounts two personal meetings with Nin, one in 1965 when she had become famous and one in 1970. Nin had visited Frieda Lawrence in Taos in the 1940s; reprints an account of this visit taken from Diary IV. "Nin's place in literary history is now secured."

39 LOTTMAN, HERBERT R. "The European Scene." Publishers Weekly, 199 (18 January), 29.
    Nin is now on the best seller list in France because of the Éditions Stock translations of her diary, volumes one and two. Ladders to Fire started her career in France, yet it was the diary which sold well. French critics hailed the diary as comparable to the memoirs of Simone de Beauvoir. Hopefully, Nin's work will someday be as popular in the United States.

40 McEVILLY, WAYNE. "The Bread of Tradition: Reflections on the Diary of Anaïs Nin." Prairie Schooner, 45 (Summer), 161-167.
    The diary functions at a deep level to communicate the "phenomenology of despair," anguish transformed by literary technique into a vision of the common human experience. Nin attempts to create beauty in order to escape dread of the

102

passing of time. Man is so wounded from living that he will
only listen to song, so Nin uses this beauty for her vision.
Diary III moves from "horror to ecstasy"; both despair and
a false sense of gaiety are rejected. The diary has the
quality of fiction, so that the ordinary is elevated. Unlike other diaries, Nin's creates intimacy by showing reality as the myth it truly is. Her diary is "a literature of
bread" which nourishes us with knowledge of the human condition as abandoned and in need of communication.

41 MARSHALL, SUSAN. "Dartmouth Holdings of AN." Under the Sign
    of Pisces, 2 (Winter), 4.
        Discuss the Dartmouth library's holdings relating to
    Nin's visit and talk in 1946.

42 NYREN, DOROTHY. Review of The Diary of Anaïs Nin, Volume
    Four. Library Journal, 96 (15 October), 3327.
        Although volume four of the diary is not as exciting as
    the earlier ones, it contains passages of beautiful prose
    which describe Nin's journeys and thoughts as she travels
    across the United States. There is too much repetition,
    diffuseness, and conceit, but the volume furnishes worth-
    while observations about many of Nin's friends: Edmund
    Wilson, Gore Vidal, James Baldwin, James Agee, and, of
    course, Henry Miller.

43 OHASHI, KENZABUSO. "The Diary of Anaïs Nin: The Inner World
    vs. The Outer World." Gakuto: Monthly Journal of Inter-
    national Biography, 68 (5 November), 12-15. [Japanese.]
        Review of Diary I and II. Nin's diary is both private
    and universal. Her diary testifies to the fact a diary
    can be a work of literature, and personal experience can
    become a public work of art. Volume one shows how the
    double nature of the diary, private and public, is deep-
    ened and complicated until the intermixture and conflict
    produce a work of art. The Miller in the diary is a Miller
    whom Nin tries to capture and reflect upon her mental mir-
    ror. Innumerable people are caught, reflected, and flicker
    fleetingly on Nin's mental mirrors. The moment a mirror is
    broken into pieces, a new one is created. The diary shows
    the duality which is an essential characteristic of a di-
    ary, the separation between the inner world and the outer.
    Nin has to expose what is strictly private to others, be-
    cause she has to test her private "island" against the
    external world. The diary becomes an obsession, but Nin
    finally transcends the obsession and heals her sense of
    division. Hereafter, obsessive words disappear completely
    from the diary, and Nin's inner world and outer worlds are
    peaceful. The schism between the inner and the outer world

represent the spiritual condition of man today and the condition of modern literature. Furthermore, the diary shows
us the mysterious and fascinating world of a woman who
tries to sustain herself in a vast, lonesome, and incon-
sistent world. The diary is a unique work of literature.

44   ORINGER, JUDY. "Anaïs Nin on Women." Ramparts Magazine, 9
     (May), 43-45.
     Interview. Nin's diary is now read by a rapidly ex-
panding audience of women, who want to trace the inner
development of a woman and her efforts to obtain liberation. Nin believes that liberation is accomplished from
within, through love and friendship, and not through sep-
arating or cutting the self off from other men and women.
The individual who frees herself creates a "oneness with
the world"; these inner changes then influence others and
eventually spread outward through the whole community.
Women will have to interest men in their total being but
this will not be possible by destroying the sexual dimension of the relationship. Nin does not advocate the uni-
sex trends favored by many feminists since she sees these
trends as narcissistic and immature for any relationship,
whether male-female, female-female, or male-male. All
relationships have tensions from differences in outlooks.
Asked for her opinion regarding variety in sexual prefer-
ence, such as homosexuality and bisexuality, Nin replied
"the only abnormality is the incapacity to love."

45   SNITOW, ANN. "Women's Private Writings: Anaïs Nin," in Notes
     from the Third Year: Women's Liberation. New York,
     pp. 131-133.
     Nin's published diary has become "a kind of cult book for
the feminist movement" although Nin's "lack of feminist consciousness is staggering." Nin seemed unaware of the treach-
ery of male psychiatrists; in her relations with Henry and
June Miller, she takes on a "painful kind of bisexuality"
but she makes June into "a kind of myth-like image of woman."
In her novels, Nin tries to be true to "Art," which she
identifies as primarily a male principle; her "diary is full-
blooded and complete" while what she calls her art is "pale,
fragmented, over-conscious." Nin wanted to be "a friend, not
an enemy of man." Women's private writings, such as Nin's
diary, are a place where they can judge others without hurt-
ing them; women are too dependent on men to afford the luxury
of self-revelation. "The diary is an opium for women" which
protects but isolates women. Nin believed "no one has ever
loved an adventurous woman as they have loved adventurous
men"; her use of male images to express her adventuring

nature is an indication of the "annihilating" difference. Reprinted 1973.B44.

46   SPACKS, PATRICIA MEYER. "Free Women." Hudson Review, 24 (Winter), 559-573.

Nin, Hellman, and Lessing, the "emancipated" women writers of this century, accepted limitation because it seemed to be freedom. Total concern with psychic and social freedom marks the works of Nin and Hellman as "peculiarly feminine." Self-sacrifice and love are Nin's means of preservation; she desires recognition for her personality and her work, but she "uses the language of self-deprecation and self-doubt." "Demanding freedom, she declares herself to have achieved it," but her need for an audience becomes a circular trap because the people with whom she surrounds herself make demands on her time. Nin, Hellman, and Lessing say the inherent problems of the feminine experience can be overcome through "direct self-preservation or fictional creation," but their victories still depend on denial or avoidance. For Nin, it is an avoidance of "self-confrontation" by means of "self-display"; she and Hellman both use "defensive narcissism"--narcissism not for the purpose of attracting attention like male narcissism, but for the purpose of convincing the self.

47   SPENCER, SHARON. Space, Time, and Structure in the Modern Novel. New York: New York University Press, 266 pp., passim.

The new architectonic novel corresponds to Nin's "novel of the future," "born of Freud, Einstein, jazz and science." House of Incest is an example of a novel with closed structure; it limits itself to one eccentric first-person viewpoint; the characters are reduced to their functions in the mind of the narrator. Cities of the Interior is an example of literary spatialization; it refuses to place itself in time, and its pieces may be read in any order. This novel is thematically conventional, but original in style and structure. It is about its characters, but Nin selects only details that reveal the core of a character or situation. Cities of the Interior, like other open-structured novels, demonstrates a desire to eradicate the division between the work of art and its source in life. Nin's books offer photomontages, engravings, collages, and artworks to furnish changing visual perspectives. Collages uses a circular motion; each of its nineteen vignettes is a variation upon the idea of the "rich creative powers of the imagination," pointing out that if love is not available one is expected to summon forth companionship and passion from imagination.

1971

48   STERN, DANIEL. "The Novel of Her Life." The Nation, 213
     (29 November), 570-572.
          Review of Diary IV. The "extraordinary emotional, sen-
     sual, and psychological impact" of the diary stems from
     the fact that Nin has been developing "a major fictional
     representation of the modern era...creating a novel in the
     form of a continuous diary." Nin's novels are "like an
     unconscious feminine glance into the universal dream
     world." The diary is a "long prose work in which all the
     major themes of our time are treated. The Artist versus
     Society...the role of the Artist and Politics...the Nature
     of Art." Nin's presentation of Gore Vidal uses "the nov-
     elist's technique at its best." The diary is a work simi-
     lar to that of Gide, Proust, and others who use their own
     sensibility as a mirror to reflect their friends and the
     history of that period. Volume four is "a self-contained
     historical novel...entirely controlled by the author's vi-
     sion." Reprinted 1974.B69.

49   STOCKING, SUSAN. "Personas Unmasked in Visit with Anaïs Nin."
     Los Angeles Times (7 November), pp. 16, 23.
          Interview. Nin is reluctant to discuss her personal
     life with an interviewer, for fear of losing the illusion
     of secrecy. She gives one the past, not the present. She
     has the ability to express warmth and destroy barriers.
     Her physical appearance reveals the essence of femininity
     in her beauty and delicateness. The diaries reveal themes
     of maternal love versus creativity, expansion versus sac-
     rifice, and romanticism versus realism. She experienced
     conflict over wanting to be the artist and wanting to be
     the woman behind artists. She sacrificed for men and was
     jeered by the critics of "free women." In the diary, she
     unmasked personas: mother, daughter, artist, muse, bohe-
     mian, friend, and caretaker. Many readers of the diary
     wrote to say she was writing their diary. Mass media pub-
     lishers have ignored her work, but the underground press
     raves about it. Nin has just become the first American to
     receive the Prix de Sevigne--France's award for autobiog-
     raphies, biographies, and letters. Nin believes readers
     of the diary are searching for stable personal values in an
     unstable world.

50   STUHLMANN, GUNTHER. "Preface," in The Diary of Anaïs Nin:
     Volume Four, 1944-1947. Edited by Gunther Stuhlmann. New
     York: Harcourt Brace Jovanovich, pp. vii-xi.
          The publication of the diary brought Nin much critical
     acclaim and many letters showing the personal significance
     of her work to readers. In Nin's own words, her life

becomes "universal, mythical, symbolic." The first three
volumes are "essentially self-contained units," each showing a stage in her growth. Summarizes the contents of
volumes one through three. Volume four is based on the
original manuscript volumes sixty-eight to seventy-four.
The basic themes of the diary are also found in volume
four: "self, femininity, neurosis, freedom, relationships,
the confluence of art and life." Discusses Nin's criticism of America: "empty," "tough," few meaningful relationships, not encouraging to art, obsessed with the
"mechanics of living." She believes changes in "inner
space" will produce changes in the individual and in
America.

51 TYTELL, JOHN. "Anaïs Nin and 'The Fall of the House of Ush-
    er.'" Under the Sign of Pisces, 2 (Winter), 5-11.
        "Under a Glass Bell" is a modern version of Poe's "The
    Fall of the House of Usher." Both explore inner conscious-
    ness and moods. Nin, however, "telescopes" the action with
    symbols, and she treats seriously the emotional states Poe
    used for sensational purposes. Each story depicts the in-
    terior of an enormous, ancient house. Nin's house, like
    her writing style, "acquires a more brittle fragility";
    Poe's house and style are more ornate. The suggestions of
    incest point to the primacy of the death wish and the fear
    of impotence. Jeanne and Usher are comparable on many
    points: her guitar links with Usher's music of stringed
    instruments; her relation to her brother, with his to his
    ill sister; they share the insulation of their worlds;
    the suggestion that each is already dead; the contrast be-
    tween the frozen silence around each character and poten-
    tial redemption through the exotic and elegant objects in
    their environments; the perceived links between death and
    nature. Both characters suggest the "logical development
    of the symbolist hero: a hysteria of hypersensitivity
    causing excesses which result in the annihilation of sen-
    sibility."

52 ULLMAN, LESLIE. "Writer Speaks on Self and Stability at Col-
    lege." Bennington Banner (21 June), pp. 1, 12.
        Review of commencement address by Nin at Bennington Col-
    lege, Vermont, in 1971. Nin spoke on the necessity of
    looking into the self for stability. She described the
    diary as the source of her knowledge that we must journey
    inward. She also noted that the diary developed from her
    curiosity about the way things grow; in the diary she was
    able to watch the growth of the self. Speaking on women's

1971

liberation, Nin advised women to focus on themselves as
individuals because personal changes can alter society.

53 VAN DER ELST, MARIE-CLAIRE. "The Recognition of AN in France:
    A Selective Bibliography." Under the Sign of Pisces, 2
    (Spring), 10-12.
        Lists Nin's books translated into French (1962-1971),
    reviews in newspapers and periodicals (1964-1970), magazine
    interviews (1970), and radio and television broadcasts
    (1970).

54 VIDAL, GORE. "Taking a Grand Tour of Anaïs Nin's High Bohemia
    Via the Time Machine." Los Angeles Times Book Review
    (26 September), pp. 1, 5, 23.
        Vidal met Nin in Paris in 1970 to approve diary entries
    about him before their publication. This meeting began
    with tension: Nin believed Marietta Donegal (1970.B67) in
    Two Sisters was a caricature of her, but Vidal admits only
    that Marietta's philosophy is similar to Nin's. Nin has a
    persistent Joan of Arc fantasy. Because she believes mind
    and feeling are always at war, Nin has "unbalanced both
    life and art" in her works. The theme of Diary IV is her
    "formidable will to power." Vidal does not recognize the
    portraits Nin draws without their names. She omits several
    of her friends from volume four, as well as "at least two
    Meaningful Relationships." The picture of Edmund Wilson is
    especially cruel because he "represents all that she hates":
    history, politics, and literature. Nin is the "subjective
    narcissist" who fails to communicate her vision; other
    people only exist to reflect her. Her solemn "hieratic
    style," and pompous prose show self-absorption. However,
    Nin does recognize her limits. Formerly, Vidal believed
    the diary would establish Nin as a "great sensibility,"
    but now he wonders. Reprinted 1972.B47.

55 WEILAND, STEVEN. "Space, Time and Structure in the Modern
    Novel by Sharon Spencer." Under the Sign of Pisces, 2
    (Fall), 2-6.
        Reviews Spencer's book, which discusses "'architectonic'
    treatments of the city, a popular model for the 'new' nov-
    el." Nin contributed to the "negation of the novel--the
    refusal to stress the imaginative reconstruction of the
    facts of the novelist's life instead of the facts them-
    selves." Agrees with Spencer's conclusion that openness
    to experiment in reading and teaching and the vigor of new
    novelists depends on the kind of criticism she has written.

1972 A BOOKS - NONE

1972 B SHORTER WRITINGS

1   ALDRIDGE, ADELE. "Report on 'Celebration: A Weekend with
      Anaïs Nin.' Coordinated by Valerie Harms Sheehan and
      Adele Aldridge." Under the Sign of Pisces, 3 (Fall), 2-6.
        "Magic Circles" weekend in Rye, New York (April 28-30,
      1972) included a group of thirty-eight artists; Nin was
      the central figure. She spoke on "Life as a Celebration"
      and read from her diary.

2   ANON. "Anaïs Nin." The Chicago Guide (March), p. 109.
        Lately public and critical attention has focused on
      Nin's diary, where she is occupied with the depths and
      complexities of relationships, the subconscious personal-
      ity, and woman's unique feelings expressed in the language
      of emotion, which differs entirely from that of the intel-
      lect.

3   ANON. "Not to Need, but To Be Needed." The Times Literary
      Supplement (12 May), p. 553.
        Review of Diary IV. This volume shows a pronounced
      developmental pattern, and one wonders how much of the
      writing was omitted merely by design. Nin is a "champion
      of omission," and to ask questions about her income or
      possible husband is to show "a lack of artistic sensibil-
      ity, the confusion of reality with realism." Nin views
      Edmund Wilson's revised opinion of her work as nothing less
      than admiration, and never considers it could be closer
      to the "recantation of a lover." The publication of Under
      a Glass Bell brought the adoration and friendship of young
      readers, many of whom were homosexuals who felt comfortable
      with Nin's love of the persona and reticient sexuality.
      She chose only those who reflected back her image. Eventu-
      ally, "all her swans turn out to be geese," however, from
      her point of view. Nin's "amateur talent" does not deserve
      admiration, but the reader can be impressed by her courage
      in getting what she wants from the publishing industry.

4   ANON. "Other New Books: The Journals of Anaïs Nin, Vol. IV."
      London, The Observer (14 May), p. 37.
        "Still beautiful, this higher bohemian surrealist cos-
      mopolite continues her marathon pilgrimmage of self revela-
      tion." The book includes some "delightfully fresh impres-
      sions" of Mexico. The most interesting friendship is with
      Edmund Wilson.

1972

5   BAILEY, ANTHONY. "Anterooms." New Statesman, 84 (4 August),
    165.
        Review of Diary IV. Nin lives in the self-centered
    world of a child. Nin notes the bombing of Hiroshima, and
    describes her life in New York City, but the book has too
    few elements which would locate it firmly in time and
    place. People become symbols to Nin, representing hunger,
    destruction, or liberation. Though she claims to explore
    the subconscious, most of her time is given to the friend-
    ship of unthreatening, "sad, emasculated young men." Nin
    describes one of her themes as self-discovery, but it is
    rather the "circular voyage of evasion," undertaken "in a
    sea of sub-Lawrentian gush."

6   BALAKIAN, ANNA. "The Diary of Anaïs Nin." The New York Times
    Book Review (16 January), pp. 28-31.
        Review of Diary IV. Nin's style in the diary unites
    inner monolog, the channel for self-analysis, with dialog.
    Although historical events are noted, her focus is on inner
    time, "the victory of Kairos over chronos." Nin's life
    among artists eliminated elitism; she offers portraits of
    both known and unkown personalities. Nin's life moves
    "towards others." The reader becomes acquainted with her
    compassion and insight, yet Nin remains hidden personally.
    She feels attraction or revulsion for people, and she con-
    stantly reassesses her relationships. Nin believes "the
    personal, if it is deep enough, becomes universal, mythical,
    symbolic." The diary offers images of the garden, the mir-
    ror, and the water, which help Nin move between dreams and
    reality. It is irrelevant to ask if Nin is "liberated"--
    she has long been "a free spirit." Her observations of the
    1940s are important for the present.

7   C[ENTING], R[ICHARD]. "Anaïs Nin Today." Under the Sign of
    Pisces, 3 (Winter), 1-6.
        Describes Nin's travels, a reception in her honor at the
    Gotham Book Mart, a lecture at the University of Wisconsin
    --Green Bay. The University of California at Berkeley
    sponsored "Anaïs Nin: A Celebration," with film, music,
    poetry, readings, and lectures. Speakers included Richard
    Centing, Evelyn Hinz, and Sharon Spencer. San Francisco
    and the Bay Area hold interest for Nin fans because Kay
    Boyle, Nin's brother Joaquin Nin-Culmell, and Robert Duncan
    live there. The new cover design of Under the Sign of
    Pisces is by Jaren Dahlstrom, a San Francisco artist.
    Notes the publication of Hinz' book on Nin (1971.A1).

8   C[ENTING], R[ICHARD]. "AN and the Feminist Movement." Under
    the Sign of Pisces, 3 (Spring), 16.

1972

Nin is on the board of advisors of the Feminist Book
Club, and advertisements for Nin's books appeared in its
first catalog.

9   C[ENTING], R[ICHARD]. "Nin Chronology: January-April 1972."
     Under the Sign of Pisces, 3 (Spring), 1-3.
          A schedule of Nin's lectures and readings January-April,
     1972.

10   CITRIN, JUDY. "Chicago Experiences Nin." Under the Sign of
     Pisces, 3 (Fall), 10-12.
          Describes the 1972 lecture by Nin on "Psychoanalysis and
     Creativity" at the Women's Committee of the Chicago Insti-
     tute of Psychoanalysis. Nin described how she made psycho-
     analysis the basis of her work. "An Evening with Anaïs Nin
     and Yevgeny Yevtushenko" was broadcast on television.

11   CLARK, ORVILLE. "Space, Time, and Structure in the Modern
     Novel by Sharon Spencer." Studies in the 20th Century,
     no. 9 (Spring), pp. 89-96.
          Spencer's book (1971.B47) is one of the most important
     studies of fiction since Nin's The Novel of the Future.
     It introduces readers to the "architectonic" novel, which
     includes Nin's Cities of the Interior, House of Incest and
     Collages. The architectonic novel achieves "the spatiali-
     zation of time" by subordinating temporal elements to "a
     new spatial sense." In this new novel, character no longer
     plays a central role; the technique of juxtaposition re-
     places narrative. Spencer's book and Nin's The Novel of
     the Future both attempt to create a new sensibility in the
     modern reader; both are concerned with the problem of
     creating a "rite of passage" from traditional literature
     to the novel of our time; both are concerned with the re-
     lationship between art and life.

12   CROMBIE, ROBERT. "Anaïs Nin Discusses the Diary of Anaïs Nin,
     1944-1947, Vol. 4." The Center for Cassette Studies, Inc.,
     Hollywood, [cassette] no. 29048.
          Crombie interviews Nin. She discusses the diary, its
     origin, portraits of her friends, relationship to her fic-
     tion. Younger writers are more resistant than older ones
     to being portrayed in the diary. Discusses her relation-
     ships with Edmund Wilson and Gore Vidal; the latter
     "changed" and they were no longer friends. Her friendship
     with Miller lasted. Discusses Maya Deren as a filmmaker.
     Nin doesn't like controversy. Feminists should work on
     themselves as individuals before trying to use groups.
     Nin is interested in women's creativity and in inspiring

1972

women. Nin talks about the presses she used to print her
books. She believes it is hard to be friends with American writers. Nin doesn't want to be rich. The diary has
now become an exchange of letters with the world. Students
are her chief readers because the ideas she had in the
1940s anticipated their feelings today.

13   DAVIS, SALLY. "The Female Angst." Pacifica Tape Library,
     Los Angeles, [cassette] no. BC9611.
         Sally Davis interviews Nin, Joan Didion, and Dory Previn
     about the pain of having a feminine psyche and functioning
     in a male-dominated world. Nin's diary is "invaluable" in
     showing the struggle of a sensitive woman wanting success
     on her own, yet wanting the approval of a man. Nin says
     she wasn't conscious when she wrote the diary that she was
     recording the difficulties of many other women. She de-
     clares that women who create are not more neurotic than
     others. However, women lack self-confidence, and gifted
     women often give up work because of the demands of rela-
     tionships. Faith in her work has helped Nin outgrow the
     need for approval from a man. Nin believes we need a bal-
     ance between female and male influence in our culture.
     Women are trying to go too far in separating themselves
     from men, but this is a transitional stage that will pass
     when women are not so threatened by men. Nin says she was
     never too threatened because she found her salvation in
     work. Nin sees women today as accelerating the movement
     toward finding and expressing themselves; the women's
     movement has been beneficial. If Nin had to relive it,
     she wouldn't want to change her life, but would want to
     accelerate such things as acceptance of her work.

14   ECKMAN, MARJA. "The Non-Legend of Anaïs Nin." New York Post
     (19 February), p. 29.
         Interview with Nin shortly before her sixty-ninth birth-
     day. Nin protests against being turned into a legend and
     gives details from her current life ("I tint my own hair.").
     Her husband was an American; they separated, and she was
     not married at the time of the interview. She has "very
     good unrivalrous relationships with women." She believes
     in analysis "completely." She weighs 115 pounds and begins
     work at 7:30 a.m. Her current heroes are Ralph Nader and
     Daniel Ellsberg, but she does not believe changing the
     system will improve life.

15   F[RANKLIN], B[ENJAMIN, V]. "AN and the Rare Book Trade."
      Under the Sign of Pisces, 3 (Winter), 11-16.
          William Young's "Catalogue 607" (1971) offers the
      largest and most complete Nin collection--22 titles. The
      high prices for scarce Nin editions reflect her high crit-
      ical standing. Gives the price of some Nin editions in
      1965, 1968, and 1972. Criticizes Young's collection for
      omissions and errors. Lists "the most difficult to ob-
      tain" books by Nin.

16   F[RANKLIN], B[ENJAMIN, V]. "New Nin Publications." Under the
      Sign of Pisces, 3 (Winter), 6-7.
          Notes publication in 1971 of Nin's Diary IV, an excerpt
      from Diary IV, and an interview with Nin.

17   F[RANKLIN], B[ENJAMIN, V]. "AN and the Swallow Press." Under
      the Sign of Pisces, 3 (Spring), 16.
          New printings of ten Nin titles by Swallow Press.

18   F[RANKLIN], B[ENJAMIN, V]. "New Nin Publications." Under the
      Sign of Pisces, 3 (Spring), 11-12.
          Lists Nin publications (1971-1972): a reprinted story
      and preface, excerpts from a speech, and a "perceptively
      sane" piece on the women's movement. Nin answered a ques-
      tion about the books that influenced her most as a teen-
      ager with the following list: "Emerson, Thoreau, and
      Whitman; then, later, Lawrence, biographies, philosophy,
      and psychology."

19   F[RANKLIN], B[ENJAMIN, V]. "New Nin Publications." Under the
      Sign of Pisces, 3 (Fall), 1-2.
          Notes publication in 1972 of an essay by Nin, interview
      with Nin, the fourth Diary, and excerpts from Diary I-III.
      A Spy in the House of Love is out of print.

20   FREEMAN, BARBARA. "A Dialogue with Anaïs Nin." Chicago Re-
      view, 24:29-35.
          Interview. The diary records Nin's concerns and atti-
      tudes at different ages; in editing, she had to be careful
      not to change the narcissism, errors, and fumblings to
      agree with her more mature state of mind. Nin knows of no
      writers today who imitate her style. Almost all Nin's
      characters were taken from real people. Lillian is Nin's
      most developed character. Miller and Nin both believed in
      writing without plan or structure. "Our lives make a pat-
      tern"; nothing is accidental once you understand it. Men
      who are brought up to believe they must control have dif-
      ficulty reading Nin. Writing comes from trusting the

1972

subconscious; the critical self is involved only in check-
ing it afterward. Nin says that if her life is not interesting, the diary won't be interesting. LSD showed her
that her aim was unity. Her key words are all in the dictionary under "trans." The writer is his own best critic,
after waiting and then looking again. It is best to write
as an individual, not as a critic, until one can distin-
guish between what one loves and does not love.

21   GALOS, PAUL. "The Mirror and the Garden, by Evelyn J. Hinz."
     Under the Sign of Pisces, 3 (Winter), 8-11.
        This book (1971.A1) is necessary for readers of Nin
     because there has been little serious criticism on Nin in
     the past. It treats Nin's writings thoroughly and pro-
     vides current information on Nin scholarship. Hinz traces
     a parallel thematic development between the diary and the
     novels, explained by Nin's desire for a "vital, inclusive
     reality." Both The Novel of the Future and D. H. Lawrence:
     An Unprofessional Study are discussed in light of Nin's
     other works. D. H. Lawrence introduced Nin's "regard for
     the intuitive-subjective direction." Hinz discusses the
     literary importance of the diary as well as its use in
     Nin's search for reality. Hinz' most valuable work is in
     supplying "lucid descriptions" of Nin's symbols, language,
     and rhythm.

22   GORDON, MERYL. "Anaïs Nin: Ending the Years of Silence."
     Ann Arbor The Michigan Daily (18 February), p. 5.
        Nin finally received acclaim when she published the
     diary. She writes "compellingly" and her work is "fasci-
     nating." Summarizes contents of volumes one through four.
     Diaries and fiction emphasize "the search of women to find
     an identity" and not merely live through men. Nin wrote
     about the struggle of women before the women's movement
     was well known. Nin spoke at Northwestern University in
     January on "Women and Women Writers." In reply to stu-
     dents' questions, Nin indicated that she discovered the
     need to write when she was put into a cast at age nine and
     could not walk. Nin thinks "woman will now probably devel-
     op her own psychoanalytical theories." She is still writ-
     ing the diary but spends more time communicating with
     others through letters.

23   HAGE, ALICE. "Always She Wanted to Write as a Woman." Chi-
     cago Daily News (February 5-6), "Panorama Pulse" Section,
     p. 8.
        Reports on Nin's talk to students at Northwestern Uni-
     versity. Nin "never allowed the admiration for men to

erase the memory of the insults she felt that her father
had delivered to her mother." Nin "brought a consciously
female approach to literature"--including her highly personal language. She associated with male writers but
"always she wanted to write as a woman." She received her
first serious critical attention on publishing volume one
of the diary in 1966. Since then she has received much
attention from young readers. She admires Joyce Carol
Oates and suspects Joan Didion of being "hard...over-
controlled." The fourth volume of her diary has won acclaim; Nin's dreams have won.

24   HARRIS, BERTHA. "Who Chose These Women, and Why?" The Vil-
         lage Voice (30 November), p. 71.
         Nin was honored at a program at the Edison Theater in
     New York. Objects to the choice of the three other women
     who were honored with Nin (Suzanne Benton, Joan Stone,
     Vinie Burrows). Says Nin merits comparison with more fa-
     mous artists like Georgia O'Keeffe and Louise Nevelson.

25   HINZ, EVELYN J. "Anaïs Nin." Contemporary Literature, 13
         (Spring), 255-257.
         Review of Diary IV. The question "What is reality?"
     lies behind each episode of the diary. Diary IV focuses
     on Nin's critique of the "objectivity" of her critics.
     Edmund Wilson is her chief opponent, but Diana Trilling is
     even more hostile. Nin asks the critic to recognize the
     subjective basis of his "agreement or disagreement with
     the premises of the work in question." Agreement leads to
     judgment of the work as real; disagreement to the label of
     "irrelevant." Volume four calls for a "humanistic philo-
     sophy of criticism," and describes the conflicts among
     critics. Nin's egotism, which resembles that of Lawrence,
     weakens the volume, yet her deep concern for literature is
     clear. Some of Nin's ideas are overly simple, and her
     critical terms are not adequate; however, the volume stands
     as a "challenge to the premises of contemporary critical
     work."

26   HINZ, EVELYN J. "Celebration, Levitation, and a New Diary."
         Under the Sign of Pisces, 3 (Fall), 12-13.
         Nin spoke on her philosophy of the "personal," which
     harmonizes with the fundamental approach of the college,
     at the 1972 commencement of Hampshire College, Amherst,
     Massachusetts. She focused on two words--"celebration"
     (because of growing freedom from bondage to objective
     standards) and "levitation" ("the ability to transcend the
     historical and social evaluation of life").

1972

27   HINZ, EVELYN J.   "'No Puedo Mas': The Paradox of a Pisces."
      Under the Sign of Pisces, 3 (Fall), 6-10.
           Discusses the Rye, New York (April 28-30, 1972) gather-
      ing in Nin's honor. Frances Steloff chided Nin for sacri-
      ficing herself to others. Quotes passages from the diary
      that show Nin giving to others to the point where she
      would cry "I can't bear any more" ("No puedo mas").

28   HINZ, EVELYN J.   "'Excuse Me, It Was All a Dream': The Diary
      of Anaïs Nin: 1944-1947." Journal of the Otto Rank Asso-
      ciation, 7 (December), 21-35.
           Nin's work focuses on the problem of "What is real?"
      The diary differs from the typical journal because Nin
      uses it to rigorously analyze intuition, "to discover the
      objective significance of a subjective response." The
      diary has thematic unity only because Nin continually re-
      tells the same story about conflicting attitudes concerning
      reality. Her conception of reality, is "poetic and intui-
      tive...the psychic (in the old as well as new sense) signi-
      ficance of the phenomenal world" as opposed to "realism."
      The conflict between realism and reality is the "surface
      dialectic" of the diary, symbolized by garden and mirror
      imagery. Analyzes the theme of realism versus reality in
      Diary I-IV. In Diary I, Miller and Allendy are "realists";
      Rank gives Nin support in her belief in the dream. The
      critics Edmund Wilson (the type who "begins with a defini-
      tion of literature") and Diana Trilling (who begins with a
      definition of reality) in Diary IV demand that the artist
      repeat the past instead of introducing change.

29   JASON, PHILIP K. "The Future of Nin Criticism, A Review."
      Journal of the Otto Rank Association, 7 (June), 82-90.
           Review of The Mirror and the Garden by Evelyn J. Hinz
      (1971.A1). It is a valuable book that clarifies Nin's op-
      position to the realist tradition. The sections on the
      fiction are too short, but the ideas are stimulating and
      usually convincing. The organization allows Hinz to trace
      character development through many works and shows "the
      complexity and magnitude of Nin's achievement." Praises
      the study of the four major women characters of the novels,
      but disapproves of the analogies to other literature. The
      chapter on Nin's use of language is "a strong, intelligent
      beginning" in an area where work needs to be done. The
      book is "indispensable," because of "its great range, its
      eminently sensible approach, its sensitivity to Nin's
      merits and importance...and its careful scholarship." Ends
      by surveying areas on Nin that still need study: the

relationship between the diary and fiction; the Villa
Seurat Circle; the influence of psychological theories
on Nin; Nin and small magazines and presses.

30 JONES, BARRY DONALD. "The Diary of Anaïs Nin, Volume Four,
1944-1947." Hanover The Dartmouth (8 November), p. 2.
Diary IV shows Nin at the center of a group of dynamic,
eclectic personalities, mostly in Manhattan. The themes
of the other volumes are expanded here: the symbolism of
the father, the struggle to know the inner life when the
outer demands constant attention, woman as artist-creator,
value for the personal and the human. The diary focuses
optimistically on the art of living; it has more of the
joy of living than of literature, but this is an unusual
treasure for a book to offer.

31 JONES, BARRY DONALD. "Nin: Some Impressions." Hanover The
Dartmouth (10 November), p. 2.
Nin spoke to a standing-room-only audience at Dartmouth.
She spoke of finding a language for nonverbal communication, going beyond an easy use of words for only cerebral
purposes. She also discussed the individual's need for a
strong "core" before being able to contribute to society.
In this discussion, Nin communicated "feeling" in Nijin-
sky's sense of the word.

32 KILLOH, ELLEN PECK. "The Woman Writer and the Element of
Destruction." College English, 34 (October), 31-38.
Rank taught Nin that woman and artist are mutually ex-
clusive categories, but Nin struggled to turn herself into
a new model: the woman artist. The writer is destructive
in refusing to compromise his own viewpoint; for the woman
writer this is a special problem, since society says her
art is secondary to her role as wife or woman. Nin
claimed that women are not destructive like men, but her
diary actually demonstrates how she herself is indirectly
destructive because she is out of touch with her demons.
Nin's diary shows growth in integrating her various roles,
"but there is no final resolution." Nin's "style at its
best...is truly dreamlike and hypnotic; at its worst it is
purple and sentimental." The diary is disturbing because
of "the emotional distance of the voice which seems to be
putting the Diary persona through its paces."

33 LAUGHLIN, JAMES. "A Note from James Laughlin." Under the
Sign of Pisces, 3 (Summer), 16.
Thomas Merton read Nin's Under a Glass Bell and quoted
from it in a journal being edited by Laughlin.

1972

34   LIPSIUS, FRANK. "Biography and Memoirs." Books and Bookmen,
     17 (August), 73-74.
         Review of Diary IV. Nin has gained fame through her
     memories, romantic stories, and images of herself as a
     beautiful, emancipated woman. For the later generation of
     American expatriate artists, she played the role that
     Gertrude Stein had played for the earlier generation. Nin
     dislikes strong opinions or judgments; therefore she is
     attracted to the childlike Gore Vidal, whose opinions are
     not yet formed. She fears Edmund Wilson, who projects a
     fatherly image of authority; she does not realize this
     fear shows weakness in herself. In this volume, Nin
     achieves public acceptance of her work through commercial
     publication. This raises the question of whether honesty
     is possible in writing intended for publication. Among
     women's liberation circles, Nin's journals are very popu-
     lar, but "her emotions seem a little too precious."

35   MOORE, HARRY T. "Anaïs Nin," in Contemporary Novelists.
     Edited by James Vinson. New York: St. Martin's Press,
     pp. 947-949.
         List of publications and brief secondary bibliography.
     Biography. Brief introduction to Nin's fiction, which
     "develops into its own remarkably special mode of utter-
     ance." The Novel of the Future is "a penetrating study."
     Praises the fiction and diary for "superb prose, their
     deep and intense projection of feminine experience, and
     their vitally imaginative reaching into unexplored spirit-
     ual space."

36   OWEN, PETER. "Anaïs Nin." The Times Literary Supplement
     (19 May), p. 577.
         Nin's publisher writes in response to a query about
     whether Gunther Stuhlmann is the editor of Diary IV or a
     Nin pseudonym. He says Stuhlmann is a distinguished New
     York literary agent and Nin's future literary executor.
     Stuhlmann has an important role in editing the diary be-
     cause of its length and the risk of offending people de-
     scribed in it.

37   RANK, OTTO. "Preface to House of Incest." Journal of the
     Otto Rank Association, 7 (December), 68-74.
         Man has traditionally viewed woman as evil for being
     "what she was essentially, namely a sexual being." Al-
     raune, the symbol of the bad woman, is "here re-created
     by a woman who was made bad by her father and who first
     wanted to win him back by becoming good." Will this modern
     re-creation reveal the "inner secret" of woman or show she

is merely what man has made her into? We should be looking
to the diary for the true self of the woman. The woman
writer shows three different roles characteristic of woman's destiny in this man-made world: the woman as good;
woman forced by man "to create and find a bad self"; "her
own self in the self-created artist who expresses this
positive evaluation of herself in the re-creation of the
Alraune tradition from the woman's point of view." "Since
man's creation of the woman type has always been in terms
of badness, creation itself became a symbol of badness to
woman while she was the real creator of man."

38   RANK, OTTO. "Reflections on the Diary of a Child." Journal
     of the Otto Rank Association, 7 (December), 63-67.
          The diary is a fragment but "rich...full and complete,"
     so our interest is captured. The diary contains Nin's
     "real self which she seemed to have lost through the loss
     of the father." An epilogue shows she began a new life
     after finding her father because she had been living her
     real life in her diary. The rest of the diary does not
     have to be known—we know her without having to hear the
     whole story. In folk tradition, there is a kind of simi-
     lar story of a girl abandoned as an infant who finds her
     father. Cosmic explanations (myths of the sun and moon)
     fit better than realistic interpretations of incest here.
     These stories seem to be written from the point of view of
     the father. The diary shows the story written by a woman.
     She becomes her father in the diary, thus uniting herself
     with him. When she finds him, only to leave him, she is
     completing the cycle and liberating herself from the "fa-
     talistic determination of her life."

39   ROBINSON, LILLIAN S. "Who's Afraid of a Room of One's Own?,"
     in The Politics of Literature. Edited by Louis Kampf and
     Paul Lauter. New York: Vingage Books, pp. 389-390.
          Objects to the suggestion Nin "writes like a woman."
     Her characters cling to neurosis and conventional feminine
     stereotypes; are self-conscious, "'superior' women whose
     nerves are very close to the surface." Like Lessing's
     characters, they are sexually experienced but think about
     whole relationships, not just the sexual side.

40   ROBINSON, VIRGINIA B. and ANITA J. FAATZ. "Editorial Note."
     Journal of the Otto Rank Association, 7 (December), 61-63.
          Explains that Rank's "Reflections on the Diary of A
     Child" (1972.B38) was written in 1935 as a preface to
     Nin's early diary, which Miller wanted to publish. Nin
     sent the preface to the Otto Rank Association. Quotes

1972

passages from Nin's diary in 1935 that clarify Rank's opinion of the diary as "invaluable as a study of woman's point
of view" and as a study of "the poetry and drama of neurosis." In 1935 Rank was becoming increasingly interested in
the psychology of women. Ideas that developed from "Reflections on the Diary of a Child" are found in "Feminine
Psychology and Masculine Ideology" in Beyond Psychology.
The pages of the diary that describe Rank's friendship with
Nin and exploration of her psychology as woman and artist
are "the most original and beautiful" in the diary.

*41   SCHULTZ, ANNE and MONDO BIZARRO. "Anaïs Nin, the Personal
Depth of a Woman. He Observes. She Perceives." The Daily
Planet (3-17 February), pp. 3-4.
    Unlocatable. Cited in Zee, Nancy Scholar. "Anaïs Nin:
Beyond the Mask." Ph.D. dissertation, Brown University,
1973, pp. 262-263.

42   SHERESHEFSKY, PAULINE M. "Rank's Contribution to the Psychology of Woman." Journal of the Otto Rank Association, 7
(June), 65-74.
    Includes discussion of Nin's relationship with Rank from
her diary and "Portrait of Rank." She sought him as a
therapist in 1933. He did not impose a definition or for-
mula on her; he understood she was experiencing a conflict
between the woman and artist and worked with her to increase
her creativity. Rank helped Nin work through her conflict
about herself as a woman and achieve harmony as an artist.
He gave Nin support in trusting her own feelings and using
them in her writings. Women's liberation groups have appreciated Nin's diary as showing women's search for self-
hood, individuality, and self-fulfillment.

43   SPACKS, PATRICIA MEYER. The Female Imagination. New York:
Alfred A. Knopf, pp. 305-307 and passim.
    Nin uses the language of "self-deprecation and self-
doubt" to record her conquests over other people. She is
obsessed with controlling her environment in order to
achieve freedom, but she is actually restricted by "endless
responsibilities to others," the need to display herself
to an audience ("defensive narcissism"), and the demands
of her many selves. Compares Nin with Lillian Hellman:
both describe themselves in "external" images; both are
writing to convince themselves of the value of their experiences. The autobiographical writing of both Nin and
Hellman is "perhaps peculiarly feminine" because of "the
obsessiveness of its implicit or explicit concern with the
question of freedom, psychic and social, and the nature of

its revelations about freedom's limitations for women."
Nin believes freedom comes from reconstructing reality in
writing, but her "real 'work' appears to be self-contem-
plation and self-display."

44   SPENCER, SHARON. "An Interview with Anaïs Nin." Shantih:
      International Writings [double issue] 1, 2, (Winter-
      Spring), 28-31.
         Nin believes the artist articulates collective uncon-
      scious feelings. Women writers will gain stature when more
      women become recognized as critics who are as objective and
      capable as men. Diary IV focuses on the need for women to
      find "their own psychology." The Four-Chambered Heart
      illustrates women's habit of being good and putting others'
      needs before their own; like Djuna, women project faults
      onto others, then feel responsible for the individuals who
      represent the "dark" side of their personalities. Women
      must learn to live both sides of themselves honestly and
      control their own destructive bent; the sublimation of
      anger is compatible with feminine identity, since women
      exist to preserve life and balance male belligerence. The
      usual desire of women to submerge themselves in a man--the
      theme of Cities of the Interior--becomes a negative way of
      achieving freedom when they choose a weaker partner. In
      the future, legal marriage will be discarded and multiple
      relationships will be granted to women as well as men. As
      women free themselves of sexual guilt, their dreams of
      violation--discussed in Diary II--will disappear.

45   STEPHEN, BEVERLY. "Anaïs Nin: Timeless and Universal Percep-
      tions." Washington Post (2 January), F, p. 11.
         Although she refuses to generalize about men as oppres-
      sors, Nin is still a heroine to the young because of her
      "timeless and universal perceptions." Feminists respond
      to the free women in Nin's novels and to Nin's own emanci-
      pation from her old-fashioned Hispanic-Catholic background.
      Many identify with her struggle to get her writings recog-
      nized. Feminists promote group struggle, but Nin believes
      many will see how the individual's efforts will enrich the
      group. Nin has no bitterness over the male-dominated past;
      she notes many men tried to understand women, and that
      breaking old patterns will liberate the male as well as
      the female. Though she is very popular, Nin protects her
      privacy in order to work. Her one experiment with LSD
      taught her it is better to have access to the creative
      realm through "inner discipline," with the integrating
      assistance of religion or art. In her dialogs with youth

1972

over drugs, Nin maintains that chemicals will ultimately
destroy, and the drug-taker is too passive in the world of
the unconscious.

46 TELANDER, RICK. "Understanding Anaïs Nin." Chicago Sunday
Sun-Times (19 March), "Midwest Magazine," pp. 16, 18, 21.
Telander traveled with Nin for four days and observed
her audiences on college campuses, where she is a "literary rage." Describes Nin as "a lady" and a "regal woman." Recounts her talk at Northwestern University on
women and literature. Nin "gives authority and authenticity to what the normal woman feels subconsciously." Nin
said that women writers have been treated as inferior for
focusing on relationships. Reports on an interview with
Nin at the Swallow Press office. Nin said she always
speaks to students about the Welsh word "furrawn," which
means the kind of talk which leads to intimacy. She believes in personal relationships rather than dogma or
politics. Her favorite authors are Proust, Djuna Barnes,
Marguerite Young, Kay Boyle. At the University of Wiscon-
sin at Milwaukee, some women criticized Nin because she is
not angry. Nin replied that we cannot change negative into
positive forces. Nin complained that students did not
realize the diary is often humorous.

47 VIDAL, GORE. "The Fourth Diary of Anaïs Nin," in Homage to
Daniel Shays: Collected Essays 1952-1972. New York:
Random House, pp. 403-409.
Reprint of 1971.B54.

48 ZALLER, ROBERT. "The Mystery of Personality." Prairie
Schooner, 46 (Summer), 181-183.
Review of Diary IV. The theme of Nin's writings is the
"mystery of personality," a personality which lives life
and does not exist to be "solved." Nin's ideas favoring
fluid response to daily change are reminiscent of Lawrence's, but she uses them in a feminine way. Lawrence
created "combative" characters who desire isolation, but
Nin sees intimacy and union as the basis for friendship and
love. The search for this union with others is the theme
of the fourth volume. In New York, Nin does not receive
literary support. The literary establishment is represented
by the conservative Edmund Wilson. Nin seeks the companionship of a circle of literary homosexuals who represent the
new sensibility of gentleness but who betray her. This
volume is a significant source for notes on the avant-garde
of New York and presents part of the philosophy behind
Nin's writing.

49   ZEE, NANCY SCHOLAR. "A Checklist of Nin Materials at North-
      western University Library." Under the Sign of Pisces, 3
      (Spring), 3-11.
           Northwestern holds works on and by Nin: unpublished
      manuscripts, galleys, holographs, published works, letters.

50   ZINNES, HARRIET. "Light in the Dark." The New Leader, 55
      (7 February), 19-20.
           Review of Diary IV. Nin believes that the personal be-
      comes "universal, mythic, symbolic." Young people agree
      with Nin that technology reaches vast numbers of people but
      cannot express intimacy. Nin sees Edmund Wilson's world
      as characterized by disguise. Wilson's opposites are Nin's
      "children of the albatross"--young writers like Gore Vidal
      --whose world is one of "doubt and intimacy." She likes
      their wit and charm, their contrast to goal-driven men, but
      they have an "inability to love, linked to noncreation."
      In volume four, Nin seeks to cure her neuroses; she be-
      lieves in awareness rather than politics. In the early
      1930s Nin knew that to be a free woman she would need dedi-
      cation to "the art of life," and responsibility for her
      destiny.

1973 A BOOKS

1   FRANKLIN, BENJAMIN V. Anaïs Nin: A Bibliography. The Serif
      Series: Number 29, edited by William White. Kent, Ohio:
      The Kent State University Press, 119 pp.
           Descriptive bibliography of primary sources, aiming at
      completeness with regard to works in English, except Cana-
      dian editions. Sections on the following: books and pam-
      phlets; contributions to books; contributions to period-
      icals; recordings; editorship of periodicals. The order is
      chronological within each section. Appendix lists letters
      to Nin from Miller and other sources that have been pub-
      lished in journals. Includes an index.

2   POTTS, MARGARET LEE. "The Genesis and Evolution of the Crea-
      tive Personality: A Rankian Analysis of The Diary of Anaïs
      Nin, Volumes I-IV." Ph.D. dissertation, University of
      Southern California.
           Chapter one: The diary is "Nin's chief means of self-
      creation"; it is "a prototype of the genesis and evolution
      of the creative personality." The diary is an artistic
      expression of Rank's theory of creativity. The creative
      personality proceeds through three phases: "self-nomina-
      tion as an artist"; identification with artistic schools

1973

or masters; "liberation" or evolving an individual style.
Reviews selected critical writing on Nin. Chapter two:
Surveys the relationship between Rank and Nin, from
analyst-patient to analyst-assistant (1933-1935). They
agree that humans are "potentially self-creative" and that
inner growth can change external reality. Chapter three:
The diary was Nin's means of union and separation from
others during the self-nomination phase. Chapter four:
The diary held Nin's demons, which she portrays as doubles.
This struggle was between life and art since the person
who rejected evil fought the artist who needed to comprehend evil. Chapter five: Studies the "liberation" from
parents and their representatives, and conflicts between
the artist and mother of artists. Nin turned from the
"drama of the father" to that of "woman in relationship to
herself" through the creation of herself as an independent
woman artist. Chapter six: Discusses confluence between
Nin's art and life. Characteristic of the modern artist,
Nin lives her art-ideology and thus becomes "a self-
creative heroine who employs the Diary for personality
construction." Conclusion: The diary has re-created Nin's
world according to her perceptions; in the diary, reality is
the relative, personal-feminine, and the unconscious.
Partially reprinted 1974.B61.

3 SCHNEIDER, DUANE. An Interview with Anaïs Nin. London:
Village Press, 35 pp.
Reprint of 1970.A1.

4 SNYDER, ROBERT. "Anaïs Observed: A Film Portrait of a Woman
Artist." Los Angeles: Masters and Masterworks Produc-
tions, Inc.
Shows scenes of Nin in Los Angeles at seventy, and many
photographs of her past, of her family and friends. Begins
with an account of Nin's first trip to America and the
origin of the diary. Nin discusses art and neurosis,
creativity, editing the diary, her writing, her correspond-
ence. Much of the film is organized around the friendships
she formed in three cities--Paris, New York, Los Angeles.
Nin recounts her decision to write as a woman in a "personal way," thus departing from Miller and Durrell. Current
scenes with Nin and Miller, and Nin and Frances Steloff.
Nin reports on artists she admires: Noguchi, Martha Graham, Harry Parch, Frank Lloyd Wright, Varda. She shows the
collage Varda sent her and notes its similarity to Ladders
to Fire. Scenes of Nin in films by Maya Deren and Kenneth
Anger. Nin describes women she admires: Lou Andreas-
Salomé, the four English women who adopted the life of the

Middle East in Leslie Blanch's <u>Wilder Shores of Love</u>.
Nin discusses <u>Diary</u> V and taking LSD; she talks with young
writers about anger and about women creating their own
freedom, talks with a young film-maker about Western
serenity, and discusses her love for and use of costume.
As a Pisces, Nin has always tried to harmonize opposites.
She concludes by saying "I like to feel that I have trans-
cended my destiny." <u>See</u> 1976.A1.

5   ZEE, NANCY SCHOLAR. "Anaïs Nin: Beyond the Mask." Ph.D.
     dissertation, Brown University.
         Introduction: Surveys critical approaches to Nin since
     the publication of the diary in 1966. Chapter one: Scru-
     tinizes Nin's work through one of her major metaphors—the
     labyrinth. This image, which resembles Nin's elusive
     style, is a metaphor "for both integration and disintegra-
     tion," since slaying the monster is equivalent to freeing
     the self or freeing the self. Chapter two: Analyzes
     Nin's "seductive" style; partly because of a fear of being
     judged negatively, Nin's writing is "a literary enactment
     of the ancient game of provocation and allurement." Chap-
     ter three: The diary shows the development of a persona
     that Nin constructed with the aim of playing the part of
     woman-artist. More of Nin's real self is in the fiction
     than in the diary. Chapter four: Nin uses the metaphor
     of the mirror for the creative process (an analog for her
     art), to describe feelings of fragmentation (the self
     divided and projected into others), and the double or
     shadow self. Chapter five: Defines the special nature
     of the struggles of the woman artist as seen primarily in
     the diary.

1973 B SHORTER WRITINGS

1   ANON. "<u>A Spy in the House of Love</u>, by Anaïs Nin." London
     <u>The Observer</u> (13 May), p. 33.
         The maddening style "makes your head ache" in this
     slender, "sickly" account of Sabina's exploits around New
     York.

2   ANON. "Paperbacks: The Journals of Anaïs Nin: First Volume
     (1931-34)." London <u>The Observer</u> (25 November), p. 35.
         Nin caused much excitement among men, but the diary was
     her chief interest. "For all its surface egotism, it's
     rooted in sensibility and strikingly well written."

1973

3   BALAKIAN, ANNA. "Introduction: The Poetic Reality of Anaïs
     Nin," in <u>Anaïs Nin Reader</u>. Edited by Philip K. Jason.
     Chicago: The Swallow Press, pp. 11-30.
         <u>Cities of the Interior</u> departed from both the realistic
     and the psychological novel written in the 1930s and 1940s.
     Unlike the realists, Nin does not show "deviations from a
     norm, but a fluidity of progression from one form to
     another." The diary and the fiction are "like two commu-
     nicating vessels, and the division is an imaginary one;
     they feed on each other constantly." Discusses Nin's re-
     lationship to symbolism and surrealism. The imagery of
     self-containment in <u>House of Incest</u> shows the world of a
     symbolist heroine. Criticism of the dream-locked world
     begins in <u>House of Incest</u> and continues through <u>Under a
     Glass Bell</u>. Jungian psychology influences the place of
     the dream ("from the dream outward") in <u>Winter of Artifice</u>,
     where the ladder becomes a key symbol. Nin's work is "very
     close to that of Andre Breton: the search for luminosity
     through the cult and realization of the dream, through the
     effort to preserve the phosphorescent child image of our-
     selves, through the expanding consciousness that love in all
     its forms creates, through art." Art gradually replaces
     music as the objective correlative of Nin's writings. Re-
     printed 1973.B4; 1974.B11.

4   BALAKIAN, ANNA. "The Poetic Reality of Anaïs Nin," in <u>Cele-
     bration with Anais Nin</u>. Edited by Valerie Harms. River-
     side, Conn.: Magic Circle Press, pp. 91-106.
         Reprint of 1973.B3; reprinted 1974.B11.

5   BATES, BETHLYN. "Toward the Meaning of 'Sexidentity.'"
     <u>Washington Post</u> (12 November), B, p. 3.
         Nin has helped to build the International Institute of
     Sexidentity, and she was honored at its founding in 1973.
     The institute is a nonprofit organization designed to col-
     lect and collate scientific data on the nature of mascu-
     linity and femininity. Nin is a "woman's woman," said
     Dr. Barbette Blackington of the International Institute of
     Women Studies, because Nin was the first person to say
     that women's feelings have not been articulated in litera-
     ture and that all previous attempts have been by men. Nin
     declared in a brief speech that society must "find out the
     role women have played."

6   BIDWELL, HELEN. "Recurring and Persistent Images: The Fourth
     Diary of Anaïs Nin." <u>Voyages</u>, 5:151-153.
         Diary IV integrates and resolves the search for the
     father so important to Nin's earlier volumes. Nin's

relationships to others likewise change as she is able to
free herself from the compulsion to mother. She sees the
world divided between the openness of the young and the
rigidity of the mature. However, she is dissatisfied with
the life styles of her "children of the albatross." In
comparison with other volumes, "volume four is more com-
pact, reflection and action are more integrated, larger
themes in her life are more apparent." "Many themes--art
versus life, young versus old, intuition or dream versus
reality--begin to synthesize."

7   B[IDWELL], H[ELEN]. "The Mirror and the Garden: Realism and
    Reality in the Writings of Anaïs Nin by Evelyn J. Hinz."
    Voyages, 5:154.
        Although her wording is sometimes too complicated, Hinz
    (1971.A1) offers an "incisive and illuminating" critique
    of Nin's entire oeuvre and explains with particular thor-
    oughness and astuteness Nin's use of eclectic references;
    Hinz focuses her critique on Nin's definition of realism
    and reality and discusses Nin's use of symbolic imagery
    (e.g., the mirror and the garden) to depict these abstrac-
    tions.

8   CENTING, RICHARD. "Anaïs Nin in 'Four Chosen Women.'"
    Under the Sign of Pisces, 4 (Winter), 14-15.
        In November, 1972, a program at the Edison Theatre (New
    York) honored Nin along with three other women artists.

9   CENTING, RICHARD. "Rochelle Holt: Poet, Painter, Printer,
    Pisces." Under the Sign of Pisces, 4 (Winter), 1-5.
        A profile of Holt. She corresponded with Nin, reviewed
    Nin's work, arranged book exhibits about Nin.

10 CENTING, RICHARD. Under the Sign of Pisces, 4 (Winter), 1.
        Nin will by 70 on February 21, 1973. Diary V, a bib-
    liography, collection of essays, and the Nin Reader will
    be published. In France she was awarded the Prix Sevigne
    for 1971.

11 CENTING, RICHARD. "Anaïs Nin at the University of Michigan."
    Under the Sign of Pisces, 4 (Spring), 6-8.
        Nin lectured about the importance of individuality and
    about women's problems, mentioning Lou Andreas-Salomé and
    Frances Steloff as two of her heroines. She noted she
    would have given fifty-six lectures from September, 1972
    to May, 1973. After the lecture she was "mobbed" by en-
    thusiastic fans.

1973

12   CENTING, RICHARD. "Blurbs by Anaïs Nin." <u>Under the Sign of</u>
      <u>Pisces</u>, 4 (Spring), 10-12.
            Nin's jacket blurbs and quotes in advertisements help
      sell books. Gives blurbs from Nin for books from 1968 to
      1973.

13   CENTING, RICHARD. "Dissertations and Theses about Anaïs Nin."
      <u>Under the Sign of Pisces</u>, 4 (Spring), 12-13.
            Cites Toinette Menashe's thesis, Reed College, 1971, as
      the only known thesis on Nin and calls for readers to send
      information on others.

14   CENTING, RICHARD. "Nin and the Otto Rank Association."
      <u>Under the Sign of Pisces</u>, 4 (Spring), 5.
            Nin spoke to the Association in 1972, noting the impor-
      tance of Rank's <u>Truth and Reality</u> to her life. Lists
      articles on Nin in the Association's <u>Journal</u>.

15   CENTING, RICHARD. "Anaïs Nin Receives Honorary Degree (Doctor
      of Fine Arts) from the Philadelphia College of Art." <u>Under</u>
      <u>the Sign of Pisces</u>, 4 (Summer), 11-12.
            In her commencement address, Nin discussed the role of
      art and the artist in transforming the future and said,
      "The artist is the one who is willing to make his dreams
      public."

16   CENTING, RICHARD. "Dissertations, Theses and Papers on Nin."
      <u>Under the Sign of Pisces</u>, 4 (Fall), 16.
            Works on Nin in 1973 range from a Ph.D. dissertation to
      an essay by a high school student.

17   [CENTING, RICHARD.] "Nin and the Otto Rank Association."
      <u>Under the Sign of Pisces</u>, 4 (Fall), 20.
            Nin's 1972 speech for the Association ("On Truth and
      Reality") was printed in the Association's journal, June
      1973.

18   [CENTING, RICHARD and BENJAMIN FRANKLIN V.] "Anaïs Nin at
      Skidmore College." <u>Under the Sign of Pisces</u>, 4 (Winter),
      13.
            Nin's lecture celebrated Skidmore's 50th anniversary.

19   [CENTING, RICHARD and BENJAMIN FRANKLIN V.] "AN to Lecture
      in February." <u>Under the Sign of Pisces</u>, 4 (Winter), 11.
            Nin will lecture at the University of Michigan (February,
      1973).

1973

20   [CENTING, RICHARD and BENJAMIN FRANKLIN V.] "Nin at Northern
      Illinois University, Dekalb." Under the Sign of Pisces, 4
      (Winter), 12.
          In a lecture, Nin discussed how books helped her but
      ultimately failed to affect her whole being because Ameri-
      can authors have been prevented from discovering new ways
      of living. Nin refused to discuss Kate Millett's criti-
      cism of Henry Miller's attitude toward women, but did
      answer questions on psychoanalysis and surrealism.

21   [CENTING, RICHARD and BENJAMIN FRANKLIN V.] "Nin Signs MS.
      Abortion Statement." Under the Sign of Pisces, 4 (Spring),
      13.
          Nin signed a statement in MS., demanding repeal of
      abortion laws and admitting, "I have had an abortion."

22   FOWLIE, WALLACE. "Anaïs Nin Reader." The New York Times
      Book Review (9 September), pp. 26-27.
          Nin has now published several novels and four volumes
      of her diary, enough work to be anthologized. The Anaïs
      Nin Reader (1973) introduces new readers to Nin's works
      and helps reviewers. The introduction by Anna Balakian
      is "sound" scholarship. Nin writes to create and change
      her world, the inner world of the psyche; she emphasizes
      the female character "caught in a fascinating labyrinthine
      reality." Critics consistently term Nin's work "feminine
      writing," dwelling on the subjectivity of women. Publica-
      tion of the Anaïs Nin Reader coincides with increasing
      critical study of Nin. Nin's books are "confessions" and
      "dreams" that convey personality through symbols. With
      Rimbaud, Nin shares "seasons in hell"; like Proust, her
      lovers create the beloved. Both the diary and Collages
      attempt to use reality and imagination in presenting por-
      traits, and the diary becomes a source of materials for
      future works. The theme of the diary is the search for
      and maintenance of freedom. Nin delivers fables which re-
      veal a person's secret reality.

23   FRANKLIN, BENJAMIN V. "Preface," in Anaïs Nin: A Bibliogra-
      phy. The Serif Series: Number 29, edited by William
      White. Kent, Ohio: Kent State University Press, pp. ix-
      xii.
          The bibliography attempts a "complete record" of Nin's
      publications in English, excluding Canadian editions of
      her books. The section on books and pamphlets is complete,
      but the deluxe editions of the Gemor Press House of Incest
      and Winter of Artifice are noted but not described. There'
      is more uncertainty about the completeness of the section

1973

on contributions to books and contributions to periodicals.
The sections on recordings and editorships of periodicals
are probably complete. Gives an account of Nin's publishing history with small presses, her own presses (Gemor
Press and the Anaïs Nin Press) and commercial presses.
Swallow editions are referred to as the standard editions
because the books issued by the Swallow Press have been in
print for as long as twelve years and because first editions of Nin's works are difficult to obtain.

24   FRANKLIN, BENJAMIN V. "New Nin Publications." Under the
      Sign of Pisces, 4 (Winter), 9-11.
          Nin publications during 1972-1973 include Paris Revis-
      ited; an excerpt from her current diary; a Harcourt boxed
      set of four diaries; excerpts from House of Incest; "Notes
      on Feminism"; and a review of a Jaglom film. Also de-
      scribes a poster of Nin.

25   FRANKLIN, BENJAMIN V. "Anaïs Nin." The University of Michi-
      gan Librarian, 4 (1 March), 1, 3-5.
          Nin spoke at the University of Michigan on "The Inner
      Voyage." Nin is now popular but was neglected for many
      years. The diary "provides the best portrait we have of
      the Paris of the 1930s" and the writers who were Nin's
      friends during those years. House of Incest is Nin's best
      work of fiction. Provides a history of the publication of
      Nin's works through private and commercial presses from
      1930 to 1972. Some of the books Nin published through her
      own Gemor Press "are among the handsomest of this century."
      Swallow was responsible for re-issuing Nin's works, and the
      Swallow Press has kept all of the Nin titles in print. Ex-
      cept for one or two stories and a novelette that were never
      reprinted, all of Nin's fiction is readily available.

26   FRANKLIN, BENJAMIN V. "New Nin Publications." Under the Sign
      of Pisces, 4 (Spring), 1-4.
          Discusses Philip K. Jason's editing of the Anaïs Nin
      Reader (1973): lists the contents; notes errors in the
      chronology and misleading citations from the texts; praises
      Jason for choosing selections that can stand as separate
      units. (See 1973.B38.) The book is "on the whole intelli-
      gently and tastefully compiled." Notes reprintings of
      selections from Nin's works in anthologies and a journal
      (1973) and a Nin foreword for a book by John Pearson (1973).

27   FRANKLIN, BENJAMIN V. "New Nin Publications." Under the
      Sign of Pisces, 4 (Summer), 16.
          In 1973, Nin published two introductions to books and
      one essay, and an excerpt from her fifth unpublished diary
      was printed.

28   [GALANA], LAUREL. "Toward a WomanVision." Amazon Quarterly;
      A Lesbian-Feminist Art Journal, 2:18-42.
          Quotations from The Novel of the Future are used to sup-
      port the thesis that male culture is negative and destruc-
      tive. Nin holds the writer responsible when he interprets
      experience in a negative way. She repudiates the "cult of
      ugliness" espoused by modern writers and the passivity of
      pop artists who resign themselves to a destructive culture
      instead of redesigning it. Agrees with Nin that "men write
      about alienation and women about relationships." Hence few
      women writers have reflected the bankruptcy of male cultur-
      al values. Discusses women writers who have experienced
      the despair of contemporary culture and the new affirmative
      vision being created by women writers. Reprinted 1975.B15.

29   GORDON, JUNE. "Anaïs Nin and Dr. Ira Progoff." Under the
      Sign of Pisces, 4 (Fall), 15.
          Progoff draws on sources Nin has used, Jung and Rank.
      Progoff uses the personal journal experience in psycho-
      therapy to help people achieve experiences of a quality
      similar to those Nin describes in her diary. Nin has rec-
      ommended study of Progoff. Lists five of his books.

30   HARMS, VALERIE. "Letters and Things," in Celebration with
      Anaïs Nin. Edited by Valerie Harms. Riverside, Conn.:
      Magic Circle Press, pp. 119-123.
          Prints letters, comments, poetry from participants who
      attended a weekend gathering with Nin. Most praise Nin:
      "Because of Anaïs' midwifery, miracles will be born of all
      of us...Anaïs truly taught me the importance of risking and
      growing." "We journeyed to Rye to meet a myth and found a
      woman, Anaïs Nin. Always and ever, in her art and in her
      life, inhaling the outer, exhaling the inner. We offered
      her a crown of adulation. She declined."

31   HARMS, VALERIE. "Magic Circles," in Celebration with Anaïs
      Nin. Edited by Valerie Harms. Riverside, Conn.: Magic
      Circle Press, pp. 12-15.
          Describes how the author and a friend, Adele Aldridge,
      conceived and planned a weekend with Anaïs Nin at Wainwright
      House in Long Island. The project was called "Magic Cir-
      cles" because of "the magical effect" of Nin's writing.

1973

Lists names of people invited: Frances Steloff, Anna
Balakian, Daisy Aldan, William Claire, Evelyn Hinz, Dr.
Beatrice Hanes. Prints some of the letters from people
wishing to attend.

32   HARMS, VALERIE. "The Celebrants Arrive," in Celebration with
     Anaïs Nin. Edited by Valerie Harms. Riverside, Conn.:
     Magic Circle Press, pp. 17-25.
         Describes the interaction among the participants during
     the first evening at "Magic Circles Weekend." "Many have
     come out of a semi-conscious need to be with Anaïs at this
     particular juncture in their lives." "Her [Nin's] presence
     is felt everywhere instantly...Throughout the Weekend I
     observe her listening to others, embracing them, constantly
     attentive." Quotes participants on their first contact
     with Nin and her significance to them. Beatrice Hanes, a
     psychologist, says: "I don't think I can describe all the
     ways in which her friendship made me grow."

33   HARMS, VALERIE. "The Cosmos of Anaïs Nin," in Celebration
     with Anaïs Nin. Edited by Valerie Harms. Riverside,
     Conn.: Magic Circle Press, pp. 4-11.
         The diary revolutionized the author's "aesthetic theo-
     ries and style of life." Recounts meeting Nin, and de-
     scribes Nin physically. Nin has "never been freed from
     domestic duties" and had only a few times in her life when
     she could devote up to four straight days to uninterrupted
     writing. Nin explored "interior landscapes" and sought
     self-discovery in the diary. Psychoanalysis liberated her
     from fears and guilts. Discusses Nin's fiction. She
     leaves out the nonessential; "she lets the form of her
     writing erupt by itself from the inner direction." In the
     fiction, "her objective is to poetically evaluate the emo-
     tions involved and attain a universal meaning, which is the
     highest form of objectivity." Men are too abstract and the
     male literary critic gives a distorted picture. To Nin,
     "Woman represents creativity and union, the physical and
     spiritual link between unconscious and the objective." Nin
     wants to speak for all women. In the novels, Nin creates
     an archetypal heroine through the use of four major woman
     characters: Djuna is perception; Stella represents the
     blind and suffering woman; Sabina, the free woman; Lillian,
     the woman who seeks liberation in aggression. Nin avoids
     explicit use of sex; she takes us further than Lawrence
     into the woman's sexual ecstasy. "Unblocking" people is
     part of Nin's power.

34   HENDERSON, BILL. "Do It Yourself Publishing." Publishers
     Weekly, 204 (13 August), 28-31.
        When Anaïs Nin arrived in New York in 1939, Winter of
     Artifice was rejected by American publishers. She set up
     her own printing press as an act of independence and cure
     for frustration. Learning how to print through trial and
     error, she printed Winter of Artifice, Under a Glass Bell,
     and books by others she admired. Edmund Wilson reviewed
     her, and finally publishers accepted her "unsaleable" style
     because of the demand for her works.

35   HINZ, EVELYN J. "The Creative Critic," in Celebration with
     Anaïs Nin. Edited by Valerie Harms. Riverside, Conn.:
     Magic Circle Press, pp. 57-65.
        The traditional novel presents characters in a social
     setting, but Nin's novels are "character studies." Nin
     explains the reason for this difference in the pamphlet
     Realism and Reality, where she questions "objective truth"
     and says that reality depends on what the individual sees.
     When Hinz began to work on Nin, there were no books on
     her. The great value of Nin's fiction is that it forces
     the reader to assess his sense of reality. In each of
     Nin's works "there is a dialogue between the character's
     social self and inner feelings, and the conflict between
     them." Defends the technique of leaving the nonessentials
     out in the novels, allowing the reader to "fill in the
     gaps with her own responses."

36   JASON, PHILIP K. "Foreword," in Anaïs Nin Reader. Edited by
     Philip K. Jason. Chicago: The Swallow Press, pp. 1-8.
        Discusses early neglect of Nin's work and her growing
     popularity after the diary was published. The selections
     in the Anaïs Nin Reader are intended to represent the scope
     of Nin's interests as well as the development of her ca-
     reer. Selections introduce the important characters and
     many of her key themes. Fiction is separated from non-
     fiction. Nin's work is distinguished from other poetic
     novelists by its "old fashioned dedication to ideas."
     "All of Miss Nin's fictional pieces may be thought of as
     charting the ebbs and flows of the disturbed self moving
     toward psychic integration." Briefly discusses House of
     Incest, some short stories, Children of the Albatross. All
     of Nin's major female characters make "an outward journey"
     into "a world of larger social context." Collages shows
     the structural method organizing all of Nin's work. Nin's
     critical prose "takes second place to her fiction." A
     short passage from the diary (the trip to Morocco) is in-
     cluded.

1973

37   JASON, PHILIP K. "Anaïs Nin at American University." Under
      the Sign of Pisces, 4 (Spring), 8-10.
           In her lecture, "The Inner Journey," Nin discussed the
      role of diary writing in her life. She talked of the im-
      portance of developing "transportable roots." Putting the
      "core self" into the diary where it could be "reconstruct-
      ed" enabled her to "risk the performance of social roles."

38   JASON, PHILIP K. "A Letter from Philip Jason to Benjamin
      Franklin V." Under the Sign of Pisces, 4 (Fall), 11-13.
           Defends the chronology of Nin's publications given in
      the Anaïs Nin Reader. The incorrect citations were done
      by the publisher. See 1973.B26.

39   JONES, BARRY DONALD. "A Dream Not Deferred: Nin Returns to
      Dartmouth." Under the Sign of Pisces, 4 (Winter), 15-16.
           Nin talked at Dartmouth College on the novel of the
      future. She said "Dreams have great vanity; when you pay
      attention to them they come."

40   RAABERG, GWENDOLYN. "Raaberg on Surrealism in Miller and
      Nin." Under the Sign of Pisces, 4 (Fall), 18.
           Raaberg's paper, presented at the Congress of the Inter-
      national Comparative Literature Association (1973), dis-
      cusses the different ways in which Miller and Nin use
      surrealism. Both of these writers have exerted great in-
      fluence on contemporary authors.

41   RAINER, TRISTINE. "Rainer Dissertation on Nin." Under the
      Sign of Pisces, 4 (Fall), 20.
           Describes Rainer's dissertation in progress at UCLA.
      "Her Own Heroine: The Diaries of Literary Women" studies
      the diary as a literary form, especially point of view.
      Studies diaries from the Heian Court ladies of Japan to
      Nin. Nin "introduced the diary as a new genre into liter-
      ature." The diary is particularly important for women.

42   RILEY, CAROLYN, ed. "Nin, Anaïs 1903-," in Contemporary Lit-
      erary Criticism. Volume 1, Detroit: Gale, pp. 247-249.
           Quotes from four critical articles on Nin.

43   SCHNEIDER, DUANE. "The Duane Schneider Press and Anaïs Nin."
      Under the Sign of Pisces, 4 (Winter), 5-9.
           The Duane Schneider Press published Unpublished Selec-
      tions from a Diary (1968) and An Interview with Anaïs Nin
      (1970). The first book contained excisions from the type-
      script of Diary I. Describes the process of printing the
      books; both sold quickly.

44   SNITOW, ANN. "Women's Private Writings: Anaïs Nin," in
      Radical Feminism. Edited by Anne Koedt, Ellen Levine and
      Anita Rapone. New York: Quadrangle, pp. 413-418. Reprint
      of 1971.B45.

45   SPENCER, SHARON. "'Femininity' and the Woman Writer: Doris
      Lessing's The Golden Notebook and the Diary of Anaïs Nin."
      Women's Studies, 1:247-257.
           Nin's diary is the "most complete record of the psychic
      life of woman as creator," and it contains "the most daring
      and powerful portraits of woman as artist." Lessing's The
      Golden Notebook is the only fictionalized work that bears
      comparison. Both works examine the same themes: the slow
      and difficult "process of confronting behavior and ambi-
      tions viewed as traditionally 'masculine'"; politics ver-
      sus art; psychoanalysis as aid in effecting change; the
      importance of nurturing relationships; whether a woman can
      be "free" sexually and emotionally for multiple relation-
      ships; whether a woman can live happily without a relation-
      ship with a man. (Both writers answer "no" to the latter
      question.) Both writers have inspired love and respect
      because of their literary merit but also because most women
      writers before them concealed themselves and concealed the
      process whereby the woman artist attempts a synthesis of
      masculine and feminine qualities. "The Golden Notebook
      and Anaïs Nin's Diary share a unique dimension; in these
      works readers can follow the process through which two
      women writers (the one fictional) gradually came to recog-
      nize and to accept the animus or the male principle within
      themselves."

46   SPENCER, SHARON. "The Art of Rag Picking in Anaïs Nin's Writ-
      ing." The Widening Circle, 1 (Summer), 20-21.
           Nin's work has always focused on creating "the new from
      discarded bits and pieces of the old" in the manner of
      Varda's collages. "Ragtime" presents this process symbol-
      ically. Collages, an "original and profound" work of art,
      demonstrates how literature can use techniques from the
      visual arts. Collages contains Renate, "the strongest and
      happiest" of Nin's women characters, and Varda, who teaches
      the "magic transformations" of collage art. The book also
      focuses on "the magic" of warm human relationships. The
      book demonstrates Nin's belief that "art is the alchemical
      process through which life is redeemed."

47   STIMPSON, CATHARINE R. "Authority and Absence: Women Write
      on Men." Confrontation, no. 7 (Fall), pp. 81-91.

1973

Nin and Doris Lessing are alike in making a woman's consciousness central in their work; neither is a dogmatic
feminist and neither uses feminism to judge men. Both
write sympathetically about some men. "A sexual ideology,
a theory of the masculine and feminine" shapes Nin's vision.
"She imposes a notion about the sexes on the sexes, and she
acts on and acts out her idea of the feminine." In much of
her writing, Nin believes in "entities" called "masculine"
and "feminine." Men are likely to be objective and impersonal; women, subjective, personal. The minds of the two
sexes differ. Nin stresses biological differences (the
anatomical difference of the womb). "Nin and Lessing con-
verge to tell us that men are creatures to whom women lie."
Men demand lies to support their self-esteem; women create
private illusions (such as dreams of a perfect lover) to
sustain the lies the men need. As she matured Nin realized
the high price of deception. Many of the men in Nin and
Lessing behave like children; Nin believes men want women
to be the perfect mother. Nin and Lessing pay homage to
the good father but show men incapable of being good fa-
thers.

*48   STONE, DOUGLAS. "Henry Miller and the Villa Seurat Circle,
1930 to 1940." Ph.D. dissertation, University of California, Irvine.
Abstracted in Dissertation Abstracts International: The
Humanities and Social Sciences. Ann Arbor: Xerox University Microfilms, Volume 34, Section 10, 6664-A.
Nin was a major figure in the Villa Seurat Circle, which
also included Henry Miller, Michael Fraenkel, Walter Lowenfels, Lawrence Durrell, and Alfred Perlès. These writers
were associated in Paris during the 1930s and 1940s. Although each group member was individualistic, they greatly
influenced each other. Nin's interest in autobiographical
writing and her intense subjectivity was communicated to
the others through Miller. She was the only woman in the
group, and the one to whom Miller most often turned for
help and advice.

49   TIBBETTS, ROBERT A. "The Text of 'On Writing.'" Under the
Sign of Pisces, 4 (Summer), 1-7.
Ohio State University libraries are developing a collection of the works of Nin. Describes a typescript of "On
Writing." Compares this typescript with one owned by Dartmouth and with the two published editions. Many changes
have been made in each typescript, changes also shown in
the published editions. Also discusses variants in the
introductory essay by William Burford in The Art of Anaïs
Nin (1947).

50 WAKOSKI, DIANE. "The Craft of Plumbers, Carpenters & Mechan-
    ics: A Tribute to Anaïs Nin." The American Poetry Review,
    2 (January-February), 46-47.
    Nin is perhaps the most important influence on twentieth-
    century letters besides Pound. Her work has taught many
    twentieth-century writers that form is an extension of con-
    tent, and that work comes "organically out of the writer's
    life." It is Nin's diaries that are "her great work of
    fiction" because they present the artist as form-maker,
    not one who makes the self conform to fit the form. Poetry
    is "as interesting as the poet who wrote it," and Nin has
    lived as if every moment were a poem--"her life is lived
    and written so fully as to seem fictional." "She is the
    closest thing to Venus living among us." Reprinted
    1974.B79 with a new title.

51 WORK, HENRIETTE. "Work Thesis on Anaïs Nin." Under the Sign
    of Pisces, 4 (Fall), 20.
    Outline of an M.A. thesis, "Anaïs Nin: The Creative
    Process as Self-Realization," California State University,
    Sacramento, 1973. Chapters: the search for identity as
    revealed in the diary; woman's search for identity as re-
    vealed in the fiction; woman's search for identity, the
    relationship between the diary and the fiction.

52 ZALLER, ROBERT. "Anaïs Nin and the Truth of Feeling." Arts
    in Society, 10 (Summer-Fall), 308-312.
    Discusses Diary I-IV. Nin is "a great and lyric master
    of English prose." There are few references to political
    figures in the diary, although it spans the years 1931-
    1947. Nin rejects politics as a solution to problems.
    Political events are a secondary reality, a colossal pro-
    jection of the individual drama. Some readers find vol-
    umes three and four less interesting, but the quiet heroism
    of Nin's efforts to resettle in New York deserves attention.
    The diary is a record of "the journey toward human love,
    the freedom, the power, the wisdom to love." It is supe-
    rior to fiction in its "utter unwavering sincerity." Nin
    has formed her style by means of her relentless examination
    of her own life, and made "the growth of one dependent on
    the growth of the other." Reprinted 1974.B85.

53 ZEE, NANCY SCHOLAR. "Towards a Definition of the Woman Artist:
    Notes on the Diaries of Anaïs Nin." Oyez Review, 8 (Win-
    ter), 49-55.
    Largely because of her personal appearances, Nin has be-
    come popular as a symbol of a woman-artist. She presents
    herself as one who integrates the roles of creator and

1973

female without the sacrifice of either, and hence audiences
often confuse the public Nin with the Nin of the diaries.
In the diary, Nin attempts to "define the specific qualities of woman's art, particularly her own" and is ambivalent about the contradictory demands of the two roles. She
most often sees herself in terms of woman's traditional
role--as a "womb" or a "labyrinth" which lures men and then
frees them to be more creative. For Nin, the metaphor of
the labyrinth serves as a "representation of both style and
personality." The labyrinth of the first four volumes im-
plies "process" and a "search for a center." It allows Nin
to express the ambiguity in her writing which she rarely
reveals in public. The self-idealized personality of the
diary manifests the deep conflicts in our cultural expec-
tations of women, and therefore represents the dualities
within the traditional woman who wants more than the conventional sphere.

54   ZEE, NANCY SCHOLAR. "Zee Completes Dissertation on Nin."
     Under the Sign of Pisces, 4 (Fall), 16-18.
        Summarizes Zee's Brown University dissertation, 1973.
     Describes courses she has taught which include Nin.

55   ZINNES, HARRIET. "Reading Anaïs Nin." The Carleton Miscel-
     lany, 14 (Fall-Winter), 124-126.
        Review of the Anaïs Nin Reader (1973). Praises the
     book for showing Nin's fiction is as important as the di-
     ary. Today when we read passages from Nin "we are used to
     the interdependence between dream and reality; used to the
     surrealism, to the irony--and to the myth." Earlier read-
     ings however produced a reaction of shock. Nin's fiction
     shows a "stunning new awareness of an existential terror."
     Collages is "a classic of our time." Cities of the Inte-
     rior is "one of the most significant literary modes of our
     time."

1974 A BOOKS

1   NIN, ANAIS and JOHN FERRONE, eds. A Photographic Supplement
    to the Diary of Anaïs Nin. New York: Harcourt Brace Jovan-
    ovich, 37 pp.
       Presents over a hundred photographs of Nin and other
    characters from her diary. Includes pictures of buildings
    and other works of art described in the diary. Divided
    into sections that correspond to the published volumes.
    Also gives sections on Nin's early years and the years
    1955-1970s. No text except for a note on the photographs
    and a "Preface" by Nin.

1974 B SHORTER WRITINGS

*1   "Anaïs Nin: Out of the Labyrinth." The East-West Journal,
      4 (August), 17, 26-27.
            Unlocatable. Cited in Madden, Deanna. "Laboratory of
      the Soul: The Influence of Psychoanalysis on the Work of
      Anaïs Nin." Ph.D. dissertation, University of Miami,
      1975, p. 187.

2   ANON. "The Journals of Anaïs Nin." London The Observer, 2
      (27 January), 26.
            Diary II features "candid, egotistic and compulsively
      readable insights into the bohemian world of the thirties."

3   ANON. Review of The Diary of Anaïs Nin, Volume Five. The
      Virginia Kirkus Service, 42 (15 February), 230.
            Review of Diary V. The qualities one either admires or
      detests in the four previous volumes are even stronger in
      volume five. Nin's poetic imagery "explodes in the Mexican
      sun." Psychoanalysis gives her further clarification of
      "the tyranny of her rejecting father." She supports medi-
      ocre writers and criticizes Edmund Wilson and Maxwell
      Geismar for not appreciating her work. The diary has be-
      come a "stage for self-dramatization" rather than a means
      for actualization of self. The diary proves human life
      cannot be treated as a work of art. Although sometimes
      illuminating, the diary is usually "spectacularly frustrat-
      ing."

4   ANON. "Briefly Noted--General." The New Yorker, 50 (13 May),
      159.
            Review of Diary V. In this volume Nin decided to stop
      spending most of her energy on ungrateful male friends and
      devote more energy to helping herself. She had a small,
      loyal circle of readers and supportive friends, but she
      could not find a publisher or a sympathetic critic. The
      most moving passages of the book describe Nin's mother and
      the tribute paid to her at her death.

5   ANON. "Nin, Anaïs. The Diary of Anaïs Nin." Booklist, 70
      (1 July), 1175.
            Review of Diary V. This volume focuses on Mexico and
      California, places with associations of Nin's Spanish
      childhood; the deaths of her parents; therapy in New York.
      Nin's first experience with drugs reveals a world already
      available to her through art. "The search for the perfect
      person/place and craving for acceptance as a writer and an
      individual are, as in the earlier Nin diaries, paramount
      themes." It is an "infinitely self-absorbed but often ab-
      sorbing diary."

1974

6   ANON. "Paperbacks--Biography and Memoirs." Books and Book-
    men, 19 (July), 112.
        Brief review of the diaries. "Crowded Paris years of
    Spanish composer-pianist's daughter, artist's model,
    dancer, novelist of Cities of the Interior, who lived in
    world of writers, painters, musicians, dancers, actors.
    A fascinating diary of self-discovery, too, rich in con-
    tacts with famous."

7   ANON. Review of The Diary of Anaïs Nin, Volume Five. Choice,
    11 (September), 943-944.
        Accusing Nin of being too preoccupied with self-inquiry
    is inappropriate criticism of the diary. She is not a
    traditional diarist merely expressing opinions on events;
    she also explores the meanings of events. One of the
    themes in this recent volume is the discovery that drugs
    are not valid sources for literary inspiration. Nin's ob-
    servation that people allow telephones and radios to sup-
    plant human intimacy is a valid defense for the importance
    of her diary.

8   ANON. "Lunatic Visions." The Times Literary Supplement
    (11 October), p. 1142.
        Review of Winter of Artifice and House of Incest. Nin
    considers House of Incest to be the germ of all her work;
    although the story appears to be ephemeral, the talent she
    expresses in this novel should not be dismissed. Winter
    of Artifice is the most polished story in the collection.
    It presents a young girl's idolization of her elegant, cold
    pianist father, and her realization that he is an "emo-
    tional cripple." Nin, using a "gossamer-like" touch,
    probes the Oedipal complex to a depth only recently reached
    by modern fiction. Her words create visual images like
    those of Klee or Chagall, with a touch of the hellish real-
    ity of Van Gogh.

9   ANON. Review of A Spy in the House of Love. Best Sellers, 34
    (15 December), 428.
        Brief note that Nin's use of sensuality in A Spy in the
    House of Love is "airy and light."

10 AYLE, FRITZI. "Novelist Nin Created Her Independence Years
    Ago." Columbus Citizen Journal (29 November), p. 21.
        Records Nin's visit to Columbus, Ohio, at age 71. Nin
    "created her independence years ahead of her time." Al-
    though she is not politically active in the women's move-
    ment, she was "active creatively in women's literature."
    Documents the history of Nin's diary; lists her literary

1974

idols (Proust, Lawrence, Giraudoux). In an interview, Nin states she is planning to write a book on growth for the people who write letters to her; that she objects to Kate Millett because "I don't like waging war on men"; that Marguerite Young is "a great neglected American writer. She will be as important to American folklore as Joyce was to Ireland." Nin is interested in women's studies programs, especially women's non-fiction. "To the academics she is a lesson in self-education." Discusses Nin's study of Lawrence, and excerpts passages from the diaries.

11   BALAKIAN, ANNA. "The Poetic Reality of Anaïs Nin," in A Casebook on Anaïs Nin. Edited by Robert Zaller. New York: New American Library, pp. 113-131.
Reprint of 1973.B3.

12   BONNIE. "Anaïs Nin: The Woman as Artist." Columbus Free Press (11 December-14 January), p. 10.
Nin spoke at a feminist-oriented film/lecture program at Ohio State University (November, 1974). She discussed differences between the sexes as reflected in their art; women's art is "introspective and relevant, inseparable from everyday occurrences." Nin declared that women's studies programs should be expanded at American universities. She asked about the program at Ohio State, which is popular but lacks administrative support.

13   BRODERICK, CATHERINE. "The Reception of Anaïs Nin in Japan." Under the Sign of Pisces, 5 (Winter), 5-7.
Nin is not well-known in Japan. It is difficult for the Japanese to understand her lack of a mother country, her self-affirmation, or her search for self. Until recently, a Japanese author concerned with the search for self, Kanoko Okamoto, was considered heretical. Analyzes A Spy in the House of Love. The Don Juan motif contrasts with the detective/psychoanalyst motif; Sabina fears not only revelation but also losing her identity in the doubling of identity. "Clarity of consciousness" is the only way to preserve individual reality. Sabina's inability to be "one woman for one man" is an expression of her ambiguous identity; Alan is both husband and father-figure; the secret she fears the Lie-Detector will find is her incestuous love for her father, the source of her guilt and fantasies. Djuna helps Sabina see she is demanding love from a fantasy father. Sabina's search for herself leads to the discovery of the "other." For Nin, "to indulge in life beyond individuality is...[the] ultimate aim."

1974

14   CENTING, RICHARD. "Emotional Algebra: The Symbolic Level of
      The Diary of Anaïs Nin, 1944-1947," in A Casebook on Anaïs
      Nin. Edited by Robert Zaller. New York: New American
      Library, pp. 169-176.
          "Emotional algebra" is Nin's own phrase to describe her
      method in Diary IV; it is associated with her goal of unit-
      ing the subjective (passions) with the scientific method.
      Nin has found "a symbolic style in Diary IV that approxi-
      mates poetry." The poetic level is the most important
      level of the diary, though reviewers have been treating it
      as primarily celebrity gossip. Agrees with Stern
      (1971.B48) that the diary is a novel which progresses from
      "death to resurrection." "She has written a religious book
      in which she is both God and mediator." Nin's Catholic
      background gives her traditional symbols which she uses to
      tell a "pagan story." A constant theme is overcoming
      guilt. Nin also uses psychoanalysis to construct her lan-
      guage of symbols from the unconscious. Examines color
      imagery, ship and water imagery.

15   CENTING, RICHARD. "Anaïs Observed Shown at GBM." Under the
      Sign of Pisces, 5 (Winter), 13-14.
          The color film by Robert Snyder, "Anaïs Observed"
      (1973.A4), shows Nin with friends, associates, other lit-
      erati; giving a lecture; at home; writing; and describes
      the "effect" of Nin and her own sense of identity. The
      film is "not strictly a chronological documentary, but
      rather an exploration of Nin's affinities, an introduction
      to her spirit." The film was shown at the Gotham Book Mart
      Gallery in New York City.

16   CENTING, RICHARD. "Dialogue with Anaïs Nin." Under the Sign
      of Pisces, 5 (Winter), 11.
          In a 1974 session entitled "Creating a Woman's Life,"
      Nin and psychologist Ira Progoff discussed the structured
      approach of the "intensive journal" taught by Progoff at
      Dialogue House and compared it to Nin's method of diary
      writing.

17   CENTING, RICHARD. "International Community College and Nin."
      Under the Sign of Pisces, 5 (Winter), 11.
          An independent study program will be offered by Nin on
      "Diary and Novel Writing" through the International Commu-
      nity College, Los Angeles.

18   CENTING, RICHARD. "Reception for Nin at U.S. Supreme Court."
      Under the Sign of Pisces, 5 (Winter), 12.

A cocktail party was given for Nin in November, 1973, by the Board of Directors of the International Institute of Sexual Identity and International Institute of Women's Studies, featuring Nin, Justice William O. Douglas, Cathy Douglas, with Barbette Blackington attending. Nin is on the Board of the Institute.

19 CENTING, RICHARD. "Anaïs Nin in Colorado, September 1973." Under the Sign of Pisces, 5 (Spring), 12-13.
 Nin talked about "The Artist as Magician" to an audience at the University of Denver in 1973. The talk focused on art as transforming reality and the necessity of faith in the creative will. Some questions afterwards showed a dogmatic stand on women's liberation. Nin attempted to focus this discussion on the integration of femaleness and maleness.

20 C[ENTING], R[ICHARD]. "Anaïs Nin in MS. and People." Under the Sign of Pisces, 5 (Spring), 16.
 Ms. published excerpts from Nin's Diary V (May, 1974), and later published a letter from Nin (July, 1974) complaining about the photograph of her in the article; hence Ms. published a better photograph. Nin's letter noted that she has worked to help women overcome the fear of age. People (June 10, 1974) published a photograph of Nin.

21 CENTING, RICHARD. "Editorial." Under the Sign of Pisces, 5 (Spring), 14-15.
 Nin scholarship, which "came of age" with Benjamin Franklin V's Anaïs Nin: A Bibliography (1973.A1), is prospering. At least twenty new Nin publications have appeared since Franklin's book. Nin is now at work on Diary VI and many articles. A number of dissertations are being done on her. Describes Nin's personal appearances, which are "creating sensations."

22 CENTING, RICHARD. "Henrietta Weigel Is a Poet." Under the Sign of Pisces, 5 (Spring), 1-4.
 Weigel appears in Nin's Diary II. Nin brought Weigel's novel Age of Noon (1947) to the attention of Dutton, who published it. Weigel reports that Nin was kind, generous, and a brilliant conversationalist.

23 CENTING, RICHARD. "New Nin Publications." Under the Sign of Pisces, 5 (Spring), 4-6.
 Benjamin Franklin V's Anaïs Nin: A Bibliography (1973.A1) will be the "standard reference work on Nin for

1974

many years." Lists seven sources that provide excerpts from Diary V. Lists Nin's current contributions to books and contributions to periodicals.

24   C[ENTING], R[ICHARD]. "Zaller's Casebook on Anaïs Nin."
     Under the Sign of Pisces, 5 (Spring), 13.
        Announces the publication of the Casebook on Anaïs Nin
     in 1974, by New American Library. See 1974.B86.

25   CENTING, RICHARD. "Anaïs Nin in the Motor City." Under the
     Sign of Pisces, 5 (Summer), 2-5.
        Nin lectured at Wayne State University, attracting a
     large crowd. Nin's talk focused on the importance of lan-
     guage and expression. Nin noted that repetitions in the
     diary are as defensible as multiple sketches by a painter.
     Nin also declared that the diary is a valid genre and that
     it is better to lose control of emotions than not have
     emotions. An interview with Nin was taped by Margaret
     Kaminski for radio and the Detroit Public Library.

26   CENTING, RICHARD. "New Nin Publications." Under the Sign of
     Pisces, 5 (Summer), 14-15.
        A list of Nin's contributions to books and periodicals
     during 1973-1974.

27   CENTING, RICHARD. "Nin and 'February House.'" Under the Sign
     of Pisces, 5 (Summer), 11-12.
        Oliver Evan's biography, The Ballad of Carson McCullers ,
     includes a chapter about February House, a literary house-
     hold of the 1940s established by George Davis in Brooklyn.
     Residents included Carson McCullers, W. H. Auden, and
     Richard Wright. Nin is described as a visitor.

28   C[ENTING], R[ICHARD]. "Sharon Spencer on Anaïs Nin." Under
     the Sign of Pisces, 5 (Summer), 16.
        Spencer's critical study of Nin's writings, "Articulate
     Dreams," is in progress.

29   CENTING, RICHARD. "A Casebook on Anaïs Nin." Under the Sign
     of Pisces, 5 (Fall), 16.
        Reviews A Casebook on Anaïs Nin, a collection containing
     twenty articles on Nin's work, some of which are reprints
     of older pieces, although most are contemporary. Only
     eight of the twenty contributors are women "but their essays
     are the most original in the Casebook." See 1974.B86.

1974

30   CLARK, ORVILLE. "Anaïs Nin: Studies in the New Erotology,"
      in A Casebook on Anaïs Nin. Edited by Robert Zaller. New
      York: New American Library, pp. 101-111.
           Nin's writing "contains a revolutionary philosophy of
      love." According to Nin, the "new erotology" is "to al-
      chemize the life of the mind into the life of the senses."
      Nin's writing enables us to experience the movement between
      dream and reality; it puts us in touch with the flow and
      sensuousness of the unconscious itself--and this is "the
      touchstone of all art." In D. H. Lawrence: An Unprofes-
      sional Study, Nin describes Lawrence's "androgynous writ-
      ing," characterized by two elements of "feminine sensibil-
      ity": sympathy, even identity with objects and other
      persons; and a profound intuitive awareness of the body and
      the senses. A similar esthetic sensibility characterizes
      Nin's writings; she reconciles "the logos of reason with
      the logos of feeling." Nin's feminine philosophy accounts
      for her preoccupation with women, a preoccupation that has
      been misinterpreted as declaring war between the sexes.
      Nin's writing is also androgynous since "it strives to
      bring about a genuine fusion between the sexes."

31   COLEMAN, WILLIAM. "Trade Winds." Saturday Review/World, 1
      (26 January), 47.
           Celebration with Anaïs Nin (1973.B31) is a well-produced
      paperback which will appeal only to Nin's followers. It is
      a record of a weekend she and thirty of her followers spent
      at a rented mansion in Rye, New York. The editing, commen-
      tary, and photography is by Valerie Harms.

32   DURRELL, LAWRENCE. "Preface to Children of the Albatross," in
      A Casebook on Anaïs Nin. Edited by Robert Zaller. New
      York: New American Library, p. 2.
           Reprint of 1959.B1.

33   ENGLISH, PRISCILLA. "An Interview with Anaïs Nin (September,
      1971)," in A Casebook on Anaïs Nin. Edited by Robert Zal-
      ler. New York: New American Library, pp. 185-197.
           Reprint of 1971.B26.

34   FRANKLIN, BENJAMIN V. "Anaïs Nin: A Bibliographical Essay,"
      in A Casebook on Anaïs Nin. Edited by Robert Zaller. New
      York: New American Library, pp. 25-33.
           Discusses the "knotty" bibliographical problems of the
      publishing history of Nin's work. Collections and books
      that have changed in content while keeping the same title
      include Winter of Artifice, Under a Glass Bell, Cities of
      the Interior, This Hunger, and Ladders to Fire. The

1974

difficulty with regard to Cities of the Interior centers
on Seduction of the Minotaur (which contains the complete
Solar Barque, originally the last novel in the series),
but also includes a lengthy coda written especially for
publication in 1961. A number of Nin's stories have had
more than one title. Some titles are used for more than
one work. Nin's publishing history is very complex. Many
bibliographical and textual difficulties remain unsolved.

35   FRANKLIN, [BENJAMIN] V. "Jaglom to Film Nin Novels." Under
      the Sign of Pisces, 5 (Spring), 13-14.
           HHH Rainbow Productions acquired four Nin novels and
      will use them for one film titled Cities of the Interior,
      to be directed by Henry Jaglom. Filming is to start in
      1975.

36   GILBERT, STUART. "Foreword to House of Incest," in A Casebook
      on Anaïs Nin. Edited by Robert Zaller. New York: New
      American Library, p. 1.
           In earlier times, Nin would have been burned at the
      stake. Her "clairvoyance" scrutinizes a "subterranean
      world." Her work required courage, skill, "a delicate
      sense of balance permitting the clairvoyant to walk the
      dangerous tightrope between self-abandon and analysis."
      Nin also has skill in using words and creating rhythms.
      Nin describes the "moments of life which resemble the ec-
      stasy of the mystics." For Nin, the lover creates the
      loved one by projection; hence love is an act of incest
      with an unreal image which is part of the lover. "Nothing
      like this [House of Incest] has ever been written."

37   GOODWIN, JUNE. "Memoirs." Christian Science Monitor
      (12 June), F, p. 5.
           Review of Diary V. Some readers' enjoyment may be
      dulled by the sheer quantity of writing, and some may feel
      they are "snooping on a surrealistic narcissistic dream,"
      but others will appreciate Nin's accurate analysis and
      skill in rendering pure emotion. Nin appeals to those who
      believe in the importance of the individual; she defends
      her diary on the grounds that one must begin with the self.
      The force of Nin's personality enables her to come through
      depression and bitterness and arrive at the faith that
      there are solutions. Her solution is to write, in order to
      taste life twice. She speaks to women through her insight
      into her mother's relationship with her father. Diary V is
      like "a flawed piece of glass"--flawed as life is flawed,
      by confusion, excess, digressions--beautiful when the light
      comes through at a good angle.

38 GOYEN, WILLIAM. "The Diary of Anaïs Nin." The New York Times
    Book Review (14 April), p. 4.
        Review of Diary V. This is the most clearly unified and
    structured volume in the series. It is also the most per-
    sonal and least narcissistic, as Nin defines herself more
    definitely and the range of her interests continues to ex-
    pand. The setting is New York, and Nin includes portraits
    of New York critics Maxwell Geismar and Malcolm Cowley.
    She mourns, complains, and turns to the diary to console
    her because, although she has published three novels and
    other works, the literary community continues to ignore
    her. Nin accepts her restlessness, and moves between Paris,
    New York, and Mexico, avoiding a fixed location. She sur-
    vives her parents' deaths, and struggles through her prob-
    lems with psychologist Inge Bogner. She tries LSD, but
    rejects it, because the experiences it brings can be found
    through art. She rejects, too, the new writers of the
    early 1950s, who lack a lust for life. This volume shows
    Nin's growth and discovery. Despite her weakness and self-
    absorption, Nin shows herself as a vital writer, strongly
    opposing the negative in modern life.

39 HARA, MASAKO. "Afterword," in Anno Nikki, 1931-34. Tokyo:
    Kawade-Shobo-Shinsa, pp. 377-382. [Japanese.]
        "Afterword" to Masako's Japanese translation of Diary I.
    The diary begins as a letter to Nin's father to bring him
    back but gradually changes to reflect Nin's obsessive
    search for truth. Paradoxically, Nin's desire for truth
    forces her away from it. Thus the diary becomes fiction;
    the diary is fiction with a specific theme: the existen-
    tial trial of becoming a woman worthy of being loved by
    the father. For Nin, becoming a woman was to become her-
    self. Nin preferred to be mother to men and art, rather
    than to children. Hence her writing did not conflict with
    being a woman.

40 HAWKINS-WORK, HENRIETTE. "An Evening with Anaïs Nin." Under
    the Sign of Pisces, 5 (Winter), 15.
        In December, 1973, in San Francisco, the Women's Collec-
    tive of Esalen Institute sponsored Nin's talk on the inner,
    psychological journey necessary for liberating women. Nin
    said, "Women who created freedom rather than waiting for
    freedom to be given, are the women to come close to and be
    acquainted with."

1974

41   HAWKINS-WORK, HENRIETTE. "Anaïs Observed." <u>Under the Sign</u>
      <u>of Pisces</u>, 5 (Summer), 6.
            Snyder's film "Anaïs Observed" (1973.A4) was shown at
      the University of California at Davis. The audience re-
      sponded with pleasure and enthusiasm.

42   HAWKINS-WORK, HENRIETTE. "'Female of the Species'--A Day in
      San Francisco Designed to Celebrate Women in the Arts."
      <u>Under the Sign of Pisces</u>, 5 (Summer), 5-6.
            At a celebration in San Francisco focusing on women in
      the arts, Nin spoke about the strong, assured woman of the
      future. This woman will not feel guilt for creating and
      will be in harmony with her strength. To the audience,
      Nin herself was a model for the "Woman of the Future."

43   HEATH, SUSAN. "Books in Brief." <u>Saturday Review/World</u>, 1
      (4 May), 52.
            Review of <u>Diary</u> V. In all her work Nin argues for the
      importance of inner experience, and the incidents that
      communicate her own inner life are found in the diary.
      <u>Diary</u> V covers the years of 1947 to 1955, when Nin's par-
      ents died and she settled in California. She delivers en-
      tertaining character sketches of her friends, but her
      writing is too self-preoccupied. She exposes her emotions
      in a search for the inner life, but the journey is shaped
      by her neurosis; her vision and dreams are weakened by fear
      and failure. The diary has been Nin's refuge, where she
      recreated herself, but this art will interest only those as
      self-absorbed as Nin. The average reader will soon become
      bored by Nin's emphasis on her neurosis.

44   HOFFMAN, NANCY. "Serialized Life." <u>The New Republic</u>, 170
      (15 June), 31-32.
            Review of <u>Diary</u> V. The diary is Nin's major work.
      Women read Nin to help them in their search for themselves.
      Nin perpetuates "female preoccupation with self at the ex-
      pense of authentic action in the outside world." Lower
      class women tend to find Nin's problems either "inconse-
      quential or boring." The fifth volume discusses various
      events in Nin's life: continued self-exploration with a
      female analyst; rejection of Marxist solutions to problems;
      anger at the limitations of American literary critics.
      These themes were treated better in earlier volumes; vol-
      ume five, covering the 1950s, adds nothing new. The "in-
      dividualizing detail" found in Nin's earlier relationship
      with June Miller is not apparent in the relationships of
      volume five. The new volume is not "memorable."

45   HOOVER, ELEANOR LINKS. "Far Out: Keeping a Journal." <u>Human</u>
      <u>Behavior</u>, 3 (May), 10-12.
           Reports a speech Nin gave on "The Therapeutic Uses of
      Keeping a Diary." Gives the history of Nin's diary, "one
      of the most complete chronicles in literature" of a woman's
      life. Some therapists have patients use journals as a way
      to "tune in to the self"; psychologist Ira Progoff uses
      the "intensive journal" as a structured discipline. Nin
      often recommends Progoff's method. Physical description
      of Nin as "a lovely woman." In the U.S., Nin had to fight
      the taboo that keeping a diary is selfish. Nin says
      therapy is not an enemy of creativity; it gave her "confi-
      dence to move...and confidence in my dreams," and she con-
      tinued her dreams in her novels. She writes with ease
      because of the "trust" therapy gave her. She would not
      have published the diary without her therapy. Nin says
      Rank was a great man, but "bourgeois" and wrong to try to
      part her from the diary. A problem is where to hide the
      diary. On one Nin misadventure, a diary was burned in
      the stove.

46   JASON, PHILIP K. Review of <u>Anaïs Nin Reader</u>. <u>Choice</u>, 11
      (April), 260.
           Hopefully, the <u>Anaïs Nin Reader</u> (1973) will introduce
      Nin's works to a wider audience, although many readers of
      the realistic tradition will probably dislike Nin. In
      discovering the "timeless, nonlinear world of real life"
      expressed in the selections, readers will encounter beauti-
      ful prose. The selections from the interior of Nin's nov-
      els may be frustrating reading. Her nonfiction and criti-
      cism best illustrate her work; selections from the diary
      are more enjoyable in the context of this collection.

47   JOHNSON, ALBERT. "Non Fiction." <u>Publishers Weekly</u>, 205
      (11 February), 59-60.
           Reading <u>Diary</u> V is a profound human experience and a
      literary pleasure. Nin writes of her life in the 1940s and
      1950s; of her many literary friends; and of her psychoanal-
      ysis and LSD experiences. Her reflections are wise and
      self-revealing, showing the climate of the times. The
      diary is fascinating in its ability "to meet truth head
      on."

48   JONES, BARRY DONALD. "A Letter Concerning the Celebration
      with Anaïs Nin." <u>Under the Sign of Pisces</u>, 5 (Spring),
      7-10.
           Reviews <u>A Celebration with Anaïs Nin</u> (1973.B31). The
      book succeeds; it shows the weekend retreat with Nin as a

new form of education. The book embodies the Russian quality of "mir," a word which suggests individuals working for
the good of the community, and suggests both "peace" and
"the world." The various sections of the book emphasize
Nin's stress on the dream. The book forms a circle thematically, structurally, and visually. "Anaïs is its dynamic
and stable center." The book proves that we are all inter-
dependent; it "becomes a part of the continuum that cele-
brates equality between and amongst the sexes."

49 JONES, MRS. E. A., JR. "Review of the Diary of Anaïs Nin,
Volume 3." Best Sellers, 34 (1 August), 225-226.
This is not a conventional diary, but the story of a
talented woman who perceptively records various locales and
well-known artists and friends. Nin's travels are bohemian,
but an awareness of deep family roots creates a sense of
guilt and unfulfillment. Her diary expresses "love of
life" on every page but simultaneously shows a sense of
sorrow. Nin's egotism is hurt by America's neglect of her,
but eventually she loses her bitterness. The illustrations
depict the beautiful "Anaïs of the Diary."

50 KUNTZ, PAUL GRIMLEY. "Art as Public Dream: The Practice and
Theory of Anaïs Nin," in A Casebook on Anaïs Nin. Edited
by Robert Zaller. New York: New American Library, pp. 77-
99.
Reprint of 1974.B51.

51 KUNTZ, PAUL GRIMLEY. "Art as Public Dream: The Practice and
Theory of Anaïs Nin." The Journal of Aesthetics and Art
Criticism, 32 (Summer), 525-537.
Nin has stressed dreams more than other artists; we can
learn much about the artistic use of dreams from her work.
Compares the diary to Winter of Artifice. The latter is
less egotistical and uses the formal pleasures of literature to get readers to accept the dream. Nin's work thus
proves Freud's theory that the artist makes dreams public
so we can enjoy them without shame. Nin's theories on
dreams are expressed in Realism and Reality and The Novel
of the Future. Defends Nin's artistic credo. The Novel of
the Future clarifies Jung's phrase "proceed from the dream
outward" in its discussion of the nature of dreaming as
free association of images; in its comparison between the
artist and therapist (both study conflicts to restore balance); and in its declaration that the artist transforms
the private into the public. Her "art is the sharing of
dream, making the most intimate aspects of our consciousness and fantasy part of the shared consciousness of

people." "Art should help man to be truthful in the existentialist sense of sincere or authentic." Reprinted 1974.B50.

52 LEE, S. P. and L. ROSS. "The Diary of Bananas Ninny, 47 B.C.-1971." Columbia Forum, NS 3 (Summer), pp. 42-43.
    Parody of Nin's diary. Extracts supposedly cover the years from 47 B.C. to 1971. Caesar visits "Bananas," asking to "draw strength" from her. Politics "bores" her during the Revolutionary War. Washington visits her. She knits beside the guillotine in the French Reign of Terror. She spouts grand statements on art: "Art is selfness; power, selfishness."

53 McBRIEN, WILLIAM. "Anaïs Nin: An Interview." Twentieth Century Literature, 20 (October), 227-290.
    Nin's style is akin to film in its use of jump-cutting, sparse dialog, and impressionistic flashbacks. To focus on non-rational emotions, Nin omits external details; she rejects colloquialism, which alienates on external grounds. The diary is "ritualistic writing which brings us back to the way we feel about things"; it uses stream of consciousness, but conveys characters' inner voices by changes in the narrator's tone. The dream life in Nin's novels draws especially on music and the fantasy created by novelists like Djuna Barnes. The modern novelist's function is to describe the "multiplicity of the human personality" and put the reader in touch with the unconscious. The garden is Nin's symbol of nature; one must fight neurosis, which separates the self from nature. Nin admits she declined to write explicitly about sex because the world is not ready for women's sexual revelations and it is not "necessary to describe everything in order to evoke it."

54 McEVILLY, WAYNE. "The Two Faces of Death in Anaïs Nin's Seduction of the Minotaur," in A Casebook on Anaïs Nin. Edited by Robert Zaller. New York: New American Library, pp. 51-64.
    Reprint of 1969.B22.

55 MAITLAND, SARA. Review of Winter of Artifice and House of Incest. The Listener, 92 (12 December), 786.
    Review of Winter of Artifice and House of Incest. This is a collection of some of Nin's earliest fiction. Nin's reputation is now growing in London, but these early stories only predict her later work. Winter of Artifice is a collection of three novelettes, all dealing with the effects of a father's desertion upon his daughter. The

second of these stories, "The Voice," is the best because
the dream-fantasy technique "eases one through the emotional excesses." House of Incest is "beautiful and strangely
emotive," but makes little factual sense.

56   MARTINEAU, BARBARA HALPERN. "Nin's Films." Under the Sign
of Pisces, 5 (Summer), 7-10.
    The sense of Nin is easily captured on film, but the
subject is threatened by the domination of the camera.
Snyder's film "Anaïs Observed: A Film Portrait of a Woman
as Artist" (1973.A4) correlates closely to the portraits
of Nin in her diary. Each scene seems to flow, but transi-
tions are occasionally bumpy. The film tries to create a
collage like the diary; to show Nin in the context of her
friends, footage is used from other films and there are
shots of old photos. Ian Hugo's "The Bells of Atlantis"
was made in 1952, with Nin as actress and narrator. The
flowing rhythm of this film is like the fiction, and is a
poetic evocation of Nin's work. Hugo's cinematic interest
in vision itself approaches Nin's intensely expressed
point of view in the diary. The film has a two-part
structure; its opening stress on the world later shifts to
the dreamer's viewpoint—from impressionism to surrealism.

57   METZGER, DEENA. "The Diary: The Ceremony of Knowing," in A
Casebook on Anaïs Nin. Edited by Robert Zaller. New York,
New American Library, pp. 133-143.
    The diary is "an archetypal voyage into the self." (Usu-
ally we follow a man into the labyrinth but women make this
voyage as often as men.) One of the major themes of Diary I
is life at its greatest intensity. The struggle toward the
high point of art." The theme of Diary II is "voyage." The
theme of Diary III is "struggle." In the war years, Nin de-
velops the idea of the responsibility of the artist, who can
create the world and hence is responsible for it. Her ob-
jection to Kenneth Patchen is "political"; she wants to "establish a counter example to destruction." By volume four,
Nin is a "warrior" who fights to create art and to know herself—but unlike men she is not deceived into hubris. Knowing there is no ultimate victory, "she is content with the
ceremony of knowing." Diary IV shows a new Nin, strong
enough to confront painful realities. Diary V seeks recon-
ciliations "relentlessly."

58   MILLER, HENRY. "Un Être Étoilique," in A Casebook on Anaïs
Nin. Edited by Robert Zaller. New York: New American
Library, pp. 5-23.
    Reprint of 1937.B1.

1974

59 PECK, ELLEN McKEE. "Section Three: Anaïs Nin, Chronicler of the Feminine Woman's Progress," in "Exploring the Feminine: A Study of Janet Lewis, Ellen Glasgow, Anaïs Nin, and Virginia Woolf." Ph.D. dissertation, Stanford University, pp. 131-314.

Studies Diary I-IV, the critical works, and the fiction. Nin, "the chronicler of the ultra-feminine woman's progress," accepted traditional definitions of women (at first, Freudian; later, Jungian). Nin emphasizes the special strengths of women's roles and promotes a feminine art which should be as positive and nourishing as the maternal role which is the essence of femininity for Nin. Many of Nin's difficulties come from the techniques she used in order to handle problems as a woman. Discusses Nin's personal development to show the connection between her literary style and biography; the fear which obsessed Nin caused her to act out female defense strategies and self-destructiveness in her own life and to portray these tactics in the actions she attributed to her female characters. The diary shows Nin's movement from dependence on role models to adult independence. By the end of Seduction of the Minotaur, Lillian has become a "virgin" in the ancient sense of "a wholeness within oneself." Nin's style is "putative," a "level of discourse which analyzes and sums up" rather than dramatizes. Nin's own life and work prove that "an emphasis on the 'feminine' warps a woman and her work as much as an opposing emphasis," but she performed valuable work in insisting that the feminine be given equal importance with the male. Some of this material was presented earlier in an article (1972.B32).

60 PELLEGINO, VICTORIA Y. "What Should You Give a Feminist for Christmas?" The Village Voice (16 December), pp. 52-53.

Brief review of Diary V. In her diary, Nin struggles with rejection, anger, and loneliness. She uses psychoanalysis and art to help her when her parents die and life is difficult. Eventually she can live for months without anxiety. She writes about uncommon characters so that we may imitate them.

61 POTTS, MARGARET LEE. "The Genesis and Evolution of the Creative Personality: A Rankian Analysis of The Diary of Anaïs Nin." Journal of the Otto Rank Association, 9 (Winter), 1-37.

Reprints parts of chapter one and most of chapters two and three of 1973.A2.

1974

62   RAINER, TRISTINE. "Anaïs Nin's <u>Diary</u> I: The Birth of the
     Young Woman as an Artist," in <u>A Casebook on Anaïs Nin</u>.
     Edited by Robert Zaller. New York: New American Library,
     pp. 161-168.
          The concept of death and birth pervades <u>Diary</u> I. The
     theme of this volume is "escape from conformity into crea-
     tivity, from death into birth." New people appear in Nin's
     life as a new side of her begins to grow; others seem to
     be dying as part of her dies. "Once the reader under-
     stands the diary as the working out of an inner liberation,
     a story of movement from life to death--then the imagery
     and characterization relate clearly to this." Nin goes
     beyond Rank to integrate woman and artist instead of see-
     ing them as dichotomies. She metaphorically achieves this
     integration in the birth story which is the climax of vol-
     ume one. "The child is stillborn but the woman artist is
     born."

63   SCHEID, ANN SALINGER. "Nin in Chicago: May 9, 1972." <u>Under
     the Sign of Pisces</u>, 5 (Summer), 12-13.
          In Nin's informal lecture at Fullerton Hall, Art Insti-
     tute of Chicago, she discussed the interrelationship between
     the arts and painting as providing growth of a new language
     fluid enough to express dreams. Art may provide solace for
     emotional shocks. Describing the unity of writers, Nin ex-
     plained "her own purpose as artist is communication which
     she sees as an opposite to power, possession and invasion
     in a global view; separation and alienation on a personal
     basis."

64   SCHNEIDER, DUANE. "The Art of Anaïs Nin," in <u>A Casebook on
     Anaïs Nin</u>. Edited by Robert Zaller. New York: New Ameri-
     can Library, pp. 43-50.
          Reprint of 1970.B63.

65   SELLERS, JILL. Review of The <u>Diary of Anaïs Nin</u>. <u>The Spokes-
     woman</u> (15 July), pp. 7-8.
          Review of <u>Diary</u> I-V. "The contradictions of the diaries
     are intensified because for Nin freshness, authenticity and
     subtlety are equally critical values." The diaries are not
     primarily literature and have no structure; they are "as
     close to raw life as can be." "The reality of the diaries
     is dialectical." Criticizes the diaries for being didactic.
     Nin "believes in the polarity of the sexes...the essential
     femininity of creation"; fears rationalism, "and positively
     dislikes it in women." She thinks healthy human nature is
     rooted in the biological and praises the simple earthiness
     of poor Mexican peasants and Harlem blacks in terms that

are embarrassing. However, it is necessary to remember
that the latest volume goes only to 1955. "Nin is part of
literary and feminist heritage."

*66   Soho Weekly News, 1 (9 May), p. 8.
          Unlocatable. Cited in Current Biography, 1975. New
       York: H. W. Wilson, p. 301.

67   SPENCER, SHARON. "Anaïs Nin's 'Continuous Novel' Cities of
       the Interior," in A Casebook on Anaïs Nin. Edited by
       Robert Zaller. New York: New American Library, pp. 65-76.
          Cities of the Interior is "the equal of many a modern
       masterpiece that is better known." It has been overshad-
       owed by the diary and been neglected because of its inno-
       vative form, because of Nin's femininity, and because of
       its lack of focus on social problems. Nin is "an expres-
       sionist," portraying the essence, not the appearance of
       the character. Most important is her characters' accept-
       ance of mutability and chance; the novel's "continuous
       structure is an approximation of the continuous, erratic,
       unpredictable process of personal growth." Cities of the
       Interior has an "open form" like a mobile; each novel is
       self-sustaining, and they can be read in any order, but
       each becomes more significant and takes on new meanings in
       context of the others. The "radical nature" of Nin's fic-
       tional themes has also gone unnoticed until recently; it
       is "decidedly and unashamedly feminine writing" with a
       boldness that is obscured by good taste and a delicate
       style. During decades when there were few serious women
       writers, Nin discussed incest, lesbianism, friendships be-
       tween heterosexuals and homosexuals, the neurotic aspects
       of women's "goodness," the dramatic problems of women as
       artists. A Spy in the House of Love is original in its
       sexually aggressive heroine Sabina. Nin poses searching
       questions about the innate differences between women and
       men.

68   SPENCER, SHARON. "The Dream of Twinship in the Writings of
       Anaïs Nin." Journal of the Otto Rank Association, 9 (Win-
       ter), 81-90.
          In her diary, Nin often expressed the desire for a twin.
       In Nin's work, twinship takes the form of two women,
       brother and sister, or father and daughter. Discusses
       connections between Rank's "The Double as Immortal Self"
       and Nin's use of the double. For Nin, twinship "provides
       the self with ways of adding dimensions to identity."
       Sabina is the woman with whom Nin's other female characters
       wish to fuse. The brother as twin symbolizes the unified

1974

hermaphrodite. Discusses the father as double or twin in
Winter of Artifice. The daughter first identifies with and
then separates from the father. Describes Nin's choice of
a "male muse" by means of her relationships with a series
of male artists. Nin's real twin is "the great Diary,
Nin's double...a duplicate of herself."

69 STERN, DANIEL. "The Novel of Her Life: The Diary of Anaïs
    Nin, Volume IV (1944-1947)," in A Casebook on Anaïs Nin.
    Edited by Robert Zaller. New York: New American Library,
    pp. 153-160.
        Reprint of 1971.B48

70 STERN, DANIEL. "The Diary of Anaïs Nin: Volume V." Common-
    wealth, 101 (25 October), 91-93.
        Superficially, Nin's work can be divided into two cate-
    gories, the surrealism of her early novels and the "de-
    tailed" reality expressed in the diary. Diary V links the
    two types because of its description of Nin's efforts to
    translate the personality of Gonzalo in the diary to Rango
    in The Four-Chambered Heart. Her surrealistic techniques
    originally won Nin a following among the young. They ad-
    mired the "reality" in the diary and "real" virtues in the
    fiction like Sabina's independence of character. Nin's own
    independence is also seen in the diary, where she is the
    central heroine. The personalities from the diary are de-
    scribed with techniques similar to those of a realistic
    novel. Nin herself is a female version of the young men in
    Balzac's novels. Nin's courage is expressed through her
    ability to endure and write in the face of neglect. The
    diary is as much a novel as a confessional, a novel in the
    mode of the "artistic bildungsroman," showing a writer
    searching for the way to maintain artistic integrity in a
    careless world. Nin's concern for authenticity and for a
    writing style which clarifies the reality people experience
    rather than objective reality explains her appeal to the
    young. Nin merges classic objectivity and subjective ir-
    rationality. Nin's attention to detail in the diary pro-
    vides "poetically moving" passages.

71 STRAUB, PETER. "Lavender Bags." New Statesman, 88 (4 Octo-
    ber), 477-478.
        Winter of Artifice examines the destructive dependence
    of women upon men; in this case, a daughter upon her father.
    Both daughter and father are trapped in emotional child-
    hood. The structure is shaped solely by the stages of the
    heroine's self-analysis. The novella exposes the powerful,
    godlike male as a weak parasite. Nin believes that life

should be harmonized with the dream; her fiction tries to
stop time through a "halting, visionary prose."

72   STRAUS, HARRIETT. "The Book Review--Literature." Library
     Journal, 99 (15 February), 489.
          Brief review of A Celebration with Anaïs Nin (1973.B31).
     The book records the weekend dialog among thirty strangers
     who came to meet Nin. Graphics, typography, and layout
     form an artistic unity to an unusual degree. This is ap-
     propriate for a book designed to study freedom, promote
     the independence needed for artistic achievement, and pub-
     licize the problems of being woman and artist. "It is an
     inspiration."

73   STUHLMANN, GUNTHER. "Preface," in The Diary of Anaïs Nin,
     Volume Five: 1947-1955. Edited by Gunther Stuhlmann.
     New York: Harcourt Brace Jovanovich, pp. vii-ix.
          Each of the published volumes of the diary is self-
     contained and explores the growth of Nin's identity. Diary
     V presents themes found in the other volumes, but the diary
     has changed in tone and purpose; what began as a letter to
     her father, then became a drug, is now a conscious form of
     art. Nin struggles between the need for a diary which
     shows how memory distorts, and the need to transcend the
     limits of the diary form. To Nin, New York is symbol of
     the outside world and activity, and California is the world
     of retreat into the self. She seeks to create a way of
     life between the two. Still governed by her father's crit-
     ical eye, she tries to eliminate disguises and be Anaïs.
     The diary is Nin's major work; in it she tries to hold on
     to the dream of a father who protects his children from
     harsh reality. Nin trusts the power of the word; to the
     question, Why does one write? she would answer: "When you
     make a world tolerable for yourself you make a world tol-
     erable for others."

74   STUHLMANN, GUNTHER. "Prefatory Note," in Winter of Artifice
     and House of Incest. London: Peter Owen, p. 6.
          This is the first publication of House of Incest and
     Winter of Artifice in England. House of Incest was first
     privately printed in 1934 and later served as the basis for
     Ian Hugo's film "Bells of Atlantis." Winter of Artifice,
     Nin's "by now almost classic exploration of a father daugh-
     ter relationship," was also first privately printed. These
     words "echo the universal and very modern themes of rela-
     tionships and experiences so forcefully explored in the
     Journals." Nin gives them "artistic, literary forms that
     are at once accessible yet wondrously different."

1974

75   SUKENICK, LYNN. "Anaïs Nin: The Novel of Vision," in <u>A Case-</u>
      <u>book on Anaïs Nin</u>. Edited by Robert Zaller. New York,
      New American Library, pp. 157-160.
              In fiction where "feeling is paramount," Nin transforms
      the stereotype that women are associated with feeling into
      a strength. She writes in the tradition of sensibility,
      using "the distillation and refinement of moments of feel-
      ing as the highest business of the novel." Nin accepts the
      archetypal sexual polarities and regards feeling and intui-
      tion as especially feminine. "A gentle but tenacious
      battle for the values of feeling and intuition is conducted
      and won by Nin." She wanted a language for intuition and
      wanted to create through her prose "that preconceptual in-
      articulate condition, that fullness of being and state of
      undissected existence." Nin uses language "as a spell to
      banish language to...awake the reader's bodily awareness."
      Nin has created a style "to awaken feeling."

76   SUKENICK, LYNN. "Chapter V: Anaïs Nin: A World of Feeling,"
      in "Sense and Sensibility in Women's Fiction: Studies in
      the Novels of George Eliot, Virginia Woolf, Anaïs Nin, and
      Doris Lessing." Ph.D. dissertation, The City University of
      New York, pp. 207-252.
              For Nin, sensitive emotional response is an absolute and
      positive value; she questions its connection with feminine
      identity less than George Eliot, Virginia Woolf, or Doris
      Lessing. "Nin is 'good at' life, the way some people are
      good at sewing or dancing or drawing—her skills in human
      relationship and acute capacity for sensation are made clear
      in the diary." Nin dignifies the diary form, using it for
      "what women always need more of—pride of selfhood." Nin
      has recently modified her views about accepting the tradi-
      tional sexual polarities; but throughout her writing she
      associates masculinity with intellect, fact, and the real-
      istic novel and femininity with intuition, feeling, and
      poetic form. She shows "a more comfortable congruity be-
      tween general expectations of women's nature and her per-
      sonality" than Eliot, Woolf or Lessing, but she often dis-
      cusses the problems of women's lives and her problems as
      a woman writer. The diary shows "Nin's female version of
      self-reliance...." Her values are subversive of American
      culture: her desire to increase sensitivity, feeling, the
      capacity for sensation. Sensibility, aliveness is "the
      touchstone" for Nin. Her struggle to intensify aliveness
      is the "central concern" of her writing. She has a connec-
      tion with the ethic of sympathy and empathy.

77 T., F.-J. "Anaïs Nin," in <u>Dictionnaire des Littératures</u>
    <u>Etrangères Contemporaines</u>. Paris: Éditions Universitaires,
    pp. 273-274.
      Biography of Nin. She married an American businessman
    (engraver and film director under the name Ian Hugo). List
    of Nin's publications (criticism, novels, diary).

78 VAUGHAN, STEPHEN. "One Damn Thing After Another." London
    <u>The Observer</u> (25 August), p. 23.
      "Tastelessness" would be no disadvantage in admiring
    Nin's "bemusing fancies" in the <u>House of Incest</u> or <u>Winter</u>
    <u>of Artifice</u>.

79 WAKOSKI, DIANE. "A Tribute to Anaïs Nin," in <u>A Casebook on</u>
    <u>Anaïs Nin</u>. Edited by Robert Zaller. New York: New Ameri-
    can Library, pp. 142-152.
      Reprint of 1973.B50 with a new title.

80 WALLACE, KEVIN. "The Diarist Who Sold Out the House." <u>San</u>
    <u>Francisco Chronicle</u> (8 April), p. 2.
      Nin--the frail, "gossamer," seventy-one year old heroine
    of the women's movement--lectured to a sold-out house at
    the San Francisco Palace of Fine Arts on the topic "Women
    and the Future." Nin, whose writing was regarded by the
    <u>avant-garde</u> in the thirties as "thin," gave reasons to
    write: to create a world in which one can live; to at-
    tract, charm, and comfort others; to serenade lovers.

81 WELCH, SUSAN. "A Magnificent Diary." <u>Minneapolis Tribune</u>
    (30 June), D, p. 11.
      Nin is the "penultimate literary seductress, the <u>femme</u>
    <u>fatale</u> of the printed word," who gives the reader a world
    heightened by her sensitivity to intimate experience and
    poeticizing of the ordinary. Her diaries aid in her at-
    tempt to give life the unity and meaning of a work of art.
    The Nin of <u>Diary</u> V has begun to preserve more energy for
    herself and to withdraw from many former assoicates. Nin
    has shown women "a magnificent way of groping with and
    growing with the world. The diary should be read in full.
    Its impact, its insight, its example, are gargantuan."

82 WILSON, EDMUND. "Review of <u>Under a Glass Bell</u>," in <u>A Casebook</u>
    <u>on Anaïs Nin</u>. Edited by Robert Zaller. New York: New
    American Library, pp. 3-4.
      Reprint of 1944.B4.

1974

*83   YOUNG, MARGUERITE. Review of <u>Anaïs Nin Reader</u>. <u>New York</u>
        <u>Woman</u>, no. 1.
            Unlocatable. Cited in <u>Under the Sign of Pisces</u>, 5
        (Winter, 1974), 14.

84   ZAIDMAN, LAURA M. Review of <u>The Diary of Anaïs Nin, Volume</u>
        <u>Five</u>. <u>Library Journal</u>, 99 (15 March), 759.
            <u>Diary</u> V lacks the "polish and organization" found in
        Nin's novels and literary studies. The volume attempts to
        link the artistic nature reflected in Nin's novels with
        the human emotional nature she shows in the diary. Despite
        the weaknesses of the volume, it provides insights into
        Nin's art that make it a necessary addition to a library
        collection. Its quality is sufficient for it to stand next
        to her previous four volumes, all noted as literary
        achievements.

85   ZALLER, ROBERT. "Anaïs Nin and the Truth of Feeling," in <u>A</u>
        <u>Casebook on Anais Nin</u>. Edited by Robert Zaller. New York:
        New American Library, pp. 177-183.
            Reprint of 1973.B52.

86   ZALLER, ROBERT. "Introduction," in <u>A Casebook on Anaïs Nin</u>.
        Edited by Robert Zaller. New York: New American Library,
        pp. ix-xvi.
            Nin's biography: It took longer for her to gain fame
        than Miller or Durrell. But "now the time has come for
        Anaïs Nin." Praises the "perfection of a style more pre-
        cise and more evocative than perhaps any other English
        prose of our age." The diary is "a masterpiece...something,
        perhaps, quite without precedent." Surveys the other es-
        says in the collection: early notices of Nin; essays on
        the fiction; essays on the diary. The fiction is likened
        to the art of collage; it has no definite order or text.
        The diary contains portraits that are both real and sym-
        bolic. It is "open," and never finished. Nin resolved
        woman's "great dilemma"--the conflict between the desire
        to create versus the desire to serve men.

87   ZINNES, HARRIET. "Anaïs Nin's World Reissued," in <u>A Casebook</u>
        <u>on Anaïs Nin</u>. Edited by Robert Zaller. New York: New
        American Library, pp. 35-41.
            Reprint of 1963.B7.

88   ZINNES, HARRIET. "Poet of the Inner Voyage." <u>The Nation</u>,
        219 (30 November), 568-570.
            Review of <u>Diary</u> V. Nin believes that America is trying
        to kill the writer in her. Nin writes that only art has

the power to aid society and restore balance between the
individual's inner and outer worlds. Psychoanalysis should
free the "strength of the inner world"; art can heal only
when "invited to do so." The world of Nin's works is unreal, for it is a world of "psychic transcendence" and
transformation through emotion. This intense emotional
interpretation creates a fusion of all sense impressions,
and allows the simultaneous experience of both inner and
outer worlds, as illustrated by Nin's descriptions of her
hospital experience and the masquerade parties of Druks and
Matthiesen. The death of Nin's father was both a loss and
a new birth for her. Nin's diary is "a world of her own
creation."

1975 A BOOKS

1   MADDEN, DEANNA. "Laboratory of the Soul: The Influence of
    Psychoanalysis on the Work of Anaïs Nin." Ph.D. disserta-
    tion, University of Miami.
        Chapter one: Studies surrealistic and psychoanalytic
    elements in House of Incest (the unconscious, dreams, hal-
    lucinations, madness, sadism, and incest and the prose poem
    form; theories of neurosis and of the dream, the ideas of
    identification and projection, and the Jungian persona and
    "basic self"). Chapter two: Examines the increased real-
    ism in Winter of Artifice: this novel focuses on fatalité
    intérieure, the gap between the real and ideal self, role
    playing and the doppelgänger. Chapter three: Explores
    the dream as either beneficial or harmful in the stories of
    Under a Glass Bell; also studies Nin's developing awareness
    of herself as a woman writer and her effort to justify the
    subjectivity of her writing. Chapter four: Examines the
    influence of M. Esther Harding's Jungian theories on This
    Hunger and Cities of the Interior. These works show the
    neurotic woman at the mercy of her unconscious and emotions.
    At this point of her career, Nin develops the concept of
    the writer as analyst and the novel as therapeutic experi-
    ence. Chapter five: Treats the theme of the richness of
    the unconscious in Collages, a work that focuses on the
    concept of the persona and the basic self and Rank's con-
    cept of the artist type.

1975 B SHORTER WRITINGS

1   ANON. "Nin, Anaïs," in Who's Who of American Women. 9th edi-
    tion. Chicago: Marquis Who's Who, pp. 654-655.
        A list of Nin's fiction, diaries, and biographical ac-
    tivities.

1975

2　ANON. "Nin, Anaïs. A Woman Speaks: The Lectures, Seminars,
and Interviews of [the author]." Booklist, 72 (15 September), 102.
　　Review of A Woman Speaks. Typical extracts from Nin are
arranged together by theme. A synthesis of Nin's ideas and
opinions presented in a way that shows Nin's "unique" manner of public speaking. "The creative spirit emerges pure
and intense in its urgency."

3　AVAKIAN, ELIZABETH. To Deliver Me of My Dreams. Millbrae,
Cal.: Les Femmes, 91 pp., passim.
　　The book focuses on the author's reflections on living
as a woman but quotes frequently from Nin and uses Nin's
ideas as a springboard. Nin was delighted that her diary
caused Avakian to write her own journal and expressed hope
that others would be stimulated to write. Nin teaches
"the value of making the personal public." Nin seems to
be able to try new ways of living without sacrificing intimate relationships or caring.

4　BOSQUE, ALAIN. "Les petits fours de l'esprit et du coeur."
Magazine Littéraire, no. 96 (January), p. 32. [French.]
　　Review of Diary V. Nin charms us and leaves us intact,
as if we have taken a cup of tea in an old-fashioned but
rich setting. Nin's two chief virtues are naiveté and rejection of complexity. For Nin, writing is a hygiene that
brings light and simplicity. In spite of her expressed
disinterest in day-to-day life, Nin's diary gives this
life as viewed by a pampered and rich woman who has satisfaction only in drawing rooms. She confuses the marvelous
with sentimental ecstasy. What she calls the infinite is
limited to a vague religiosity harmonized with good taste.
Nin is a being of civilized pleasure. One should not complain because she offers us the small cakes of the spirit
and heart. She is so disarming that the reader succumbs
to her delicate chatter.

5　CENTING, RICHARD. "Nin in Columbus, Ohio, November 26-27,
1974." Under the Sign of Pisces, 6 (Winter), 2-6.
　　Describes Nin's visit to Columbus. Centing introduced
her, noting that Nin's diary shows her playing "a thousand
roles." Snyder's film "Anaïs Observed" (1973.A4) was
shown; Nin answered questions and attended a reception.

6　C[ENTING], R[ICHARD]. "Omission from Franklin's Nin Bibliog-
raphy." Under the Sign of Pisces, 6 (Winter), 16.
　　Nin's review of Marguerite Young's book Angel in the
Forest is missing from Benjamin Franklin V's bibliography

162

of Nin (1973.A1). Asks for other omissions in order to print them in <u>Under the Sign of Pisces</u>.

7   C[ENTING], R[ICHARD]. "<u>Anaïs Observed</u> Shown on Camera Three." <u>Under the Sign of Pisces</u>, 6 (Summer), 16.
    Snyder's color film of Nin (1973.A4) was edited to a thirty-minute version for the television program <u>Camera Three</u> in 1975.

8   C[ENTING], R[ICHARD]. "Capra Press <u>Paris Revisited</u> Goes O. P." <u>Under the Sign of Pisces</u>, 6 (Summer), 16.
    The chapbook of Nin's <u>Paris Revisited</u>, 1972, is out of print, but copies can still be found in bookstores.

9   CENTING, RICHARD. "New Book on Alan Swallow." <u>Under the Sign of Pisces</u>, 6 (Summer), 14-15.
    <u>Publishing in the West: Alan Swallow; Some Letters and Commentaries</u>, edited with an introduction by William F. Claire, was printed in 1974. Nin benefited from Swallow's publication of her fiction, and contributed an essay to the book on him.

10 C[ENTING], R[ICHARD]. "New Nin Publications, Reprints and Interviews." <u>Under the Sign of Pisces</u>, 6 (Summer), 2-7.
    Lists editions of books, contributions to books, and contributions to periodicals by Nin for the years 1973-1975.

11 C[ENTING], R[ICHARD]. "Nin in <u>Newsweek</u>, <u>MS.</u>, <u>Cosmopolitan</u>." <u>Under the Sign of Pisces</u>, 6 (Summer), 16.
    Cites brief mention of Nin in popular magazines. She appeared in <u>MS</u>. as a signer for repeal of laws restricting sexual orientation.

12 C[ENTING], R[ICHARD]. "Nin Promoted in Libraries, East and West." <u>Under the Sign of Pisces</u>, 6 (Summer), 15.
    <u>Diary</u> IV is cited in a special bibliography, <u>The New York Public Library Reader</u> (1975), distributed for International Women's Year. Nin is also pictured on a poster created for the San Francisco Public Library.

13 CENTING, RICHARD. "New Nin Publications." <u>Under the Sign of Pisces</u>, 6 (Fall), 8-9.
    Updates Benjamin Franklin V's 1973 bibliography of Nin by noting new work published by Nin.

1975

14   CHASE, KATHLEEN. "Anaïs Nin--Rumor and Reality: A Memoir by
       Kathleen Chase." Under the Sign of Pisces, 6 (Fall), 1-8.
          Traces the contacts between Nin and Kathleen Chase, who
       was related to Nin by marriage. Chase was very impressed
       by Nin, and Nin "nervously" served as godmother to Chase's
       second child. When Chase told Nin she was writing stories,
       Nin urged her to give up everything for writing and sent
       her a copy of Under a Glass Bell. Chase was fascinated by
       the book, the first work she had seen by Nin; she sent Nin
       a note of praise and received a reply stating how pleased
       Nin was that her work could help others to rid themselves
       of fears and inhibitions.

15   [GALANA], LAUREL. "Toward a WomanVision," in The Lesbian
       Reader. Edited by Gina Covina and Laurel Galana. Oakland:
       Amazon Press, pp. 189-211.
          Reprint of 1973.B28.

16   GETZOFF, CAROLE. "A Spy in the House of Nin." The Village
       Voice (6 January), p. 17.
          At 71, Nin is reconciled to age and now has the reputa-
       tion of a woman who always found pleasure in doing what she
       wanted. She speaks like one who is glad to have survived
       "at the top." She dates her present period in life from
       1966, when the first volume of her diary saw publication
       and elicited response from other women who saw themselves
       in her work. During the years of rejection by critics,
       Nin missed solidarity with other women writers; yet her
       world has always been identified with the male artists she
       maternally supported. She believes she was portrayed as
       more frail and feminine than she really was. Throughout
       the many roles she played, from psychoanalyst to Spanish
       dancer, she used her diary to help express what she really
       felt. Unfortunately, the edited version of the diary shows
       an "exalted" creature. Nin states she never has lived
       alone, but the woman who emerges from the diary is independ-
       ent and free from mundane duties. Widening acceptance of
       her works by the young supports Nin's belief that she re-
       flects the changes America underwent in the 1950s, a new
       consciousness and sensitivity, an attempt at creating a
       climate where feeling and intellect can coexist. Nin is
       neither an appropriate symbol for the women's movement nor
       a hopelessly feminine character, just very much herself.

17   HARDY, JOHN. "Nin at Hofstra University, November 22, 1974."
       Under the Sign of Pisces, 6 (Winter), 1-2.
          Nin spoke on the influence of surrealism on her work and
       was presented the Distinguished Author Medal at Hofstra's

conference on Dada and Surrealism. The film "Anaïs Observed" (1973.A4) was shown and Nin said that Anna Balakian, present in the audience, was responsible for America's understanding of surrealism.

18 HARMS, VALERIE. "Anaïs Nin, Witch of Words," in <u>Maria Mon-
    tessori, Anaïs Nin, Frances Steloff: Stars in My Sky</u>.
    Riverside, Conn.: Magic Circle Press, pp. 82-118.
        Nin is a "witch of words" who uses words to "transform,
    heal, and teach wisdom." Nin's diary makes her "the
    most important representative of the questing female
    writer." Examines unpublished material (Nin's diary and
    fiction) at Northwestern University Library. Quotes pas-
    sages of the diary that have not been published. Nin's
    first novel (written when she was nineteen) is about a
    girl who poses for artists. Quotes from it and summarizes
    the story. Discusses its major theme: "being a <u>mere</u>
    woman." Discusses and quotes from the next novel, which is
    also about a woman in relation to male artists. The style
    of the third unpublished novel shows progress as a writer.
    In this novel, "Nin has chronicled death in a relationship
    and followed it further than she had ever gone before...."
    In much of Nin's writing there is ironic humor ignored by
    critics. Analyzes this humor in a number of stories Nin
    wrote in her twenties. (Northwestern has about sixteen
    unpublished stories.) In these stories, women characters
    recognize the importance of work to their lives more than
    in the novels. Quotes from Miller's notations in the mar-
    gins of Nin's manuscripts and quotes unpublished passages
    from early versions of <u>House of Incest</u>. Compares earlier
    drafts of <u>House of Incest</u> to the published version.

19 HINZ, EVELYN J. "Introduction," in <u>A Woman Speaks: The Lec-
    tures, Seminars, and Interviews of Anaïs Nin</u>. Edited by
    Evelyn J. Hinz. Chicago: Swallow Press, pp. vii-xv.
        <u>A Woman Speaks</u> is an attempt to recreate the effect of
    Nin's presence through excerpts from her public lectures,
    seminars, and informal speaking engagements during the
    years 1966 to 1973. Nin emphasizes her struggle to develop
    into an articulate speaker and maintain her integrity dur-
    ing public appearances; success, she tells her audiences,
    usually comes through "exceptional stubbornness" not "ex-
    ceptional talent." Nin raises the issues of racial injus-
    tice, the status of women, and technology and art. She
    invites her audiences to ask her questions, is concerned
    to understand each question correctly, and makes sure the
    questioner understands her answer. She approaches every
    subject in a "distinctly feminine idiom," and believes

1975

there is a strong need for more women who feel free to
speak their minds. She hopes other women will be encour-
aged and concerned enough to express what the word "woman"
means to them.

*20 HOY, JODY. Interview with Anaïs Nin. East-West Journal
      (August).
         Unlocatable. Cited in Biography News, 2 (July-August),
      854-855.

21 JOHNSON, ALBERT. "Non Fiction." Publishers Weekly, 208
     (1 September), 65.
        Review of A Woman Speaks. The publication of Nin's
     diary created a demand for Nin as a speaker. A Woman
     Speaks compiles excerpts from lectures, seminars, and in-
     terviews from 1966 to 1973, organized into "characteristic"
     lectures and followed by question and answer sessions. The
     subjects are immediate and universal: faith, the future,
     the quest for the new, and creativity as opposing negation.
     The book shows Nin's wisdom.

22 KRAFT, BARBARA. "A Woman Speaks: A Review by Barbara Kraft."
     Under the Sign of Pisces, 6 (Fall), 12-14.
        A Woman Speaks is "ethereal" in the medieval sense, giv-
     ing the pure essence of Nin's wisdom. Unlike the diary,
     which was written in a state of transformation, this book
     portrays "the culmination of a lifetime of personal and ar-
     tistic growth." Nin records personal dialog in a universal
     language directed to women, since they are the ones who are
     listening. "A personal life lived deeply," creatively, and
     begun with an inner journey to free the soul, will take one
     beyond the personal, says Nin. Art functions as the search
     for essence, and the artist is the one who helps us to re-
     gain our vision after shattering experiences. The diary
     tells the reader that Nin's life and art are unified, a con-
     stant quest for transformation and integration; this book
     is "the purity of that effort."

23 LOUIT, ROBERT. "Anaïs Nin: Le roman est un rêve dirigé."
     magazine littéraire, no. 96 (January), pp. 31-32. [French.]
        Interview with Nin. Until 1966, she did not believe her
     diary would be published; she tried to give the essence of
     it in her fiction. She distrusts memory and has always de-
     scribed important events in the diary on the day they hap-
     pened. The diary approaches truth by describing the moment
     of existence. Collages doesn't resemble her other books in
     structure because she wanted to imitate the style of Var-
     da's collages. She differs from Varda, who is interested

1975

primarily in fragments, because she always seeks to synthesize the fragments of life. She is interested in the dreams
of her fictional characters. Seduction of the Minotaur begins with Lillian's dream, and the rest of the book is a
tentative elucidation of the dream. Psychology aids one to
pass from one phase to another, so the inner life does not
stay trapped in the same conflict. Nin has direct access
to the dream through intuition and doesn't need the passive
experience of drugs.

24 NYE, ROBERT. "Ms. Nin's Diary." Manchester Guardian Weekly
    (11 January), p. 19.
        Miller's claim that Nin's diary would stand beside Au-
    gustine's confessions was harmful, but the publication of
    her diary was worse--it ended the legend that Nin had "all
    the goods" on herself as well as on the rest of a famous
    coterie in Paris of the 1930s. As the basis for her five
    "hectically overwritten" novels, the diary reveals "just a
    middling Freudian Cinderella" condemned to mother artists
    and psychiatrists. The grief over her parents' deaths in
    Diary V is momentarily moving, but Nin returns to self-
    approving introspection, which she vulgarly calls "psycho-
    logical deep-sea diving." The entire diary is "artificial-
    ly involuted...paranoid" and narcissistic.

25 O'CONNOR, MARGARET ANNE. Review of A Woman Speaks. Library
    Journal, 100 (15 October), 1926.
        A Woman Speaks is not an attempt to preserve Nin's words
    for scholars but an attempt to disseminate her words as
    widely as possible. It is not a comprehensive work since
    it contains only transcripts from public statements made
    between 1966 and 1973. Passages on specific topics are
    grouped under particular titles, providing a "characteris-
    tic lecture" on a specific topic. The book is valuable
    because it provides material unavailable from other sources
    and accurately reflects the spirit of Nin's writings.

26 SCHOLAR, NANCY. "Cities of the Interior Revisited." Under
    the Sign of Pisces, 6 (Fall), 9-12.
        Reviews a new edition of Cities of the Interior. "Cit-
    ies of the Interior is a portrait of woman in the process
    of discovering who she is." Examines the symbols of mir-
    rors and labyrinths. "The inward-turning coils of the
    labyrinth are a powerful emblem of woman's traditional
    inner-directedness. But the labyrinth lacks exits, and the
    coils of its shape can be a source of confusion as well as
    enlightenment." For Sabina, the mirror is a sign of stasis;

1975

for Djuna, it symbolizes objectivity. In Seduction of the
Minotaur, self-acceptance brings Lillian "the means of
liberation from the prison of self-reflection."

27   SMITH, CRAIG. "Harold Norse Reflects on Anaïs Nin." Under
      the Sign of Pisces, 6 (Summer), 8-10.
          Summarizes Norse's reminiscences of a twenty-year ac-
      quaintanceship with Nin. Nin's letters to Norse gave him
      "a lot of strength to go on," and he was encouraged by her
      faith in his work. Nin's London publisher, Peter Owen,
      refused Nin's request that Norse write the introduction to
      Diary I. Norse believes the critics "never understood"
      Nin and admires Nin's ability to transcend psychological
      problems through work.

28   SPENCER, SHARON. "The Art of Collage in Anaïs Nin's Writing."
      Studies in the 20th Century, no. 16 (Fall), pp. 1-11.
          "Collage as a concept underlies Anais Nin's sense of
      art, both as a theory and as a process." Collage is de-
      pendent upon juxtaposition. In Nin's writing the degree of
      displacement caused by juxtaposition is usually slight.
      Examines "Ragtime" (a dream piece, first published in
      1938) as a symbolic presentation of the artist as collage
      maker. Examines Collages (1964), which shows the adapta-
      tion of a technique from the visual arts to literature by
      fusing apparently unrelated materials into one composition.
      Renate (the "strongest and happiest" of Nin's women charac-
      ters) is the artist who shows balance between work and re-
      lationships. The description of Varda is central to the
      book; he teaches the art of collage, "piecing together the
      ...visions that are called collages." Nin's "desire to re-
      claim whatever has been discarded" and to revitalize it
      by using it in a composition (her "ragpicking") relates her
      art to collage composition.

29   STUBBS, JEAN. "Private View." Books and Bookmen, 20 (April),
      56-58.
          Review of Diary V. The journals are preferable to Nin's
      novels because the former present men as characters in
      their own right and give a full picture. Sketches Nin's
      early life. Volume five gives the final pieces in the pic-
      ture of Nin's life. Nin strives to harmonize her penchant
      for collecting and nurturing the lame and savage--a trait
      she inherits from her mother--and her wandering and fear
      of being confined, inherited from her father. She pursues
      the goal of changing what can be changed and accepting what
      cannot be changed. Cites topics in the current volume:
      Nin's work on anger with Dr. Inge Bogner; sorrow that she

has no children; her reaction to her mother's death; a
tumor operation; rejection of LSD experience as "passive
dreaming." The diary shows Nin's philosophy that life
should be a search for permanent sources of joy and ecstasy.

30   STUBBS, JEAN. "Woman and Love." Books and Bookmen, 20
      (June), 57-58.
          Review of Winter of Artifice and House of Incest. Nin
      "is a caviar-and-oysters sort of writer, a rare luxury
      rather than a steady diet." She plays on the minute
      stages of the individual; the effect is "illuminating,"
      but "claustrophobic." Winter of Artifice contains three
      interconnected novellas depicting the father-daughter re-
      lationship. "Winter of Artifice" is the meeting of a
      daughter with her adored father. He is afraid of being
      rejected, makes possessive demands but the daughter frees
      herself. "The Voice" is a psychiatrist father-figure who
      listens to the confessions of two lesbians, Djuna and
      Lillian. When Lillian persuades the Voice to confide in
      her, he becomes a jealous child, the mirage of "perfect
      union" disappears, and her love for him dissolves. House
      of Incest moves into the subconscious. Jeanne loves
      Sabina "like a shadow kissing, without hope of reality."
      Nin has a unique talent, and there is more to discover
      each time one reads her work. It has taken four decades
      to realize she speaks for more than an elite and private
      circle.

31   TRABA, MARTA, "El 'Yo' monumental de Anaïs Nin." [Mexico]
      Dialogos, no. 63 (May-June), pp. 27-29. [Spanish.]
          Nin's diary is unique for both its size and the "idio-
      syncracy of the writing." All Nin's descriptions of her
      environment are written to praise her, and everyone around
      her is her mirror. Nin never yields, for nothing is
      greater than herself. She does not say this, but her
      friends say so; she is indispensable to their existence.
      Nin's own "'I' neither affirms nor feigns nor performs with
      any arrogance." Nin is the "authentic senorita" who re-
      jects her "normal" mother. She seeks out Rank to justify
      her passion for her father from a "heterodox Freudian" per-
      spective; after acknowledging the resemblance between her
      father and herself, she turns him into a caricature to save
      herself as the "untouchable person." "She becomes the
      father of her father," even as she exercises paternity over
      Miller, Allendy, June, and Rank. As Nin realizes that her
      literary ambition outweighs her capability, she "converts

1975

> literature into an appendix" to the monumental diary. Nin
> "incarnates literature"--that is "what makes her tremen-
> dously original." She pretends to exalt all women and the
> feminine condition, but "she herself is all women"; she is
> "the great incarnator." Nin sees herself unmasked in her
> relationship with Artaud, so she dissects him into soul
> and body and keeps only the soul. The diary is dangerous
> reading for women, but suitable for men who are poets,
> writers, and analysts. See 1976.B40 for translation.

32   ZAIDMEN, LAURA M. Review of Cities of the Interior. Library
> Journal, 100 (15 March), 603.
> Highly recommends Cities of the Interior, which unites
> five previously published Nin novels; praises the creativ-
> ity and continuity of the individual pieces. The quality
> of "timelessness" in this fictional cycle is also apparent
> in Nin's diary. Cities of the Interior attempts a psycho-
> logical study of three female characters, Sabina, Djuna,
> and Lillian, in an effort to expand upon Nin's theme of
> "'the quest of the self through the intricate maze of mod-
> ern confusion.'"

1976 A BOOKS

1   SNYDER, ROBERT. Anaïs Nin Observed: From a Film Portrait of
> a Woman as Artist by Robert Snyder. Chicago: The Swallow
> Press, 126 pp.
> Shows still shots from scenes in the film (1973.A4) and
> uses basically the same script and organization. Includes
> some additional material: a weekend "furrawn" at Berkeley;
> Nin as dean of the master of arts program at the Interna-
> tional College in Los Angeles; a dialog between Nin and
> Lawrence Durrell. Also adds material on how Snyder met
> Nin, his early relationship with her, her encouragement of
> his film on Henry Miller. Unlike the film, the book dis-
> cusses what was covered in the various sessions of film
> making. Adds a discussion of cutting and editing the film
> and the first public showing.

1976 B SHORTER WRITINGS

1   ANON. Review of In Favor of the Sensitive Man and Other Es-
> says. Publishers Weekly, 209 (8 March), 68.
> Nin never aligned herself with particular groups or
> limited herself intellectually. The Sensitive Man shows
> Nin's thoughts on eroticism in women and women's artistic
> efforts. The book enables one to get acquainted with a

woman too busy praising what she likes to waste time lamenting what she opposes.

2   ANON. Review of The Diary of Anaïs Nin, Volume Six. Publishers Weekly, 209 (29 March), 54.
Diary VI lets the reader "plunge headlong into the mysteries of living" and gain insight into Nin's own character. For those who enjoy reading about celebrities, there are many in this volume. The greatest value is the information on the human condition supplied through Nin's moving pictures of her own life.

3   ANON. "Literature." Booklist, 72 (15 April), 1156.
Diary VI reminiscences over Nin's newly achieved recognition as a writer. The "agonies of stringent self-analysis" are accompanied by accounts of friendships and journeys and an experiment with LSD.

4   ANON. Review of The Diary of Anaïs Nin, Volume Six. The New Yorker, 52 (21 June), 120.
When Nin's books were beginning to be published and read, she recorded all the long-awaited public recognition in her diary. Diary VI covers her new public life and the private life in which she finally rejected the passivity of traditional femininity with the aid of psychoanalysis. Nin's increased sensitivity and freedom from defensiveness make this volume more entertaining than the others.

5   ANON. "Recent Arrivals." Christian Century, 93 (21 July), 668.
"In-people are sticking with this multivolume miscellany of high-class chatter on the part of Nin, who has known everyone, been everywhere, and seldom bored anyone."

6   ANON. Review of In Favor of the Sensitive Man and Other Essays. Choice, 13 (July–August), 649.
In this collection of essays, Nin expresses her ideas on men and women, the arts, and travel. There are several lectures and two interviews. The first section of the book, titled "Women and Men," discusses feminism, the new woman, and the title subject, the new sensitive man. The second section, "Writing, Music, and Film," covers film and book criticism, with comments on the creative process and on Nin's experiences setting up her own printing press. The final section, "Enchanted Places," discusses her travels to Fez, Bali, Morocco, the New Hebrides, and New Caledonia. The book offers good specimens of Nin's latest essays.

1976

7   ANON. "Language and Literature: English and American."
     Choice, 13 (October), 984.
          Review of A Woman Speaks. It is a good collection of
     Nin's lectures, seminars, and interviews. Even Nin fans
     may find a 262-page "lecture" too long, but the book pre-
     sents an appealing, courageous and astute woman who gives
     a powerful analysis of the "woman problem." Nin's
     "Emerson-like optimism" sees art as "anti-toxin" for modern
     society. The book is "highly recommended."

8   ANON. "Language and Literature: English and American."
     Choice, 13 (November), 1138-1139.
          Review of Diary VI. This volume resembles previous ones
     in Nin's focus on herself. It is sometimes marred by items
     of little interest, such as letters or reviews and also by
     "a sort of continual whistling in the dark" as a way of op-
     posing the neglect Nin felt she suffered from American
     critics. However, the diary is "a sensitive and eloquent
     document" and "one of the most significant personal jour-
     nals kept in our time." It is "recommended."

9   BRODERICK, CATHERINE. "Abstract of Speech and Article:
     Structural Similarities in the Work of Anaïs Nin and Nat-
     sume Soseki." Under the Sign of Pisces, 7 (Spring), 19-20.
          Abstract of a paper given for the Japan Comparative
     Literature Society, 1974. "Structural patterns of juxta-
     position and repetition of motifs are the backbone of Nin's
     and Soseki's novels." In Kojin and Ladders to Fire, mad-
     ness (neurosis) leads to destructiveness in intimate rela-
     tionships. The two novels can be compared by comparing
     "the structural patterns of their motifs and the resulting
     thematic similarities."

10   CARNES, VALERIE. "Author Tries Distillation of Anaïs Nin's
     Voluminous Diary." Lost Generation Journal, 4 (Winter),
     11-13, 21.
          Few critics have focused on Nin's diary as belonging to
     the literary genre "journal." Discusses the first three
     volumes of the diary as serving the following functions:
     Providing an interior "room of one's own" where Nin can be
     more open and honest than she can be in fiction; providing
     a means for self-analysis and self-discovery for resolving
     her conflicts and unifying her fragmented selves; providing
     a place where she can present her life as representative of
     other women's lives. Nin develops an aesthetic theory
     based on a belief in woman's unique gifts for subjectivity
     and the personal. The diary form is genuinely feminine
     (even "feminist") because its spontaneous quality shows
     woman's experience and true nature.

11   [CENTING, RICHARD.] "Nin in The American Heritage Dictionary
      of the English Language (1970)." Under the Sign of Pisces,
      7 (Winter), 16.
          Nin is quoted to help define "sumptuous."

12   [CENTING, RICHARD.] "New Nin Publications." Under the Sign
      of Pisces, 7 (Spring), 5.
          Nin's "The Swallows Never Leave Noumea," inspired by her
      visit to New Caledonia, is published in the periodical
      Westways (January, 1976). Nin recreates the place and its
      culture and uses two women as symbols of New Caledonia.

13   [CENTING, RICHARD.] "Diary Mss. Sold to UCLA." Under the
      Sign of Pisces, 7 (Fall), 16.
          Expresses willingness to publish an article on the sale
      of Nin's diary manuscript to UCLA and a checklist of the
      items deposited at UCLA.

14   [CENTING, RICHARD.] "Les Femmes Poster of Anaïs Nin." Under
      the Sign of Pisces, 7 (Fall), 15-16.
          A poster of Nin in the Distinguished Women series is
      available from Les Femmes Publishing, Millbrae, California.

15   [CENTING, RICHARD.] "Quote of the Quarter." Under the Sign
      of Pisces, 7 (Fall), 12.
          "The works of Doris Lessing and Anaïs Nin are deliberate
      expressions of female humanity that furnish models for
      feminist identification." Yates, What Women Want: The
      Ideas of the Movement, 1975.

16   COSSEBOOM, RAY. "From 'Letters to Anaïs Nin,' a Chapter in a
      Novel in Progress called Anaïs Nin: This New Woman: Bos-
      ton and Beyond by Ray Cosseboom." Under the Sign of
      Pisces, 7 (Spring), 17-18.
          Furnishes a sample fictive letter.

17   DAVIDON, ANN MORRISSETT. "Anaïs Nin vs. Gore Vidal: Bon Mots
      and Billets Doux." The Village Voice (17 January), pp. 80-
      82.
          The battle between Nin and Vidal transcended personali-
      ties to become a struggle of "reason vs. intuition, objec-
      tivity vs. subjectivity, order vs. chaos...." Traces the
      relationship between Nin and Vidal as recorded and reflect-
      ed in their writings. Their intense early friendship is
      seen in Nin's Diary IV (1944-1947) and reflected in Vidal's
      letters and novels of this period. At this time Nin was
      already disturbed by Vidal's cynicism and inability to
      trust his emotions. Her growing disillusion with Vidal

1976

caused Nin to place him in "The World of Reality" rather
than "The World of the Artist." Nin's later diaries deleted all but a few negative remarks about Vidal. Vidal's
chief attack on Nin is in The Two Sisters (1970.B67); the
character Marietta who represents Nin is accused of an
"insatiable appetite for glory and sex."

18 DUNCAN, ERIKA. "Anaïs Nin--Two Views by Susan Manso and
    Erika Duncan." New Boston Review, 2 (Fall), 27-28.
        Prints a speech delivered to the Woman's Salon, "an
    alternative literary structure" to support writers not yet
    known. Nin is "one of this century's great defenders of
    largeness and innovative risk-taking in others." Her writ-
    ing is "a deliberate quest for beauty and transcendence."
    It took the world a long time to recognize her work, but
    Nin did not turn bitter. Instead, she created a whole
    movement, a "support system" that has greatly influenced
    "impassioned writing." Because of Nin's friendships, she
    is "a role model for working relationships."

19 FOOTE, AUDREY C. "Her Own Best Work of Art." The Washington
    Post Book World (29 August), M, p. 4.
        Review of Diary VI. The diary reveals Nin's life has
    been one long struggle for recognition and publication.
    In this volume, Nin is unchanged: seeking spiritual close-
    ness with artists; revealing her psyche but hiding her
    daily life; arrogant about her writing, obsessed with pro-
    moting it and recording praise. Perhaps it is this exces-
    sive praise from Nin's partisans which has caused critical
    indifference and even attack. Oddly, this romantic,
    nineteenth-century lady has great appeal for the young.
    Nin suggests the possibility of being both elegant and
    liberated; she focuses on woman's fulfillment in art and
    love rather than sports or career; her passion is for free-
    dom, not equal opportunities. Nin's egotism and her gen-
    erosity with praise for others is a paradox. Volume six
    indicates Nin is a better person than many writers and,
    appropriately for a diarist, it is her finest work of art.

20 FULLER, EDMUND. "A Feminist Writes without Hostility." Wall
    Street Journal (13 April), p. 20.
        Nin is now at the height of her influence with a new
    generation of readers. She claims not to know what a radi-
    cal feminist is, but letters she receives make her realize
    the large number of lonely women who have no way of devel-
    oping their potential and are apt to give to others the
    faith they should have in themselves. Nin believes hostil-
    ity is a refusal to take responsibility; if we cannot find
    inner nourishment, we shift the blame to society or men.

1976

Those who bring private neuroses to women's movement groups
will not solve their problems through political action.
Nin teaches the necessity for developing a sense of identity and creative living latent in oneself. Women should
work at liberation with men. Woman's gift for the personal
is not a weakness but a strength. To write, for Nin, is
"to love twice."

21   GRAHAM, P. "A Response to Under the Sign of Pisces (Winter
      1976): In Response to the Monumental I of Marta Traba."
      Under the Sign of Pisces, 7 (Summer), 1-4.
           Point-by-point disagreement to 1976.B40. Nin is not a
      strange woman; she is "intimate and whole." Even in her
      earlier, more fragmented period she was intimate and whole
      in every fragment. The length of the diary is necessary
      for Nin's development; if it appears maniacal, this may be
      necessary to help her, like others, to create. Nin does
      not see herself as a self-worshipping goddess; the diary
      is about being human and relationships of mutual exchange.
      Nin's portraits show much beyond herself: the gentleness
      of Miller, the beauty of June. Nin did not lie in her
      diary, for if she had, it would not have lasted. Her "ex-
      cessive literary zeal" is exalting; she transforms ordinary
      life in her life and art. Even if she had not made her
      father temporarily a saint, she would have written. She
      is not indifferent to the outside world, for she has lis-
      tened to others and helped them for over fifty years. The
      diary is not an apology for her literature, but rather
      true revelation. See 1975.B31.

22   HALL, JOAN JOFFE. "The Diary of Anaïs Nin, Vol. VI, 1955-66."
      The New Republic, 175 (21 August), 35-36.
           The diary is basic to Nin's quest for self. Discusses
      the woman-artist problem, Nin's struggle against anarchic
      impulses, biography from the diary, and A Woman Speaks.
      Younger women now flock to see Nin; "she has reassured
      many women that it is possible for a female artist to sur-
      vive in the face of male antagonism." This new volume
      shows less mystery, less narcissism, more harmony and wis-
      dom. Nin's fiction and the diaries seek "both 'the truth
      of the moment'...and the 'sense of continuous change.'"
      "The interior drama is the source of her strength."

23   HARTY, JOHN III. "Thesis in Progress on Anaïs Nin." Under
      the Sign of Pisces, 7 (Spring), 6-7.
           Describes an M.A. thesis in progress: "Under a Glass
      Bell: From Interior Fatality to Psychological Motion,"
      University of Richmond. Under a Glass Bell presents "the

moment of the interior fatality" and shows that movement
away from this crisis is through self discovery. Psychological movement is divided into two periods: the pro-
tagonist is controlled by his inner fatality or is able
to move out of this control. An ambivalent period occurs
between interior fatality and psychological motion.

24   HENKE, SUZETTE. "Anaïs Nin: Bread and Wafer." Under the
     Sign of Pisces, 7 (Spring), 7-17.
          Nin's fiction allows her to live out multiple selves
     and establish a symbol-system archetypal for women social-
     ized in a patriarchal environment. In Ladders to Fire,
     Lillian represents the "ego," aggressive and seeking lib-
     eration; Sabina is the "id," a free woman living spontane-
     ously but not personally independent; and Djuna is the
     "superego," the character who transforms ordinary "bread
     of life" into the "sacramental wafer of art." Lillian is
     a combination of Nin with the destructive characteristics
     she perceived in June Miller. Lillian meets male demands
     for altruism, self-sacrifice, and maternal solicitude be-
     cause she believes herself unworthy. Djuna is the "artist
     of life" who most nearly represents the biographical Nin.
     She becomes a prophetess and dares to explore the "cities
     of the interior," where she learns that women must create
     themselves. She lives a self-sufficient and nearly andro-
     gynous life, holds chaos in check by force of discipline
     and will, and is the mother-goddess in the guise of the
     virgin Diana.

25   HOLT, ROCHELLE. "Review of Maria Montessori, Anaïs Nin,
     Frances Steloff: Stars in My Sky." Under the Sign of
     Pisces, 7 (Fall), 13-15.
          Harms' book (1975.B18) is a "unique" biographical work
     "because it not only relates the meaningful lives of three
     individual women, but does so in the context of the author's
     own personal life." The section on Nin is of special in-
     terest because of the excerpts from the childhood diary
     and unpublished drafts of fiction. Praises Harms' discus-
     sion of Nin as a young writer.

26   HOLT, ROCHELLE. "The Vitality of Life: A Response to Marta
     Traba." Under the Sign of Pisces, 7 (Fall), 10-12.
          A reply to 1976.B40. Traba was deeply affected by the
     first volume of Nin's diary and recognizes Nin's ability
     to "tell things" rather than merely describe; yet Traba
     criticizes Nin's diary for not being like other diaries.
     The diary moves beyond description to create empathy for
     the artists and writers who are Nin's associates. Nin's

work teaches that all war and attacks on people are opposed
to life. The diary is a spiritual autobiography. Nin can
communicate the essence of being alive and feeling. The
diary reaches out to many women and men, who see Nin's efforts as a model for their own lives. We need more books
like Nin's, concerned with literature as a means of sharing
perception on all levels. Emotions can be shared only when
transformed into art. "The Monumental 'I' is a living
'eye' looking on life and seeing its vitality and meaning
in relating all to the individual which is exactly what we
all do."

27   JENSEN, CRUZ. "Writing Releases Her—Cruz Jensen on Anaïs
      Nin." Times Educational Supplement, 23 (11 June), 3184.
          Review of Diary I-V. Nin's diary is "exciting" because
      of her interest in the "singular and the individual" in-
      stead of the commonplace. She vividly recreates a long
      list of characters and also describes places with creative
      skill. Most important is her exploration of "every corner
      of her being." "She has all the resources for self reve-
      lation, a bottomless memory, language which expresses every
      shade of meaning, and willingness to broach the big themes,
      love, suffering and death...." She "hides nothing" and has
      easy access to her unconscious. "She is at her most per-
      ceptive writing about physical delight, the alchemy of in-
      teraction...." Nin has much to teach about creativity and
      about women's needs.

28   KIRSCH, ROBERT. "Anaïs Nin Extends Her Family." Los Angeles
      Times (19 February), Section 4, pp. 4-5.
          Review of A Woman Speaks. Nin's readers identify with
      her struggles for love, independence, and self-expression
      without paternal validation; they see her battle as a kind
      of "symbolic odyssey of autoemancipation." Nin received
      many requests for personal appearances from readers who
      wished to link Nin the writer with Nin the woman expressed
      in the diary. Though Nin may appear a high priestess to
      the public, she is actually more of a teacher, speaking of
      life in terms of faith and the refusal to despair, con-
      cerned with the contemporary issues of psychology, preju-
      dice, technology, and the problems of women. Her lectures
      show her moderation and common sense, her well-read criti-
      cal background, and her impatience with clichés and cant.
      Nin rejects the role of priestess for the women's libera-
      tion movement, for she believes groups and movements
      "bleach out" individuality and "possibly substitute for
      faith in self." Hinz has done a good job of arranging this
      volume, using excerpts from tapes organized around the

1976

issues and themes of Nin's speeches to give a sense of
Nin's public speech and presence. The book is an "extraordinary evocation of a remarkable woman," rounding out in
another form the intimacy of the diary and the novels.

29 McKINVEN, MARY JANE. Review of In Favor of the Sensitive Man
and Other Essays. Booklist, 72 (1 May), 1241.
Nin's essays from the 1970s have been loosely organized
around the themes of woman (including views on the feminist
movement and Nin's vision of the "new woman"), artists, and
travel. The book is representative but not very challenging because Nin's belief in the importance of instinct and
emotion in the creative life is repeated too often.

30 MANSO, SUSAN. "Anaïs Nin--Two Views by Susan Manso and Erika
Duncan." New Boston Review, 2 (Fall), 27-88.
The size of Nin's diary is matched only by its "vacuity."
She stupefies the reader by her "monotonous voice" and her
utterly "self-enclosed system." Nin lacks the intelligence
to write a modest diary; instead she makes a parody of the
diary with her large claims. In addition, her conception
of the "Artist as Modern Woman" is "banal." Nin lacks the
irony and humor that accompany genuine self-scrutiny. Her
"deep meanings" and idea of "woman as a shortcut to the
psyche" are narcissistic and exhibitionistic. "She offers
herself a crown and then looks in vain for her kingdom."
Nin accepts sexual stereotyping, but since she values what
was formerly conceived of as women's limitations, some
feminists support her. Nin distrusts ratiocination and
shows "complete epistological confusion." Nin "needs
Nabokov's caution that reality always requires quotation
marks."

31 MYERS, CAROL FAIRBANKS. "Nin, Anaïs," in Women in Literature:
Criticism of the Seventies. Metuchen, N.J.: The Scarecrow
Press, pp. 141-143.
List of secondary sources on Nin (dissertations and
journal articles, reviews, and mimeographed papers) from
1970 to 1975.

32 OATES, JOYCE CAROL. "A Gigantic Plea for Understanding: The
Diary of Anaïs Nin, 1955-68 and In Favor of the Sensitive
Man and Other Essays." The New York Times Book Review
(27 June), pp. 4-5.
Diary VI is the most successful volume so far. It concerns Nin's love relationships and disillusionments, and
offers the insight--common to many who live in the imagi-
nation--that her highly-praised intuition is not always

1976

reliable. In this volume Nin forms her material along the
lines of art; she says she has finished with the character
Anaïs Nin, and the intensity of personal relationships
flows over into the universal. This volume ends with the
publication of Diary I and Nin on the verge of international fame. It is ironic that Nin's novels were rejected
by the critics and that this "seductive" form, the diary,
should succeed. Occasionally there are embarrassing passages that should have been deleted. It is puzzling that
Nin believes the poetic novel originated by Lawrence,
Woolf, and Joyce is still new and must make its way against
tremendous odds. In Favor of the Sensitive Man is a collection of Nin's "graceful," concise, and usually timely
essays. They touch themes developed at greater length in
the diary and Nin's fiction, so they introduce the reader
to her longer works.

33   O'CONNOR, MARGARET ANNE. "Literature." Library Journal, 101
      (July), 1532.
          Review of Diary VI and In Favor of the Sensitive Man
      and Other Essays. Nin enhances the importance of the diary
      genre with her argument that it is both therapeutically
      valuable to the individual and of literary worth to soci-
      ety. Volume six adds to Nin's portrait but lacks the
      "anecdotes of interaction" with prominent figures found in
      earlier volumes. One more volume is planned for this se-
      ries. In Favor of the Sensitive Man is a collection of
      essays, reviews, lectures, interviews, and diary entries
      previously published in popular magazines. Nin remains
      consistent regardless of the audience she addresses. She
      defines feminism through her discussion of "the woman of
      the future," a person who is "in harmony with her own
      strength." Time should not be wasted in negative rebel-
      lion, or in imitating men and their tactics while denying
      woman's femininity. The collection is uneven, but some of
      the essays supply valuable information about Nin's work
      and her ideas on human relationships.

34   RILEY, GLENDA. Review of In Favor of the Sensitive Man and
      Other Essays. Best Sellers, 36 (July), 130.
          The selections in In Favor of the Sensitive Man are
      representative, but depth and dimension are lacking. The
      book is a convenient collection of scattered fragments of
      Nin's work, occasionally charming and stimulating, but the
      overall effect is uneven and lacks continuity. An essay
      on Nin's work or a key essay would improve the book.

1976

35   SCHWEITZER, LEA. "A Response to Anaïs Nin's Review of <u>At a
      Journal Workshop</u>." <u>Under the Sign of Pisces</u>, 7 (Winter),
      5-8.
           Nin and Ira Progoff believe the basic purpose of keep-
      ing a diary is the "harmonization of all aspects of the
      self, which should lead to self-actualization and develop-
      ment." Both believe the diary should be as creative and
      innovative as the person who keeps it. Progoff's system
      divides life into sections and places diary entries in
      specific sections depending upon the particular event or
      problem. Nin emphasizes writing from the "flow" of the
      psyche without division into categories.

36   SPENCER, SHARON. "<u>Cities of the Interior</u>--Femininity and
      Freedom." <u>Under the Sign of Pisces</u>, 7 (Summer), 9-16.
           Nin's writing focuses on the question of woman's essen-
      tial nature, her sexuality, and her need for both freedom
      and stable relationships of passion. "Birth" is a naked
      account of how procreation threatens a woman's identity.
      In the diary, Rank helps Nin develop from a dependent,
      unformed child to a maternal figure. Being mother to oth-
      ers made Nin feel like a woman. In <u>Cities of the Interior</u>,
      however, Lillian and Djuna struggle against the compulsion
      to mother; they find that using the maternal role to gain
      security thwarts their sensual and emotional pleasure in
      relationships. Sabina is the least conventionally "femi-
      nine" character, for she gives nothing. With the option
      of rejecting or limiting motherhood, woman has as many
      life choices as man, including the "challenge of maintain-
      ing multiple relationships." However, as long as all women
      are conditioned to mothering, the woman who rejects or
      modifies the role will suffer "from the unconscious convic-
      tion that her life is in some way abnormal or wrong." Nin
      writes in the diary, "I see Sabina as a portrait of a
      modern woman, seeking to break taboos but still a prey to
      guilt."

37   STONE, LAURIE. "Anaïs Nin: Is the Bloom off the Pose?" <u>The
      Village Voice</u> (26 July), p. 43.
           <u>Diary</u> VI has been published, and it is time to assess the
      diary as a whole. It is weak in recreating "life as it is
      really lived." <u>Diary</u> I shows a frankness that probably
      stems from its being written for private purposes rather
      than publication. Nevertheless, "edited versions of the
      diary nearly all appear to be concealing more than they
      reveal." Nin frequently fails to really reveal herself or
      to make her life of concern to the reader. The diary has
      "gossip appeal" but this is not what Nin hoped to be valued

for. The diary is weakened by Nin's lack of awareness of
her own anger and resentment and the fact that she is
threatened by political involvement. Moreover, Nin is
"unaware of the degree to which, like it or not, all of
her perceptions, tastes, values, and ideas are functions
of her social class." Many women critics harshly attacked
Nin because she seemed a threat to women who chose "to be
intellectual, concrete, and political as a way of being
new and free." The diary is "still a unique and frequently engaging document." "The full value of the diary will
not be measurable until, if ever, we see it in its unex-
purgated form."

38 STUHLMANN, GUNTHER. "Preface," in The Diary of Anaïs Nin,
    Volume Six: 1955-1966. Edited by Gunther Stuhlmann.
    New York: Harcourt Brace Jovanovich, pp. ix-xvi.
        Nin's diary began as an open letter to a lost father,
    but became a private drug. It grew in secrecy, although
    she occasionally showed portions to friends. Nin feared
    publishing the diary because it might hurt others, expose
    her candid revelations, and harm her self-esteem. The
    diary was Nin's most natural writing, and the key to her
    fiction; it reveals the shifting of personalities and in-
    finite potential for growth. Nin's recorded emotions
    flowed between herself and this alter ego. Nin wanted to
    relieve her isolation by revealing her essential lifework.
    In reviewing her diaries, she applied critical standards
    to a once spontaneous undertaking. Her emotional depend-
    ence on the diary lessened; she stopped focusing on her-
    self as the major character and sought a "new objectivity"
    about others. She minimized damage to the privacy of her
    relationships by editing the diary to eliminate some char-
    acters and make others anonymous or pseudonymous.

39 SUKENICK, LYNN. "Notes on The Diary of Anaïs Nin, Volume V."
    Under the Sign of Pisces, 7 (Fall), 1-9.
        Nin inspires her readers by showing them the conflicts
    and mistakes she surmounted to achieve harmony. Diary V
    is full of psychic and geographical change; Nin tries to
    resolve her restlessness, to develop a practical, almost
    domestic self quite unlike the Anaïs of volume one. Her
    duality of spirit is pronounced, and she is challenged to
    choose between writing and ecstatic living, between her
    desire for candid revelation and her need not to harm any-
    one. Her mother's death inspires examination of Nin's own
    maternal impulses, and their conflict with her fears of
    female "servitude." Like Woolf's Mrs. Ramsay, Nin is in-
    tuitive and sympathetic; but Nin escapes the demand for

1976

modesty and obedience because assertiveness is necessary to the artist. The diary shows Nin's continual struggle towards perfection. She takes herself seriously, not in a narcissistic way, but as one capable of recognizing and encouraging the potential for growth in others.

40 TRABA, MARTA. "The Monumental 'I' of Anaïs Nin." Translated by George C. Hart. Under the Sign of Pisces, 7 (Winter), 8-14.
    Translation of 1975.B31.

41 TYLER, RALPH. "The Diary of Anaïs Nin, Vol. 6." Saturday Review, 3 (29 May), 38-39.
    Nin is now receiving long-awaited recognition, since feminists and other women are eager to share her interest in inner worlds. In Favor of the Sensitive Man, however, suffers from a characteristic fault. Nin's rarefied writing, a corrective against the harsh, anti-poetic environment of her youth, is monotonous, like a diet of only lime sherbet.

42 WAKOSKI, DIANE. "Trivia into Myth: A Woman Speaks." The New York Times Book Review (4 January), pp. 3-4.
    "A Woman Speaks is a manual for anyone who cares for the artist inside his or her own beautiful self." It expresses Nin's "articulate insightfulness about the interior processes of the artist" and "the deep love for people and life which she and all of her work possesses." This is not a book of rhetoric, for it goes beyond the politics of women's liberation with hopes for a world where "we can all be human, not simply members of partisan groups." Hinz has constructed the book so that there is an organized and coherent view of Nin's esthetics and philosophy. Each chapter begins with one of Nin's lectures, and ends with a question and answer session. The introduction gives a sense of Nin's belief in "lived literature," her insistence that life goes "beyond the autobiography into the myth of self." Nin took an old, personal form of writing, the diary, and turned it into "a rich public art form." The artist desires not "to glorify trivia but to use the trivia of daily occasions to make art." A Woman Speaks should be required reading for creative writing workshops.

43 WATSON, FRED. "Allegories in 'Ragtime': Balance, Growth, Disintegration." Under the Sign of Pisces, 7 (Spring), 1-5.
    The major theme of "Ragtime" is the balance of control between the consicous mind (symbolized by the narrator)

and the subconscious mind (symbolized by the ragpicker).
The surreal setting is the irrational world of the mind
filled with "psychic debris." The ragpicker represents
forces which must be integrated in order to produce change
and growth, yet he is fragmented and unable to renew himself. The narrator is also fragmented; as she goes deeper
into the ragpicker's world, she loses control over him, and
the balance between conscious and unconscious is upset.
Hope of growth and integration are symbolized by the man-
dolin and the dancing.

1977 A BOOKS

1   SPENCER, SHARON. <u>Collage of Dreams: The Writings of Anaïs
     Nin</u>. Chicago: Swallow Press, 188 pp.
        Chapter one: Argues that "collage as a concept under-
     lies Anaïs Nin's sense of art, both in theory and as proc-
     ess." Analyzes "Ragtime" (1938) and <u>Collages</u> to show how
     Nin adopts the collage technique to literature. Chapter
     two: Studies the influence of dance, painting, and music
     on Nin's art. Music had the greatest influence on Nin's
     style, especially on <u>A Spy in the House of Love</u>, the "most
     musical" of Nin's works. Chapter three: Examines Nin's
     use of the dream; her later work stresses the usefulness
     of the dream in experiencing the unconscious world. Her
     fictional characters show her desire to present the uncon-
     scious, hidden self. Chapter four: Surveys Nin's explo-
     ration of woman's role as mother as presented through
     fictional characters (Lillian, Djuna, and Sabina) and
     personal experiences recorded in the diary. Nin learned
     to redefine the image of woman to include the power of
     destruction as well as the power of nurturing. Chapter
     five: Examines Nin's work on woman as artist. "Nin's
     development as an artist shows both sides of the process
     of moving toward self-realization by bringing both mascu-
     line and feminine components of the self into awareness."
     Chapter six: Analyzes <u>Diary</u> I-VI; in <u>Diary</u> I, "the ab-
     sorption with self seems unprecedented." By <u>Diary</u> VI, Nin
     has shifted emphasis to the outer world. Chapter seven:
     Compares Nin's diary to Proust's <u>A la recherche du temps
     perdu</u>; both works show the process by which "consciousness
     creates art." Chapter eight: Defends Nin from the charge
     of narcissism by arguing that Nin's life work "gives us
     both books that exonerate the artist from the charge of
     selfishness and the history of a life devoted to the actu-
     alization of all its capabilities, not the least of which
     is the gift of love for others." Includes a selected bib-
     liography.

1977

1977 B SHORTER WRITINGS

1   ANON. "Obituary Notes." Publishers Weekly, 211 (24 January),
     256.
         Nin died at 73, on January 14 in Los Angeles, from can-
     cer. Quotes John Ferrone, her editor at Harcourt Brace
     Jovanovich, saying Nin was one of the pioneers of women's
     liberation: "Miss Nin wrote from the point of view of a
     woman and artist struggling to perfect herself, but her
     work has a universal appeal." The publication of the diary
     brought Nin critical recognition. Lists forthcoming publi-
     cations (a seventh volume of the diary and Delta of Venus).
     Brief biography and list of publications.

2   ANON. "Nin, Anaïs: Delta of Venus: Erotica." The Virginia
     Kirkus Service, 45 (1 April), 377-378.
         The client who paid Nin to write erotica in the 1940s
     "got his money's worth and to spare." Nin gives both
     pornography and "class." Using Krafft-Ebing and the Kama
     Sutra, Nin writes erotica with skill: "slightly tongue-
     in-cheek, supremely unabashed--a woman of good family kick-
     ing up her French heels."

3   ANON. "Fiction." Publishers Weekly, 211 (11 April), 73-74.
         Review of Delta of Venus. In spite of the injunction to
     "leave out the poetry" from her commissioned erotica, Nin
     "simply couldn't do it. Beauty of language was too much a
     part of her." Erotica has limits, and the poetry and oc-
     casional female language do not offset the weaknesses of
     the work. "Redemption comes in that she could never manage
     to separate sex from feeling."

4   ANON. "Fiction." Booklist, 73 (15 May), 1400.
         Delta of Venus is a "literary curiosity" which Nin wrote
     in the 1940s. By today's standards, "the sex isn't all
     that explicit, but, more importantly, Nin's unique sensi-
     bilites as an artist glimmer distantly in a repressed and
     nascent state."

5   ANON. "The Incredible Contents of Anaïs Nin's Pornography:
     Queen of American Avant-Garde Literature from Nouveau Roman
     to Jazz: Sex Hunter Who Taught Henry Miller How to Love."
     Weekly Playboy, 12 (24 May), 149-151. [Japanese.]
         Includes personal memories of Nin by Japanese writers
     Koji Nakata and Kazuko Sugisaki. An unorganized collection
     of excerpts from Nin's novels and descriptions of her asso-
     ciates. Nin explored sex from the woman's point of view
     and made women equal to Henry Miller in eroticism.

1977

6   ANON. "Acquisitions." College and Research Libraries News,
     no. 8 (September), p. 234.
         Nin's papers were acquired by the University of Califor-
     nia, Los Angeles, and will be housed in the University Re-
     search Library's special collections. The papers include
     Nin's diaries, correspondence, manuscripts, and related
     papers covering the years from 1913 to the present. "The
     Nin papers are of major importance and will significantly
     increase the corpus of research materials available to
     scholars."

7   ASHTON, ELIZABETH. "Nin's Erotica: A Distinctly Female View."
     Houston Chronicle Zest Magazine (17 July), p. 9.
         In 1940 a book collector asked Henry Miller to produce
     pornography for him at the rate of a dollar a page. Miller
     declined and gave the job to a group of writers which in-
     cluded Nin. Nin's contributions are collected in Delta of
     Venus, an uneven work that contains unrelated episodes
     lacking story resolution. What makes the book unique is
     its "distinctly feminine view through the keyhole." Female
     anxieties, frustrations, and needs underlie the erotica.
     Recurrent themes deal with the sexually unfulfilled woman,
     the detached woman, the challenging woman, and the woman in
     love.

8   BLOCH, ALICE, KIRSTEN GRIMSTAD, VALERIE HARMS, et al. "Waste
     of Timelessness and Other Early Stories, by Anaïs Nin."
     Chrysalis: A Magazine of Women's Culture, no. 3, p. 81.
         Familiar Nin themes include feminism, the exceptional
     and creative child/woman living in fantasy, the "alchemy"
     of art, conflicts between truth and deception. The stories
     show an ironic humor that "tends to be bitter, and almost
     cold; the compassion of later works is nearly absent." The
     book is "of great interest to those who wish to see the
     complete progression of Nin's development as a writer, and
     of little interest to others."

9   BRIANS, PAUL. "Sexuality and the Opposite Sex: Variations on
     a Theme by Theophile Gautier and Anaïs Nin." Essays in
     Literature, 4 (Spring), 122–137.
         Compares the heroines of Gautier's Mademoiselle de
     Maupin (1836) and A Spy in the House of Love (1954).
     Through the adventures of heroines who break the restric-
     tions of traditional sex roles, Gautier and Nin explore
     bisexuality and homosexuality, as well as "the fragmenting
     nature of sex roles and their theatrical character, the
     tendency of such roles to limit the individual comprehen-
     sion of others, and the beneficial or harmful results

1977

which derive from efforts to break out of the traditional
patterns." Gautier's heroine "forges a new self free of
the confining limits prescribed for a proper young girl,"
but she is a "male fantasy figure" rather than a model
liberated woman. Nin's work is "much more authentic."
Sabina sees herself as a female Don Juan, "playing one role
after another, taking one lover after another, admiring and
achieving the ability to experience intense sex without
love, like a man." Sabina's goals are exposed as neurotic;
sex without love is viewed as weakness rather than strength.
"It is to Anaïs Nin's credit that she has explored the com-
plexities and profundities of sexuality and love with a
skill and an insight few others can match."

10   CAMPOS, JULIETA. "Anaïs Nin (1903-1977)." <u>Vuelta</u>, 1 (March),
     49-50. [Spanish.]
        The diary is now closed, for Nin died in January. But
     rereading it proves that it is still alive and fluid.
     Nin's writing is passionate, showing her awareness of joy
     and anguish. She believes that adventures of the body
     are also adventures of the spirit; she explores ways of
     achieving harmony with the self and universe. Nin probed
     the significance of dreams. She is a romantic in the
     tradition begun by Rousseau. The diary is "magical," a
     monumental account of the labyrinth of a normal day. Early
     in life, Nin realized that words could create a habitable
     world and offset loss. Gives impressions of Nin's last
     hours when she was weak and had a failing memory. Not even
     death can diminish Campos' sense of kinship with Nin.

11   CENTING, RICHARD. "<u>Anaïs Nin Observed: From a Film Portrait
     of a Woman as Artist</u>, by Robert Snyder." <u>Under the Sign of
     Pisces</u>, 8 (Winter), 1.
        Nin died in Los Angeles on January 14, 1977, of cancer.
     She was cremated and her ashes scattered over the Pacific.
     She will be remembered in her works and friends; in her
     recorded voice; her influence on writers, and in Snyder's
     film "Anaïs Observed" (1973.A4). Swallow Press has re-
     leased a book of the film's highlights with commentary by
     Snyder (1976.A1).

12   [CENTING, RICHARD.] "Book Dedicated to Anaïs Nin." <u>Under the
     Sign of Pisces</u>, 8 (Winter), 14.
        Bill Henderson's <u>The Pushcart Prize: Best of the Small
     Presses</u> (1976) is dedicated to Nin and cites her as found-
     ing editor.

13   CENTING, RICHARD. "International College Tribute to Anaïs
      Nin." Under the Sign of Pisces, 8 (Summer), 3-6.
          Nin was a tutor at International College (Los Angeles),
      which was founded as an alternative to traditional higher
      education. She offered an independent study program on
      the diary and novel writing. International College of-
      fered a tribute to Nin on February 21, 1977 (which would
      have been Nin's seventy-fourth birthday), combining music,
      poetry, song, film, photographs, and spoken commentary.
      Christopher Isherwood hosted the program and a number of
      guests (including Dory Previn and Stephen Spender) offered
      personal tribute to Nin. The International College has
      established an Anaïs Nin Scholarship Endowment. Under the
      Sign of .Pisces hopes to publish more about the tribute and
      welcomes articles by those who attended.

14   EKBERG, KENT. "The Importance of Under a Glass Bell." Under
      the Sign of Pisces, 8 (Spring), 4-18.
          "Under a Glass Bell (1944) represents a turning point in
      the life and career of Anaïs Nin." Nin regards this book
      as her best work and its theme is that of all of Nin's fic-
      tion: "self-realization through the spontaneous expression
      of emotions in relationships with other human beings." Di-
      vides the stories into three groups, those where: (1)
      people are thrust together trying to understand each other
      and need freedom to seek their own individuality; (2) the
      individual is left alone to his own devices for sustenance
      and survival; (3) the theme of self-discovery is moored in
      a firm "I." "Birth" is the best story in the collection
      and clarifies the whole work. Examines a typescript of the
      stillbirth story in the Northwestern University Library;
      the paragraphs Nin deleted show that "Birth" is about the
      birth of the narrator as well as about death. Changes Nin
      made in this draft show her artistic control. Unity is
      achieved in Under a Glass Bell by means of the dream image
      or motif, the use of twins, doubles, and parallel situa-
      tions.

15   EKBERG, KENT. A Report of the 1976 Special Session on the
      Writings of Anaïs Nin." Under the Sign of Pisces, 8
      (Spring), 1-4.
          The session was held at the Modern Language Association
      annual convention, 1976, with Valerie Carnes as discussion
      leader and four participants. Papers included: Kent Ek-
      berg, "The Importance of Under a Glass Bell" (See 1977.B14);
      Stephanie Demetrakoponlos, "Anaïs Nin and the Feminine
      Quest for Consciousness: the Quelling of the Devouring
      Mother and the Ascension of the Sophia," is original

1977

because of its "new stress" on the importance of Nin's
mother in her life and work and the implications this has
for Jungian depth psychology; Nancy Scholar, "Persona:
Two Variations on a Theme," compares House of Incest and
Bergman's "Persona" because of "their mutual obsession with
the psyches of women"; Harriet Zinnes, "Anaïs Nin: The
Poetry of Her Vision," focuses on the use of the unconscious and dream in transforming life into art and also
"the necessity for the poet to link self and other success-
fully through the finished product of art." Sharon Spencer
commented on the papers and called for feminist revision of
classical psychoanalytic theories.

16   EKBERG, KENT. "Waste of Timelessness and Other Early Stories
      by Anaïs Nin." Under the Sign of Pisces, 8 (Summer), 12-
      17.
         Waste of Timelessness and Other Early Stories contains
      stories from Northwestern University's collection of pre-
      viously unpublished stories written by Nin in her twenties.
      Valerie Harms convinced Nin to publish these stories
      through Harms' Magic Circle Press; Harms also supplied the
      first significant critical comment on them in a previous
      book (1975.B18). Nin feared adverse criticism, but readers
      who like the later Nin will like this collection. In these
      stories, Nin "has not yet fully learned the art of abstrac-
      tion and condensation" that characterizes her later work.
      The importance of the dream to Nin's work is apparent in
      the stories. The title story is the most important; it
      deals with a circular journey centering on a dream of a
      boat in a garden. Some of the women characters are proto-
      types of the unconventional women of Cities of the Interior.
      Many of the stories deal with love triangles and fidelity
      and infidelity in marriage. The book is important because
      the stories share similarities with later Nin work, because
      of autobiographical elements, and because it is art.

17   ESMONDE DE USABEL, FRANCES. "Nin, Anaïs. Waste of Timeless-
      ness and Other Early Stories." Library Journal, 102
      (15 September), 1868.
         The stories are "long on introspection, short on plot,
      and tenderly depict heroines who are projections of the
      author." The collection is "worth reading on its own
      terms."

18   FERRE, ROSARIO. "Anaïs Nin: 'Escribo para enamorar, encantar
      y consolar a los otros.'" Siempre!, no. 1234 (16 February),
      pp. ix-x. [Spanish.]

Nin is dead at 74 [sic]. According to Nin, life is a
series of deaths culminating in a final encounter; she did
not fear death, believing she had lived fully. She de-
tested mass-produced men and women. Her life was greatly
influenced by her friendship with Henry Miller. After
meeting Miller in 1931, she abandoned a life of wealth in
the upper class to join the world of artists. She also
studied psychology with Otto Rank. She viewed writing as
the instrument a writer uses to create a world of retreat.
She placed the greatest emphasis on dreams, which for her
supercede all reality. She possessed a unique passion for
life, and this perhaps explains why she so often allowed
herself to be exploited without feeling resentment.

19 HALL, JOAN JOFFE. "Starving Artist." Houston Post Spotlight
   Magazine (7 August), p. 33.
      In 1940 and 1941, a group of writers, including Nin,
   wrote pornography at a dollar a page for a collector.
   Delta of Venus contains Nin's contributions. She felt her
   style was influenced by men's works and that she "'had
   compromised my feminine self'" in following the collector's
   urgings to be more specific and less poetic. However, Nin
   later felt that she used the woman's point of view and
   language because women "'have never separated sex from
   feeling, from the love of the whole man.'" For the most
   part, the selections in the book support this observation.
   Throughout the episodes Nin stresses the ideal of "two
   bodies in love with each other...." These selections do
   not differ much from scenes in contemporary novels by either
   men or women.

20 HARA, MASAKO. "My Last Visit with Anaïs Nin." Gakuto:
   Monthly Journal of International Biography, 74 (3 March),
   12-15. [Japanese.]
      The diary shows Nin's struggle to live. Describes Nin's
   last struggle to live while suffering from cancer and mel-
   ancholy. Nin's womanhood was a source of strength. She
   fought everything that blocked being a woman. Her greatest
   contribution to the American novel is in her introduction
   of the womanly principle to a literature which had been
   dominated by the male focus on power. The diary was popular among women, more so than feminism. Both the diary and
   feminism are motivated by the search for a true father.

21 HARA, MASAKO. "First, You Have to be a Woman: Anaïs Nin's
   Daughters." Bokushin, 9 (May-June), 8-21.
      The "daughters" of Nin are offspring such as Barbara
   Kraft and Erica Jong who help clarify the meaning of the

1977

diary. "Lolitaism" is basic to Nin's self-portrait and
her pursuit of womanhood. Nin shows two conflicting "Lolitas": the loving Lolita who loves her father, and the
creative Lolita who identifies herself with her father.
In the diary Nin tried to liberate the two Lolitas. Nin's
experience of a stillbirth made her give up physical
motherhood and turn to abstract motherhood that focuses on
loving men and creative activities. However, the "daughters" of Nin still show the struggle between devoting
themselves to art or men.

22 HOLDER, ORLEE E. "A Response to Courtenay P. Graham's Response." Under the Sign of Pisces, 8 (Spring), 18-21.
Criticizes the manner in which Graham (1976.B21) defends
Nin from Traba (1976.B40). "It is time Anaïs Nin and her
work...stand up to even harsh criticism." It is not necessary to be a "Nin-ite" or "Ninnie" to appreciate Nin.
Traba's essay is valuable and challenging if sometimes
wrong. Graham descends to name-calling. Nin's work can
withstand scrutiny without apology.

23 HOLT, ROCHELLE L. "On the Life of Anaïs Nin--To Assert Her
Aliveness." Birmingham, Alabama Independent Press (9 February), p. 2.
Nin the person was intimate, approachable, caring; she
even answered postcards from undergraduate admirers.
Whether lecturing or talking at home, she delighted her
audience with her vibrancy, refusing, even when dying of
cancer, to give up her "sensibilities," her "vibrations"
and her "continuous aliveness."

24 KLUGMAN, ELANA. "Stars in My Sky, by Valerie Harms." Chrysalis: A Magazine of Women's Culture, no. 3, p. 80. An
"inspiring biographical tribute" to three women (Monte-
sorri, Nin, Steloff). Harms shows that the three women are
important to her personally and that readers can get "en-
couragement and strength" from viewing the lives of the
women. See 1975.B18.

25 LINGEMAN, RICHARD.R. "New Nin." The New York Times Book
Review (10 July), p. 47.
Nin has two posthumously published books: Delta of Venus
and Waste of Timelessness and Other Stories. The latter is
a collection of the first stories Nin wrote. Nin at first
refused to publish the stories in her lifetime because she
felt them to be immature but later decided to allow publication.

26   MARCINCZYK, REESA. "A Checklist of the Writings of Anaïs Nin,
      1973-1976, compiled by Reesa Marcinczyk." Under the Sign
      of Pisces, 8 (Winter), 2-14.
           Extensive list that attempts to be as complete as pos-
      sible. Books, contributions to books, contributions to
      journals, tapes, films, letters, bibliographies (1973-
      1976).

27   MILLER, HENRY. "Anaïs Nin" Cómo morir ante un espejo."
      Translated by Benito Lacave: La Cultura en Mexico [Sup-
      plement to Siempre!] (1 June), pp. 2-6. [Spanish.]
      Translation of 1937.B1.

28   MITGANG, HERBERT. "Behind the Best Sellers: Anaïs Nin." The
      New York Times Book Review (28 August), p. 24.
           Review of Delta of Venus. Quotes from Nin's editor,
      John Ferrone of Harcourt Brace Jovanovich on Delta of Ve-
      nus: Nin "tended to dismiss the erotica as imitative and
      a betrayal of her true feminine self, but I was able to
      persuade her that it contained superb writing and that she
      had not obliterated her own identity." Upon rereading,
      Nin agreed that she had produced a woman's work in an area
      previously dominated by men. Delta of Venus put Nin on
      the best seller list for the first time.

29   NAKADA, KOJI. "Anaïs Nin." Eureka, 9 (April), 230-245.
      [Japanese.]
           A tribute to Nin after her death. Mentions personal
      meetings with Nin at Tokyo and Los Angeles. Compares Nin
      to Henry Miller. Both Nin and Miller show that women do
      not collapse under humiliation and defeat but instead show
      a strong desire to live. The delicacy of Nin's style can
      be a defect; however, the novels in Cities of the Interior
      are as fascinating as Nexus with regard to the theme of
      strong human desire.

30   PERHAC, PEGGY KAY. "The Restless Spirit. By Barbara Kraft."
      Under the Sign of Pisces, 8 (Summer), 18-19.
           Review of a journal by Barbara Kraft, a student of Nin
      when she wrote The Restless Spirit. The journal shows
      Nin's influence in its "fluid style and imagery." Kraft
      says of Nin: "After creating the myth she actually became
      it." It is this mythic quality which particularly dis-
      tinguishes Nin's writing.

1977

31   SELIG, NEENA HUSID. "Delta of Venus." Austin The Daily Texan
     (14 July), p. 12.
       Nin's "literary conscience" troubled her when she wrote
     the erotica in Delta of Venus as commissioned pornography.
     Recounts the battle between Nin and the man she was writ-
     ing for. He kept demanding "less poetry." Nin later was
     surprised at how much poetry remained; she believed her
     work was saved from pornography because she was "intui-
     tively using a woman's language" and "never separated sex
     from feeling." Delta of Venus, is "well-written" and
     shows "the beautiful and sensitive coupling of physical
     desire and spiritual need."

32   TIBBETTS, ROBERT A. "A Spy in the House of Love: A Note on
     the First Printings." Under the Sign of Pisces, 8 (Summer),
     1-4.
       Collates the first two printings, Dutch and American,
     of A Spy in the House of Love. Twenty-two variants are
     listed, most of them obvious misprints which were corrected
     for the American impression. Contrary to Franklin's bib-
     liography (1973.A1), the Amsterdam printing was the first,
     and the American printing the second. The Ohio State Uni-
     versity Library has a letter from Nin indicating that the
     first (Dutch) printing was full of errors.

33   WALKER, ALICE. "Anaïs Nin: 1903-1977." Ms., 5 (April), 46.
       Describes a personal meeting with Nin; she seemed like-
     able even though her personal beauty seemed "carefully
     presented." Reprints a "fan letter" from Nin to Walker in
     which Nin praises Walker's short stories. The erotica in
     Delta of Venus shows "Nin's erotic imagination set free in
     an explicit and personal way." Delta of Venus is "the
     boldest, most useful of her books" because it is "so dis-
     tinct an advance in the depiction of female sensuality."
     Nin's lack of interest in politics was "self-indulgent and
     escapist." However, Nin "made of her own mind and body a
     perpetually new frontier, enlarging our consciousness by
     exploring and presenting the many and varied exposures of
     the same Anaïs Nin."

34   ZINNES, HARRIET. "Collector's Item." The New York Times Book
     Review (10 July), pp. 11, 26.
       Along with others, Nin wrote erotica for a collector who
     admonished the writers to omit poetry and write more ex-
     plicitly of sex. Nin's Delta of Venus includes the "first
     American stories by a woman to celebrate sexuality with
     complete and open abandonment." Although Nin thought her

work was influenced by male writers, she eventually came
to believe she used woman's language and point of view by
concentrating on the pleasure of sexual surrender rather
than on aggression. Nin describes sex as a creative and
joyous human experience in which nothing is abnormal so
long as mutual pleasure exists.

Index

Index

Review of <u>Winter of Artifice and
House of Incest</u>, 1974.B55
"Reviews by Anaïs Nin," 1971.B16
Reviews by Nin, 1971.B16, B32
Reyes, Barbara, 1971.B25
Richardson, Maurice, 1970.B62
Rider, Laura, Nin and, 1970.B9
Riley, Carolyn, 1969.B14;
    1973.B42
Riley, Glenda, 1976.B34
Robinson, Lillian S., 1972.B39
Robinson, Virginia B., 1972.B40
"Rochelle Holt: Poet, Painter,
    Printer, Pisces," 1973.B9
Rolo, Charles J., 1950.B11;
    1954.B2
Rosenfeld, Isaac, 1945.B1
Rosenfeld, Paul, 1942.B2
Ross, Alan, 1963.B6
Ross, L., 1974.B52
Rowe, William, 1969.B27
"Ruined Raj," 1968.B12

S

Sayre, Nora, 1966.B28
Scheid, Ann Salinger, 1974.B63
Schlesinger, Marian C., 1969.B28
Schneider, Duane B., 1967.B20;
    1968.B16-B17; 1969.B29;
    1970.A1, B63; 1973.A3, B43;
    1974.B64
Scholar, Nancy, 1975.B26
Schultz, Anne, 1972.B41
Schweitzer, Lea, 1976.B35
"Second Installment," 1967.B12
"<u>Second Wave</u>: Interview with
    AN," 1971.B22
"Secret Vice," 1970.B4
"Section Three: Anaïs Nin,
    Chronicler of the Feminine
    Woman's Progress," in "Ex-
    ploring the Feminine: A
    Study of Janet Lewis, Ellen
    Glasgow, Anaïs Nin, and Vir-
    ginia Woolf," 1974.B59
"<u>Seduction of the Minotaur</u>,"
    1962.B5
<u>Seduction of the Minotaur</u>,
    1961.B1-B4; 1962.B5; 1968.A1;
    1969.B22-B23; 1970.B29, B46,

B56, B66; 1974.B59; 1975.B23;
    <u>characters in</u>, 1961.B4;
    1968.A1; 1969.B22-B23;
    1970.B56; <u>"female" writing</u>,
    1962.B5; 1969.B22-B23;
    1970.B56; <u>style</u>, 1961.B1-B4;
    1962.B5; <u>theme of woman</u>,
    1962.B5; 1970.B50; <u>use of
    the dream</u>, 1975.B23
"Self behind the Selves, The,"
    1966.B13
Selig, Neena Husid, 1977.B31
Sellers, Jill, 1974.B65
"Serialized Life," 1974.B44
"Seven Veils, The," 1967.B17
Sex Roles, Nin on, 1973.B5, B28,
    B33, B45, B47; 1974.B30,
    B65, B75
"Sexuality and the Opposite Sex:
    Variations on a Theme by
    Theopile Gautier and Anaïs
    Nin," 1977.B9
"Shadow Dance," 1947.B7
Shapiro, Karl, 1966.B29;
    1967.B21
"Sharon Spencer on Anaïs Nin,"
    1974.B28
Shereshefsky, Pauline M.,
    1972.B42
Sherman, John K., 1966.B30
Simon, Marion, 1966.B31
Slotnikoff, William, 1970.B64
Smith, Craig, 1975.B27
Smith, Harrison, 1946.B5
Snitow, Ann, 1971.B45; 1973.B44
Snyder, Robert, 1973.A4;
    1976.A1
<u>Solar Barque</u>, 1960.B3; 1962.B2
"Soothsayers," 1968.B10
<u>Space, Time, and Structure in
    the Modern Novel</u>, 1971.B47
"<u>Space, Time, and Structure in
    the Modern Novel</u> by Sharon
    Spencer," 1971.B55; 1972.B11
Spacks, Patricia Meyer, 1971.B46;
    1972.B43
"Special Notices," 1963.B6
Spencer, Sharon, 1971.B47;
    1972.B44; 1973.B45-B46;
    1974.B67-B68; 1975.B28;
    1976.B36; 1977.A1